BASEBALL BETWEEN THE LINES

BASEBALL BETWEEN THE LINES

Baseball in the '40s and '50s
As Told by the Men Who Played It

Donald Honig

Introduction by Red Smith

COWARD, McCANN & GEOGHEGAN, INC.

NEW YORK

SBN: 698-10725-X

Library of Congress Cataloging in Publication Data

Honig, Donald.
    Baseball between the lines.

    Includes index.
    1. Baseball—Biography. I. Title.
GV865.A1H618   1976   796.357′092′2   75–34477

PRINTED IN THE UNITED STATES OF AMERICA

For Stanley Honig and David Markson

CONTENTS

[dates in brackets indicate major-league playing career]

ILLUSTRATIONS

LEGEND FOR ENDSHEET

1. Carl Furillo, Jackie Robinson, Roy Campanella, Pee Wee Reese, Duke Snider, Preacher Roe and Gil Hodges of the 1951 Dodgers.
2. Harry Brecheen. 3. Bucky Harris. 4. Joe Medwick. 5. Jackie Robinson. 6. Al Rosen. 7. Al Simmons. 8. Cookie Lavagetto.
9. Monte Irvin stealing home in the 1951 World Series. 10. Pete Reiser. 11. Monte Irvin. 12. Willie Mays. 13. Sal Maglie. 14. Willie Mays leaping for a fly ball in Wrigley Field. 15. Warren Spahn.
16. Tex Hughson.

ACKNOWLEDGMENTS

The author would like to express his gratitude to the following:

The Card Memorabilia Associates, Ltd., Amawalk, New York, for assistance in photo research.

The National Baseball Museum and Library, and to the indefatigable Jack Redding, in particular, for assistance in photo research.

In addition, the author would like to note the contributions of his editors, Bill Henderson and Cathy Rossbach, Joan and Theron Raines, Allan J. Grotheer, Stanley Honig, the invaluable counsel of David Markson and Larry Ritter, as well as the generous assistance offered by members of the Bobo Newsom Memorial Fan Club.

Thanks also to my wife, Sandy, and daughter Catherine.

Above all, the author wishes to express his heartfelt thanks to the ballplayers who so generously and good-naturedly shared their memories with him, as well as allowed him to use pictures from their personal albums.

INTRODUCTION

When Tommy Henrich was declared a free agent and sold himself to the Yankees, he took a train to New York and checked into the Hotel Commodore. Upstairs, the bellhop carrying his bag said: "You're Hendrichs, ain't you?" Tommy glowed.

"Yes," he said.

"Boy," the bellhop said, "I'd hate to be in your shoes."

Up to then, Tommy had been comfortable in his shoes. As a kid in Massillon, Ohio, he had been a Yankee fan. Now he was a Yankee, already recognized in the big town from his picture in the paper. As a free agent, he had collected a bonus of $25,000 or $30,000, a gang of money in 1937.

"The Yankees," the bellhop said, "have DiMaggio, Powell and Selkirk. Boy, I'd hate to have to break into an outfield like that!"

"Well," Tommy said, not bravely but because he had to say something, "remember you haven't seen me play."

"And I have to admit," Tommy said years later, "it was a long time before he did." Before the bellboy had a day off, Henrich was in Newark, and even though he was soon recalled it was a while before he shook off the fear that his future might lie in New Jersey.

"Tommy," Joe McCarthy said that first summer, "they're making a sucker out of you with that outside curve. I want you to lay off that pitch."

About a week later McCarthy said: "Tommy, I told you to lay off that curve. Either you do it now, or you'll learn to hit it in Newark."

"When he put it that way," Tommy said later, "you got the message."

I'm glad Don Honig led off this book with Tommy Henrich because Tommy got more pure joy out of baseball than any other player I ever knew, and this comes through when he talks about the game. That line of his about the contributions Judge Landis and Babe Ruth made to the game ought to wind up in Bartlett's *Familiar Quotations:* "Landis cleaned it up and Babe Ruth glorified it."

Baseball Between the Lines is the third member of a noble triumvirate. First Larry Ritter charmed us with *The Glory of Their Times*, the reminiscences of men who played when Ty Cobb and Honus Wagner were riding high. Then Ritter's friend Honig interviewed stars of the nineteen thirties and delighted us with *Baseball When the Grass Was Real*. Now Don moves a decade closer to today, and if I think this is the best of the three it is probably because I am a prejudiced witness; I know many of these men as friends and saw all of them play.

There is hardly a page that doesn't bring back memories. Al Simmons, Tommy Henrich says, "was one angry man when he strode up to home plate."

"You know," Al told me when he was a coach with the Philadelphia Athletics, "when I was hitting I hated pitchers, I wanted 'em dead. Them sonabitches were trying to take the bread and butter out of my mouth."

"Do you feel that way about hitters?" I asked Early Wynn years later.

"Just the same way," that angry pitcher said, "and most of all I hate the guy who hits back through the box. He's not only taking the bread and butter out of my mouth, he's trying to cut the legs from under me."

"That space between the white lines," Early said, "that's my office. That's where I conduct my business."

I envy the reader picking up this book for the first time. He's going to spend time with Ewell Blackwell, who looked like a flyrod with ears unless he was pitching on your side; then he looked like the Angel Gabriel. He'll meet Dick Wakefield, enormously likable, incurably spoiled, who never fulfilled his potential and blames the press for that.

He will hear from Kirby Higbe about Ernie Lombardi, who could rub the shine off a new baseball with one hand. If the reader ever saw Bob Feller pitch, he will treasure the advice Bucky Harris gave the Washington Senators:

"Go up and hit what you see, and if you don't see it come on back."

November 1975   RED SMITH

PREFACE

The nineteen men interviewed for this book are essentially players of the post-Depression era, their baseball careers spanning the end of the Depression, the war years, the postwar years. Only two—Buddy Hassett and Billy Werber—played the bulk of their big-league careers before 1940.

Technological, economic and social upheavals generated by the war dictated a changing world, and nothing, including baseball, remained unaffected. For example, night baseball, infrequent before the war, came to dominate the playing schedule, its popularity unquestioned. It looked like the same game, but it wasn't quite. To this day some veteran ballplayers will insist the record books should have been closed with the advent of night ball because of the advantage to the pitcher pitching under the lights (just as today many insist the designated hitter rule will eventually make all existing lifetime batting records meaningless).

In 1946 Branch Rickey and the Brooklyn Dodger organization breached baseball's decaying racial barriers. A year later Jackie Robinson became the first black to play in the big leagues. The reaction to Robinson's entrance into a hitherto-segregated field was watched closely, and no one watched with more interest and concern than Monte Irvin, who two years later was to cross the color line on the New York Giants. "There was a lot at stake," Irvin says, "and not just for Jackie, not just for the other black ballplayers, not just for baseball; it went beyond that."

Jackie Robinson's success—as a man and as an athlete—was undoubtedly the single most significant event in baseball's postwar history. It gave the game its greatest lift since Babe Ruth's unprecedented distance hitting raised the sport from its scandal-ridden uncertainty some twenty-five years before.

When he was a boy, Robin Roberts says, he listened to the games over the radio, and a career in professional baseball "was all a dream. We just couldn't imagine ourselves as major-league ballplayers, whereas today you can see it on television and it has greater reality to kids." While it is true that the first television relay of a big-league game occurred in August, 1939, at Ebbets Field, it was not until the late forties that the camera's eye began dissolving the "dream" and establishing for the at-home fan the "reality" of the game.

The impact of television on baseball had its negative effect. While the revenue for permission to televise was considerable, the expansion of coverage was reflected at the gates of minor-league teams by gradually diminishing returns. One by one minor-league communities and eventually entire leagues disappeared from the baseball roster, parching the proving grounds where young players were taught and developed. In 1947 there were fifty-two minor leagues in operation; today the number is approximately one-third that.

The postwar years also introduced the bonus player. The big-league clubs indulged in spirited checkbook competition for the talents of gifted young players. This style of corporate gambling proved extremely risky and unpredictable. Many youths who commanded enormous bonuses never played an inning of big-league ball. On the other hand, investments in untried players like Robin Roberts, Curt Simmons, Herb Score and others were more than justified. It is ironic now to note the comments of Dick Wakefield who, in 1941, was the first of the "bonus babies." Wakefield signed a Detroit Tiger contract for a $52,000 incentive, a sum considered by many at the time to be almost immoral. A few years later a bonus of that amount was barely noted.

Inevitably, the war years saw a deterioration in the quality of baseball. Total strangers appeared in big-league uniforms, along with aging veteran players prolonging their careers in an acute talent shortage. Wartime service interrupted the careers of many of the players included in this book. But wherever they went—whatever the distant front line or obscure outpost—American soldiers brought baseball with them. Enos Slaughter played on Saipan (as diehard Japanese soldiers emerged from their caves to watch), Kirby Higbe pitched in the Philippines, and Mickey Vernon was the finest first baseman the atoll of Ulithi ever had.

For the fan, two of the game's most enduring attractions are statistics and memories. Statistics are duly and imperishably recorded in guides, record books and encyclopedias. Memories, however, are perishable. So, following the intent of a first volume, *Baseball When the Grass Was Real*, which recorded the memories of stars of an earlier time, I sought out some of the men who played during this transitional era. Some of them have now drifted away from the game; others still retain their ties, in one capacity or another: Ralph Kiner and Herb Score are broadcasters; Tommy Holmes works for the New York Mets' group sales department; Enos Slaughter coaches Duke University's team; Monte Irvin is special assistant to the commissioner; Mickey Vernon is batting instructor for the Los Angeles Dodgers. But even those no longer connected with baseball still maintain an avid interest in the box scores, the standings and the players who are today on the mound, at bat, in the field, creating the excitement and the drama and shaping the memories of tomorrow.

DONALD HONIG

January, 1976

TOMMY HENRICH

Thomas David Henrich
Born: February 20, 1913, Massillon, Ohio
Major-league career: 1937–50, New York Yankees
Lifetime average: .282

One of the most popular players ever to wear the Yankee uniform, Tommy Henrich earned the nickname "Old Reliable." Part of the famed Keller-Henrich-DiMaggio outfield of the late thirties and early forties, Henrich was considered one of the game's most intelligent players. He had a career high of 31 home runs in 1941 and in 1947 and 1948 led the league in triples.

I was born and raised in Massillon, Ohio, the middle one of five children. You know what Massillon is—it's a football town. Everybody says, "How'd you get started playing baseball?" Well, my dad didn't like football. He thought you could get hurt at it. So as soon as I was old enough, I was throwing a ball. I had a very natural talent for throwing a ball and catching it and hitting it. It was no fluke. You couldn't have kept me away from baseball. It was all there, right from the beginning.

At that time, growing up, I didn't have any ambition about making baseball a career. Never thought about it. I never dreamed I could be good enough to play professional baseball.

I played a lot of softball. The town seemed to go in for that. I think that was because there weren't enough good fields for baseball, and not enough equipment. Softball was more convenient, and it was an easier game to play. I played all the way through high school and for a year after I was out of high school.

How did I finally get into hard ball? Well, I can tell you just how that happened. I'd been playing softball for a team around here for two years. And we had a great team. We won 80 out of 87 games in 1932. At the end of the year we had a bazaar. We sold chances on Indian blankets and things like that, to get some money together to buy team jack-

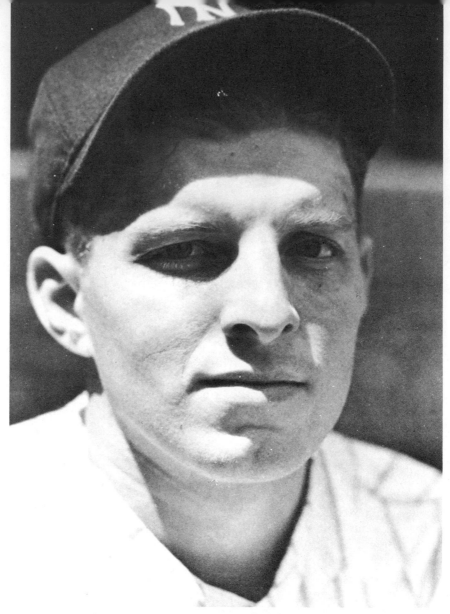

Tommy Henrich in 1937.

ets with. We took in $200, and then the manager told us that by a strange coincidence the expenses just equaled that amount. It left a sour taste, and that was the end of the ball club.

During the winter somebody asked me if I'd like to play hard ball. I said all right, I'd give it a whirl. So I joined this team in the spring and was doing all right. One day in June a scout from Detroit named Billy Doyle showed up. He wanted to see the game against Canton. It was a six-mile ride out to the ball field from town and Doyle wasn't about to go for the cab fare, so some of us invited him to ride along. On the way he told us he'd come down to scout the guy who was pitching for Canton that day.

"What about some of the boys on our team?" somebody asked him.

"I came to see the fellow on the Canton club," he said.

"We've got some good ballplayers, too," we told him.

"Maybe you do," he said. "But I came to see the fellow on the Canton club."

He seemed pretty definite about that.

Well, I hit two screamers in that game and around the eighth inning I'm sitting on the bench and I feel somebody tapping me on the shoulder. I turn around. It's Billy Doyle.

"How would you like to play pro ball?" he asked.

I think my eyes must have popped. "Are you kidding? I asked. "You're doggone right I would."

"Okay," he said. "I'll send you a contract. You sign it immediately and send it back."

Sure enough, the contract came in the mail. It called for me to report in 1934. Now, this was June of '33. I said to myself, "Gee, I sign up now but don't do anything until next year." I wasn't so sure I wanted to sign it. So I filed it away, and at the same time told myself that maybe I ought to get serious about baseball. I started getting in some batting practice every day and played as much as I could. I figured that after having played softball for so many years I had some lost time to make up.

Then in September down comes Bill Bradley of the Cleveland Indians and he offers me a contract. He stayed around for a while and I got to know him and to like him. So I signed a contract with Cleveland, to go to Zanesville, Ohio. I eventually wound up playing for Monessen, Pennsylvania.

The funny thing was, Cleveland was more or less the local big league club, the closest one to Massillon, but I'd never been a Cleveland rooter. Never rooted for them a day in my life. At that time I was a New York Yankee fan. I'd been a Yankee fan since 1921, when I was eight years old. I was a Babe Ruth man. When I look back now I wonder how lucky a guy can be—to be in love with baseball, to love the New York Yankees and Babe Ruth especially, and to end up not just with the Yankees but playing out there in right field where Ruth had played, and winning pennants every year to boot. What more can a guy ask?

I played three years in the Cleveland organization. At the end of 1936 I was sold to Milwaukee in the American Association. Milwaukee was also a Cleveland farm. In other words, I was being shifted around the Cleveland organization. Now, in my three years in the minors I'd hit .326 in D ball, .337 in C, and .346 in AA. I was hitting better the higher up I went, and I was beginning to ask myself when I was going to get a shot at the big leagues. At that time Cleveland had Jeff Heath in the organization and Heath was a particular favorite of Cy Slapnicka, the general manager. I heard that they were bringing Heath to spring training with them in 1937, even though he'd played only Class C ball. Jeff Heath sure turned out to be a fine slugger, but at that time I felt a little put out, feeling that I'd earned the shot.

Early in 1937, right after the new year, I read in the paper where the Boston Braves are interested in buying Henrich from the Milwaukee Brewers. I also read where the Cleveland Indians are toying with the idea of trading Joe Vosmik to the St. Louis Browns, with Henrich as a throw-in. So at about this time I started saying to my dad, "For heaven's sake, who in the heck do I belong to? Milwaukee wants to trade me to Boston, and Cleveland is talking about trading me to St. Louis."

After thinking about it for a while I decided to write to the commissioner, Judge Landis, and try to get the situation clarified. What the heck, he was a ballplayer's commissioner, wasn't he? I knew I'd get a fair decision from him.

So I wrote the letter. It reached Landis somewhere in Florida, where he was on vacation. Well, I got a telegram back from him, about fourteen lines deep, the biggest telegram I ever saw in my life. I wish I could remember his exact words, but it went along like this: "You say so-and-so. Prove it. You say so-and-so. Prove it. You say this and that. Can you prove it?" And on and on like that.

I went through everything I had, trying to make as strong a case as I could, and wrote back to him. When I heard from him again he told me to report to the Milwaukee training camp, which was at Biloxi, Mississippi, that year. So I went down there. By this time it was around March first. Cleveland was training in New Orleans, not far away.

Landis called a meeting in the Roosevelt Hotel in New Orleans, and over I go, with the top executives of the Milwaukee ball club. I was scared to death. I thought Landis was going to be my lawyer in the matter, but I was wrong; he was the judge, he was taking the evidence. So I had to be my own lawyer.

What I had was mostly hearsay, but Landis was familiar with the kind of shenanigans that were going on and he went after those guys. I don't think he liked Slapnicka, anyway. Nevertheless, he made his decision strictly according to baseball law, as it existed at that time. Cleveland was definitely directing my progress through the minor leagues, which, according to Landis, they had no legal right to do. So it was a clear violation, although hardly an uncommon one. It was an everyday thing in baseball back then. The judge could have let it go, but because he didn't like Slapnicka, and because I think he got a kick out of me writing to him and standing up for my rights, he declared me a free agent.

So I went back to Massillon. I got back there on a Thursday night. By Saturday I'd heard from eight clubs, including the Yankees. Jacques Fornier, the old Brooklyn first baseman, was scouting for the Browns, and he kept hammering away. I think he was ready to top the Yankee offer, but I thought to myself, "Gee, I don't want to belong to the Browns." I knew where I wanted to play.

My dad said, "Do you think you can make the Yankee ball club?"

"Well, I don't know," I said. I figured if I wasn't a good ballplayer it wouldn't make any difference where I played; but if I was a good ballplayer, then I wanted to be with the Yankees. And that's where I went.

I joined the Yankees at the beginning of the season in '37, stayed with them for two weeks and then was shipped to Newark. I was there for about ten days and was hitting around .440. Then McCarthy got rid of an outfielder and I was recalled.

On one of our first trips into Chicago I was standing at the batting cage and an usher comes walking up to me.

"Are you Henrich?" he asks.

"That's right," I said.

"Well, the commissioner wants to see you."

I took a look and there's Landis sitting in the front row, staring at me. Oh-oh, I thought, what's this all about? What have I done wrong?

I walked over to him and said, "How are you, Mr. Commissioner?"

He's still staring at me, very sternly.

"How are they treating you?" he asked.

"Just fine," I said.

"Well," he said, "they'd better."

I loved Judge Landis. He was quite a man. I've always said that the two greatest names in baseball are Babe Ruth and Judge Landis. Landis cleaned it up and Babe Ruth glorified it.

I remember right after I joined the Yankees in '37 Al Simmons beat us with a home run off of Lefty Gomez into the right-field seats. That was my first look at Simmons, and what a smasher he was. He's got to be the most vicious man I ever saw at home plate. He was starting to go downhill when I came into the league, but I saw him look real good. Oh, but he was one angry man when he strode up to home plate. He hated that pitcher with a vengeance, and showed it.

Bill Dickey told me a story about Simmons one time. In 1928 the A's were the coming team. Connie Mack had put together that great team and was challenging the Yankees. The A's came in for a big series and

Judge Kenesaw Mountain Landis during the 1933 World Series at the Polo Grounds. "I've always said that the two greatest names in baseball are Babe Ruth and Judge Landis."

the Yankees were wondering what to do about some of those big hitters like Foxx, Cochrane, Haas, Simmons. Somebody thought it would be a good idea to rough Simmons up, to knock him down a little.

"So we rough him up," Dickey said. "In a four-game series he had eleven base hits, ten of them for extra bases." Yeah, they roughed him up all right, and he returned the compliment. He hated the Yankees, but I liked him. I liked him for the way he would bear down against us.

He hung around as a coach after he was through playing. I used to yell to him during batting practice, "Hey, Al, get in and hit a few." He'd push out his lip and shake his head. "Go on, Al," I'd yell. "Go on and hit a couple." The guys would hear it and they'd let him get in. The reason I'd do that was just to watch him step in there. It was something to see. When Al Simmons would grab hold of a ball bat and dig in he'd squeeze the handle of that doggone thing and throw the barrel of that bat toward the pitcher in his warm-up swings, and he would look so bloomin' *mad.* In *batting practice*, years after he'd retired! I'd watch him and say to myself, "Tom, old boy, *that's* the mood you ought to be in when you go to home plate."

Joe McCarthy? I loved him. One of the greatest men I ever knew. I don't know where in the heck he learned all his psychology about ball-players. He could handle almost anybody. And if he couldn't handle them he'd trade them, I'll tell you that. Fellows like Ben Chapman and Johnny Allen. He traded them. But I don't think anybody was ever able to handle Johnny Allen. He was a case all by himself.

But that McCarthy, he seemed always to know just how to talk to you. He knew when to jump on you, when to be your friend, when to give you a pat on the back, when to leave you alone. Best manager I ever knew or heard about. That's the way I felt about him, and I know quite a few other fellows who felt the same way.

He had a phenomenal memory for facts and figures and for a ball-player's strengths and weaknesses. I don't think that guy ever forgot anything. He told me a story one time, after he'd retired. Red Rolfe was managing the Tigers and Joe was managing the Red Sox. The Tigers were doing all right, but they might have been doing better. The Red Sox came in for a ball game and Rolfe invited McCarthy into his office to sit down and talk a little bit. Rolfe idolized McCarthy.

"So I went over to his office," Joe said, "and we sat and chatted for a while. Then I noticed he had a lot of clipboards hanging around the office. I asked him what they were. He said they were records he was keeping. Records of what? I asked. Oh, he said, various things that had happened in ball games during the year. He liked to keep those records so he could refer back to them."

After telling me that, McCarthy looked at me and said, "That's what his trouble is as a manager."

"What?" I asked.

"He's got a lousy memory."

McCarthy didn't need any clipboards; he had it all upstairs, all the time. I'll tell you another story about him. Remember Jimmy Wasdell? He came up to the major leagues with Washington in 1937, in the middle of the season. Now, I knew him; I'd played with him in the Mid-Atlantic League in 1935. He hit .357 that year. That guy could hit. He was a good friend and I was delighted when he came up.

The next time we played Washington Charley Ruffing was the pitcher. He's sitting in the clubhouse looking at the Senators' lineup.

"Who's this guy Wasdell?" he says. "What do we know about him?"

Well, as far as I knew, I was the only one on the club who had ever played with Wasdell, who knew anything about him. But I'm not that dumb; I'm not going to tell these wise guys how to pitch to Jimmy Wasdell. I've seen too many outfielders give well-meaning advice that exploded in somebody's face. But while I'm keeping quiet, McCarthy says, "I know who he is. He's that kid that pinch-hit against us in Chattanooga when we came through there in the spring. He can't hit a change-up." This is what McCarthy says.

I looked at him. I couldn't believe it. To this day I can't believe he's that sharp, that he could size up and remember a man in one appearance in an exhibition game. The truth was, Wasdell *couldn't* hit a change-up. But I still don't believe a man can have that kind of memory. He *must* have called and got a scouting report on Wasdell when he heard Jimmy was joining the Senators. And if he did do that, then he was shrewd enough to sell us on the idea that he did indeed remember Wasdell from one at bat in the spring.

Anyway, so now we have the lowdown on Wasdell, right? Change-ups. Ruffing is the pitcher. Do you know what Wasdell did that afternoon? He was 0 for 4. Didn't get the ball out of the infield. After the game I went around to the Washington dressing room to wait for him. When he came out he was pretty upset.

"Let's get out of here," he said.

"What's the matter, Jim?" I asked.

"Big leagues my foot," he said. He was really disgusted.

"What's the problem?" I asked.

"Smart guys," he said. "Big leaguers. I asked those guys before the game, 'Who's pitching?' They say Ruffing. 'What do you look for with Ruffing?' I asked. 'Seven out of eight fastballs,' they tell me."

Well, they were right, because Ruffing did throw a lot of fastballs. But I haven't told Jimmy to this day what happened over on our side, how he got double-crossed.

That was McCarthy. What a cagey man. He knew everything that was going on, and when he didn't want you to know something, well, you just didn't know it. Art Fletcher was our third-base coach in those days and McCarthy would flash signs out to him. And do you know that no Yankee ballplayer ever knew what those signs were? Now, on any ball club, after a while the players know what signs the manager is using with the coaches. Not only did we never know them, but he never told anybody what they were and I don't suppose he ever will.

Now, Gomez was pretty cute. You know all about the Great Gomez. One day he's sitting a few feet down the bench from McCarthy, watching out of the corner of his eye to see if he could pick up those signs. All of a sudden, without even looking at him, McCarthy says, "Gomez, pay attention to the ball game. You can't get my signs."

Joe McCarthy (left) and Tommy Henrich (right).

Yes, you look back and talk about those great old names. At one time we had on the team seven guys who went into the Hall of Fame. Do you suppose any other team ever had that? We had McCarthy, Earle Combs, who was coaching; Lou Gehrig, Joe DiMaggio, Gomez, Dickey, and Ruffing. Pretty good gang, wouldn't you say?

I roomed with Gomez for three years. One of the wittiest men I ever met. He told me a story once that happened when he was just breaking in. He recognized that he pitched like Grove—a lefthander who got by with a fastball. So he figured he'd talk to Grove.

"Hey, Lefty," he said, "what do you do when you get down to about the eighth inning and you've got to get a guy out?"

"Oh," Grove said, "when it gets down to the eighth inning I just give 'em a little extra."

"Okay," Gomez said. "now what would you do if it was the ninth inning and you really got to get a guy out?"

"Oh," Grove said, "if it's the ninth inning I just blow it by 'em."

Gomez looked at him and said, "Thanks, Lefty. Now I'm a smart pitcher."

Of course when I came into the league Grove didn't have that great fastball anymore. Dickey said he was the fastest he ever saw. He said one day they knocked the Athletics' pitcher out of the game. Dickey was the next batter and he's standing up there looking out to the bull pen to see who they're bringing in. "Wasn't anybody coming in from the bull pen," he said. "Grove walked out of the dugout, threw three pitches and said he's ready. Then he threw three more and I haven't swung at them yet. Don't ever tell *me* about a guy throwing fastballs."

But that didn't happen too many times to Dickey. He was one of your best money players. Take that first game of the 1939 World Series, against Cincinnati. We're tied 1—1 going into the last of the ninth, Derringer against Ruffing. Charlie Keller hits a ball between Harry Craft and Ival Goodman into right-center field. Either one could have caught it, but they couldn't get together and it drops. So Keller's on third, one out, and up steps DiMaggio, followed by Dickey and Selkirk. What do you do? Walk DiMaggio? Never a bad idea, and that's what they did. Then what do you do, walk Dickey to set up a force at any base and pitch to Selkirk? You don't like to pitch to Dickey in a spot like that, but you don't like to pitch to Selkirk, either.

So they pitched to Dickey. When I saw that—and this is the absolute gospel truth—I turned around and picked up my glove, because I knew the game was going to be over right now. And it was. Dickey singled into center field. One way or another, he was going to get that run in. No doubt about that.

Gehrig was still there when I came up, and I saw a pretty good Lou Gehrig for a couple of years before he got sick. What kind of guy was he? Live and let live. Very, very nice and friendly man. Always in good humor. Of course, when you can hit like he could, it's not hard to be in good humor. When I joined the club in '37 he was in a slump. You could see he wasn't making good contact. Then one day in Philadelphia he came out of it. All of a sudden I saw Gehrig hit four line drives to all parts of the ball field. Four for four. I said to Dickey after the game, "I never saw such line drives in my life." And Dickey said, "Wait awhile. You haven't seen anything yet. Those were *soft* ones." What a smasher! That's what Gehrig did. He just went up there and smashed that ball to all fields. A mean, vicious hitter. Like Simmons. Medwick was another one. They just whacked that ball all over the lot, didn't care where it went.

Gehrig was the perfect team man. Never created any problems, always hustled. Where McCarthy used to have some problems with Ruth—who didn't have problems with Ruth?—he never had any with Gehrig. They respected each other, to the extent that as sad as Gehrig looked in 1939 McCarthy still wouldn't take him out of that lineup. It was going to have to be Gehrig's decision.

Lou was pathetic that spring. He couldn't move, couldn't hit the ball hard, couldn't do anything. Nobody knew he was sick; we just thought he was through as a ballplayer. I remember a game in Clearwater that spring. Gehrig tried to go from first to third on a single and when he went around second it looked like he was trying to run uphill at a forty-five-degree angle; he was running as hard as he could and not getting anywhere. But he never complained. I never, never heard him complain.

Then finally he had to take himself out. That was in Detroit, early in May. He went up to home plate to hand in the lineup, then came back to the bench and sat down and began bawling. The public-address announcer saw the lineup cards, realized that here was baseball history in the making, and made the announcement: "Ladies and gentlemen, Lou Gehrig has taken himself out of the lineup for the first time in 2,130 games." There was a tremendous ovation for Lou, while he was sitting there bawling. Now, what do you do? That's a very sad and delicate situation. Well, here's what happened. After about fifteen seconds Gomez got up and walked down past Gehrig, looked at him and said, "What the heck, Lou, now you know how we feel when we get knocked out of the box." Everybody laughed, including Gehrig, and that broke the tension.

Lefty Gomez. A sweetheart of a guy and a sweetheart of a pitcher. You know, there wasn't that much difference between him and Ruffing, but for some reason Ruffing was always looked upon as the ace. He seemed to have that stature. But for most of those years in the thirties you couldn't have chosen between them, one was just as tough as the other, the way Raschi and Reynolds were ten or so years later.

You know, you bandy these names around and then you stop to realize why there was such a thing as a Yankee dynasty. Just stop and look at how some of those players came up and took each other's place. DiMaggio's last year was 1951, which was Mantle's first year. Dickey retired in 1946, and Berra came up at the end of that year. When Crosetti began to slow down, Rizzuto came up. They got rid of Lazzeri and replaced him with Joe Gordon. And so on. The farm system was inexhaustible in those days.

I played on five pennant winners in my first six years. The only year we missed was 1940. That 1941 Series stands out in my mind; that was the first one the Yankees and Dodgers ever played against each other, the first of many. Some of the wildest things ever to happen in a World Series occurred between the Yankees and the Dodgers. I was right in the middle of a couple of those things.

I was up at bat when Mickey Owen let that third strike get away. Is that the most famous strikeout in baseball history? I don't know; it could well be. Whatever it was, it wasn't a very good time to strike out, since it was the top of the ninth, two out, nobody on, and we're losing, 4–3. Hugh Casey threw me a heck of a pitch. Everybody says it was a

"Then finally he had to take himself out." Detroit, May 2, 1939. Lou Gehrig. Number 11 is Lefty Gomez.

spitter, but I don't buy that. I listened one time to Mickey Owen describe what he thought the pitch was and he described it exactly as I remembered it. He said it was the best curveball Hugh Casey ever threw. Casey didn't have a good curve, but this ball exploded.

The count was three and two, and I'm up there guarding the plate—poorly. In comes this pitch, and if I were a Johnny Mize or a Ted Williams or a Paul Waner I would have waited a little longer on it, because they were great waiters. But I had committed myself too quickly and too far and when I realized that was a bad ball I couldn't hold back. It broke down so fast I knew it was going to be ball four. You see, he didn't start it out chest-high; he started it out belt-high. It looked like a fastball. Then when it broke, it broke so sharply that it was out of the strike zone. So I tried to hold up, but wasn't able to. There's that famous picture you see all the time—that's the end of my swing, right out in front of me; I never wrapped that bat around me; I never finished that swing; I was trying to hold up. But I knew, too, that I'd committed myself and that it was going to be strike three.

But even as I was trying to hold up I was thinking that the ball had broken so fast that Owen might have trouble with it too. Yes, sir, that went through my mind. There's another picture—I'm looking for that ball, I'm looking in a hurry. And I saw that little white jackrabbit bouncing, and I said, *Let's go.* It rolled all the way to the fence. I could have walked down to first.

When people talk about that top of the ninth inning all they seem to remember is Hugh Casey, Mickey Owen, and me. I always say, "Wait a minute. You're forgetting a few guys. What about DiMaggio coming up and hitting a screaming line drive to left for a single? And then what about Keller coming up and doubling off of that right-field screen to score us? And then Dickey walking, and Joe Gordon doubling to left for two more." That's what happened. We won it, 7–4. We beat them again the next day and ended the Series.

I guess one of the nicest things ever to happen to me took place in September, 1942. I was playing my final game before going into the Coast Guard. When I came up for my last time at bat the public-address announcer got on his microphone and told the fans that this was my last appearance for the duration. Well, it was a pretty good-sized crowd and jee-minnies did they let loose! They just rose up and cheered and cheered. It was a tremendous feeling for me, knowing they felt that way; though I'm sure that part of that outpouring was for all the fellows who were in or going in the service at that time.

I was embarrassed. I stepped out and tipped my hat. They kept cheering and applauding. Then I stepped back in and was ready to go. We were playing Detroit and Dizzy Trout was the pitcher. But he wasn't about to pitch. He just stood out there looking at me, saying, "This happens once in a lifetime. Enjoy it." He wouldn't pitch. He was a rough, tough guy, but I guess a sentimentalist at heart.

Finally the cheering died down and I stepped in and got ready. I figured now I've got to hit one to the moon for these people, after that. That's the way it should happen, right? Well, I took a few and missed a few, and the count went to three and two. I said to myself, "Forget about the moon—just hit the ball." Well, the next one came in and I hit a line drive to center for a single. And I'll tell you something—you'll never hear me say a word against Dizzy Trout, because he knew I was a fastball hitter, and he gave me six fastballs. That's some kind of class, isn't it?

Bob Feller once said that I was one of the toughest hitters for him, and I think that's a tremendous compliment, because he had as much super-stuff as I ever saw in my life. Why I got as many hits off of him as I did I'll never know.

As I said, I was a fastball hitter, and I don't know why Bobby gave me as many fastballs as he did, because he also had that remarkable

Heroes of the fourth game of the 1941 World Series. Tommy Henrich, who struck out, and Joe DiMaggio, Charlie Keller and Joe Gordon, who didn't.

curveball. I never asked him about it. Maybe he was a little bullheaded and was saying to himself, "You son of a gun, I *will* throw this by you." Because if he was, I was saying to myself, "Oh, no you won't."

I'll tell you something else. I'll show you how good Feller was. For two years we knew every pitch he was making with nobody on base. I'm not sure what the record shows for those two years, but I'd say we were around .500 with him. And these were years when he was right at the height of his greatness. You see, when he was going to throw his fastball his arms would be separated; when he was going to throw the curve he'd cover the ball with his glove. So for two years we knew every pitch he was going to make, with nobody on base, and still couldn't do better than .500 against him. That's how good Bob Feller was.

Talking about stealing those little advantages, Detroit had a guy coaching for them in those years who was as skillful at picking off the opposition's signs as anybody you can name: Del Baker. Not every hitter likes to get those signs, you know; they're afraid they might be crossed up and step into a pitch thinking it's a curve and find themselves face to face with a fastball. But Hank Greenberg didn't mind getting the signs when they were available.

One time Hank was in a slump, and at the same time Baker was having trouble picking up the other team's signs.

"Come on, Del," Hank says to Baker. "What's going on here? You're not giving me any signs."

Del says, "I'll tell you the truth—I'm not getting any."

And Greenberg, who's pretty frustrated by this time, says, "Well, *guess.*"

Hank was a great one. Power to burn. You know, back then, in the late thirties, when there was trouble in the eighth or ninth inning the cry always went up: "Bring in Murphy." Johnny Murphy, our great relief pitcher. One day we're in the bottom of the ninth, it's a tight game, and Greenberg is up. "Bring in Murphy." And that means Murphy is going to curve him, that's all there is to it. So here he comes, walking across the center field grass—in those days the bull pen in Briggs Stadium was out in center field. He passes by DiMaggio, and for the only time in his life that I ever heard of, DiMaggio has a thought for the pitcher. Joe has a brilliant idea.

"Why don't we fastball this guy once?"

Murphy thinks it over and by the time he reaches the mound he's saying to himself, "That's not a bad idea. Change the pattern."

So Johnny changed the pattern. And on the second pitch, *Pow!*, in the seats. That's the end of the ball game. We get into the clubhouse and Murphy's sitting there with his head in his hands, and DiMaggio's saying nothing. All of a sudden, after about five minutes, DiMaggio gets up and walks over to him.

"Let me tell you something," Joe says. "Don't you *ever* listen to anything I ever have to say again."

That was pretty funny, for Joe.

Joe of course was always in a class by himself. A very quiet and unassuming man. His performances out on that field day in and day out were hard-boiled and businesslike, and I don't think he ever looked upon himself as being anything special. In 1941 the team got together and bought Joe a gift, a sterling silver humidor, engraved with all our autographs. It was our way of paying tribute to him. Murphy presented it to him in the Shoreham Hotel in Washington. It came as a complete surprise to Joe and he was deeply moved by it. Joe didn't show emotion easily, but this was one occasion when he did. He said later that it was one of the nicest things ever to happen to him. Joe was surprised that his teammates thought that much of him.

Jimmie Foxx? A wonderful man. I loved him. You know, I saw Jimmie Foxx hit a home run in my hometown of Massillon when he was just a kid, about seventeen years old. He was with the Athletics then;

Joe DiMaggio, rounding first base after he tied and broke George Sisler's consecutive-game-hitting streak, June 30, 1941, in Griffith Stadium, Washington, D.C.

Connie Mack had just signed him up. They were playing an exhibition game against a semipro team, the Massillon Agathons. Must have been around 1925. Well, he tagged one, way out into the left-field corner and sprinted around for an inside-the-park home run.

Many years later, when I came up to the Yankees, we were playing the Red Sox and I got on first base. Jimmie walked over to hold me on. He was a great, good-natured, outgoing man.

"Well, Tommy," he said, "how's everything going?"

"Just fine, Jimmie," I said. Then I said, "You know, I remember a home run you hit in Massillon, Ohio, when you were just a kid with the A's. A home run inside the park."

"I remember that," he said. "Man, I belted that ball, didn't I?"

"You sure did," I said. "And you legged it around pretty good, too."

"Hey, I could run," he said. And he could, too.

In 1938, on Decoration Day, we played the Red Sox a double-header. We had the biggest crowd in the history of Yankee Stadium that day, around 80,000 people. Grove is pitching for them and they're ahead. Then we start to get to him. Lefty began to lose it and was getting wild. He came close to a couple of guys. McCarthy, our master psychologist, wants to get Grove out of there. He turns to Jake Powell and says, "You see what he's doing to us, Jake? You see how close he's coming? You going to let him get away with that stuff?"

Jake, who was a rough, aggressive character, says, "No sirree. He ain't gonna get away with throwing at us."

Now, when it becomes Jake's turn to hit, the Red Sox have taken Grove out of the game and brought in Archie McKain, another left-hander. So Jake is up there full of fire.The first pitch McKain throws is a curveball, inside. Well, now, that's enough for Jake. He's not going to stand for any more of this nonsense. So on the next pitch he's going to bunt the ball; you know, push it down to first, make the pitcher cover and spike him when crossing the bag. That good old play—which I've never seen happen. The next pitch is a curve that breaks too far inside and hits Jake. Well, that's all he needs. Jake drops his bat and goes for Archie McKain. But before he gets there Joe Cronin intercepts him, and they go at each other. They roll around on the grass, and then both of them are thrown out of the game.

McCarthy sends me in to run for Powell. I'm standing on the bag, next to Jimmie Foxx, while Cronin and Powell are leaving the field. In those days you had to leave through the Yankee dugout, which was on the third-base side then. They went through the dugout, and then went at each other again, underneath the stands. Our team found out about it and suddenly the whole bench empties and disappears down the runway. The Red Sox see that and naturally they go storming across the field, into our dugout and down the runway. Everybody is gone. There are two guys left on the field. Henrich and Foxx, at first base. Well, you know what he looked like—he had to turn sideways to get through a door; he was just a mountain of muscles. He looks at me and says, "Well, looks like they're choosing up sides."

For a minute I thought he was serious. Then I said, "Are you kidding? Get out of here, you big gorilla, you." And he laughed. He was a great man, a great, wonderful guy. And could he hit that ball!

Somebody once asked Gomez who hit the longest ball off of him.

"Foxx," Gomez said.

"Where'd he hit it?" the guy asked.

"He hit it in the upper deck of the left-field corner in Yankee Stadium. Way back in the upper deck."

"How far is that?" the guy asked.

"I don't know how *far* it is," Gomez said, "but it takes you forty-five minutes to walk up there."

I'll tell you another one on Foxx. He's out in Comiskey Park one day putting on a show in batting practice, pumping one after the other into the upper deck. Finally somebody says, "Ah, for Pete's sake, you're so doggone big and strong; what would you do if you had to hit-and-run like we do?"

Jimmie was indignant. "I can hit-and-run," he says. "I can hit behind the runner anytime I want to."

The guy is skeptical.

"I'll prove it to you," Jimmie says. "I'll hit-and-run today."

So, sure enough, during the game he comes up with a man on first. Jimmie gets the sign to hit behind the runner. The pitch comes in, the runner takes off, Jimmie chokes up and punches the ball—on a line into the right-field seats. He hit behind the runner all right; he hit behind the outfielder, too.

I remember the year Ted Williams came up, 1939. Early in the season he and I were sitting in Yankee Stadium talking about hitting the long ball. He'd already hit some clouts, one out of Briggs Stadium, one out of here, one out of there.

"Did anybody ever hit a ball out of Yankee Stadium?" he asked.

"No," I said, "and don't get any dumb ideas either."

"Why?"

"It's further than you think."

He looked out toward right field. Sort of measuring it. I just knew what he was thinking.

So the next time they came to New York I was watching them take batting practice. Ted caught hold of one; it was a beauty. Man, he drilled that thing up into the third deck, right into an exit. Quite a shot.

But still not out. I yelled, "Hey, Ted." He turned around. "You give up?" I asked. He grinned and yelled back, "Hey, don't tell anybody I said that, huh?" But he had ideas about doing it.

I saw Ted for the first time in spring training. Of course he looked good up there, but you never know how good a guy really is until you've seen him for a while. But Ted was always confident. And to say the least, he knew the strike zone.

We had a clubhouse meeting before our first series with the Red Sox. We talked about Cronin, Foxx, going down their lineup. We get around to Williams. What do we know about Williams? Spud Chandler wants to know. He's pitching. Well, the consensus was pitch him high and tight, low and away. The old words of wisdom. So we went out and played. And Ted had a pretty good day. The next day we're talking again. What did we learn about Williams? Chandler speaks up.

"Well, I'll tell you what I found out," he says. "High and tight is ball one, and low and away is ball two."

Then Bill Dickey, in his own quiet way, said, "Boys, he's just a damned good hitter."

And that sizes up Ted Williams. That's what we found out, after one look. And it stuck.

I'll tell you another great man with that bat—Buddy Lewis of the old Washington Senators. Talk about bat control, he was an artist. I used to drool watching Buddy Lewis handle a ball bat. He could hit a pitch just about anywhere he wanted. They had another guy with Washington at that time, Cecil Travis. My first year up I hear the guys moaning about Travis. Ruffing especially. There weren't too many hitters who gave Ruffing trouble, but you mention Travis and he just shook his head. I'm watching him pitch to that guy and Travis is slicing line drives to left field like it's the easiest thing in the world.

"Hey, Charlie," I said to him one time, "how come you never change up on Cecil Travis?"

He smiled. This was my first year up, remember. "We did that, Tom," he said. "Believe me, we tried it. We pitch him fast balls to get him to single to left; when we change up he triples to right."

The '47 Series? Well, I was the man in the middle again, wasn't I? That's right, I was out there in right field when Cookie Lavagetto hit that line drive to break up Bevens' no-hitter and win the ball game. I would say that those were the toughest five seconds of my life.

Remember now, it's the last of the ninth, the Dodgers have men on first and second, there are two out, and we're winning by a run. On top of that, of course, Bill Bevens has the no-hitter going.

While Lavagetto hits the ball I know immediately it's a good line drive. As an experienced outfielder, I know the ball is tagged very well

Ted Williams.

and that it's going to reach the wall. What I don't know is if it's going to be too high for me to go to the wall and catch, and if it is then I have to get set to play a rebound. But if it's only six feet high and I decide to stay off of the wall to play a rebound, then I've booted it. Now don't forget, I don't have much time to get there. As it turned out, I couldn't have gotten there anyway; so there's no way for me to second-guess myself. In the meantime, I lose that ball for a fraction of a second—don't ask me how. This is beautiful, right? What a spot. Then I pick it up again, and now I find it's too high for me to catch. But I had been going to the wall, playing it like I can catch it. But when it comes out and I see it I know I *cannot* get that ball, and I tell myself, "Get the heck off that wall as fast as you can."

It was going to happen fast, you see. I was so close to the wall that I knew the ball was going to rebound to me on the fly. It's going to be bang-bang and my glove had better be there. There wasn't much time, but actually I lined up pretty well. The ball came back and hit my glove—but it hit the heel of the glove while I was pulling toward the infield to get set to throw. So the ball drops down, and now I've got to stop and come back and get it. You know how long that takes? A good three seconds. And that's the second run. If I catch the ball cleanly and throw it in, Eddie Miksis, who's carrying the winning run from first, will have to stop on third. But because I have to turn around and go back for the ball, that's one more base for him. It was no contest for him; he scored easily. That's where I lost it, because the ball dropped.

Now, you might say I should have got off the wall and played for a rebound to begin with. Well, that's fine—but suppose the ball was six feet high? What does Bevens think? I gave away a no-hitter. But as I say, it all happened in five seconds, and I won't second-guess myself. Not in that kind of situation. And I also say those are five seconds I could have lived without.

But I can tell you what happened the next day. We're still in Ebbets Field. Frank Shea has them beat 2–1 in the last of the ninth. There's a man on first and two out, and we know that Lavagetto is going to pinch hit. You wonder: Can that guy do it again? I was standing near DiMaggio in the outfield, and we look at each other. Would you believe that he said to me, "For Christ's sake, say a prayer"? That's exactly what he said. DiMaggio.

Shea strikes Lavagetto out. We run into the clubhouse and I go over to Crosetti. "Get a load of this," I said. "What do you think the big guy said when Lavagetto came up?" And I tell him. Crosetti's reaction is, "Why didn't you tell him to pray?" That's pretty good, right? So I go over to DiMaggio. "What do you think Crosetti said?" And I repeat it to him. And Joe says, "I *was* praying. I wasn't sure if I was getting through."

We won it again in '49, after a heck of a battle with the Red Sox. They came into the stadium for the last two games of the season needing only one to clinch it. We beat them on Saturday, on a home run by big John Lindell. That put us in a tie, so it came down to the last game of the season.

The Red Sox started Ellis Kinder. Rizzuto led off for us with a double, and Williams had trouble on the wall in left field and played it into a triple. So we've got a man on third in the first inning, nobody out, and I'm up. And I can't hit Ellis Kinder nohow. I take a look to see how they're playing me, and they're giving us the run. The right side of the infield is playing back, which means if I can hit a ball on the ground to the right, we've got a run. Well, that was about how good I was against Kinder—about a ground ball's worth. I knew one thing: I was not going to pop up. I made up my mind that I was going to put that ball on the ground. And I did. I hit about a fourteen-hopper to second base and Rizzuto scored.

That run held up to the eighth inning, when they had to take Kinder out for a pinch hitter, because they hadn't scored yet, with big Vic Raschi mowing them down. Now they bring Mel Parnell in to pitch to us in the last of the eighth. I'm the lead-off hitter. And I get lucky and hit one in the seats, so now we're ahead 2–0. Then we get three more and we go into the ninth ahead by five runs.

They got a few base hits and the next thing we knew they had three runs. DiMaggio had been sick with the flu all week, and he took himself out of the game in that inning because he felt he was hurting us in the field. Cliff Mapes took his place in center. Somebody flies out to Mapes for the second out. I'm playing first base and I position myself at the mound to take the throw in. Mapes throws it over my head to Yogi at home plate. Raschi is backing up Yogi. So I'm standing at the mound. Yogi come out and we wait there for Vic. And here he comes, scowling; he's all business. Vic Raschi was always all business. I know Yogi is going to give him the old, "Come on, Vic old boy, just one more." That's what I'm going to say, too. As Vic gets close to us he says, "Give me the damned ball and get the hell out of here." We left. And as I walked to first base I said to myself, "We're in."

Birdie Tebbetts is the batter. He hits a foul ball in the air down to first base. I didn't have to move more than a few feet. But I hear Jerry Coleman yelling behind me: "I got it! I got it!" Jerry called for everything. "Get out of here!" I yelled. He wasn't taking that one. That was my ball. That was the one I'd been looking for all year long.

So we went into the Series, against the Dodgers again. That first game was as good a pitching duel as you'll ever want to see, Allie Reynolds against Don Newcombe. Nobody got close to a run until the bottom of the ninth. I led off that inning. Newcombe tried a fastball and missed outside. Then he came back with kind of a slider and missed outside again. Now it's two balls and no strikes. He hasn't walked anybody all game, and nobody wants to start an inning with a base on balls. So I say to myself, "This is going to be a good ball." I was ninety-nine percent certain he was going to throw his fastball and that it would be over the plate.

So I'm geared for the right speed now. Everything was my way, right? Hitting the ball was something else again, but at least I knew I had every advantage. If I had been anything less than positive about it I would have sacrificed part of that advantage. Newk came in there with it and I tagged it good and solid. I knew it was hit hard enough, but sometimes that kind of ball sinks before it has a chance to go out. As I ran down the line I looked at Furillo and as soon as I saw his head go up a little bit I said to myself, "*That's all.*" I knew it was going to go out.

That got us going in that Series. We won it in five games. You know, I participated in eight World Series, as a player and a coach, and was never on a loser. Never saw the losing side of a World Series. That's pretty good, isn't it?

Riding the train in 1950. As usual, the Yankees of those years had a lot to laugh about.

EWELL BLACKWELL

Ewell Blackwell
Born: October 23, 1922, Fresno, California
Major-league career: 1942-53, 1955, Cincinnati Reds, New
   York Yankees, Kansas City Athletics
Lifetime record: 82 wins, 78 losses

In 1947 Ewell Blackwell put together one of the most remarkable seasons a pitcher ever had. In addition to leading
the league with 22 wins, 23 complete games, and 193 strikeouts, Blackwell startled the baseball world with a 16-game
winning streak that included a no-hitter and a near miss of a
second consecutive no-hitter. After suffering an arm injury
in 1948, Blackwell returned to have several more successful
years for Cincinnati.

I was pitching for an aircraft company team in Downey, California,
in 1941 and a lot of big-league scouts were coming to my front
door. I signed with Cincinnati and I can tell you exactly why. They
had a farm club in Ogden, Utah, where my mother originally was from.
Well, we thought it would be nice if I went there to pitch. So, when the
Reds promised they'd send me to Ogden, I signed with them.
   They took me to spring training with them in Florida, and I was
throwing the ball pretty good. One say a front office guy walked up to
me and said, "Blackie, you're not going to Ogden."
   "Listen," I said, "that was the deal."
   "It's all changed," he said.
   I didn't like the sound of it until they told me they were tearing up
my contract and signing me to a big-league contract. Well, I sure
wasn't going to complain about that, was I? I got into a few games for
the Reds but spent most of my time with Syracuse in the International
League. I won fifteen games. Then I went into the service. This was
1942.
   I was supposed to go to Norman, Oklahoma, to join the Navy. Had

my railroad ticket and was all set to leave. Then that afternoon President Roosevelt came on the air and said all enlistments were canceled. A week later I went into the infantry.

I was in the service for three years, three months, and three days. Went through France, Germany, and ended up the furthest east of any ground troops, in Austria, where we met up with the Russians. I was with the Third Army, Patton's army. Old Blood and Guts. Our blood and his guts.

I was discharged in the spring of '46 and headed for Tampa, where the Reds were already in training. I had played a little ball in Europe before leaving, so I was in pretty good shape and had every intention of making the club. Bill McKechnie was managing the Reds then, and he was a man who knew every aspect of baseball, frontwards and backwards. He helped me tremendously. I made the club all right. I won nine and lost thirteen that year, and led the league in shutouts with six.

Even though I'd had a losing record, I still felt pretty good about things. I was confident I was going to do better in 1947.

Things seemed to be happening pretty quickly for me—first year in Triple A and then out of the service and right into the big leagues. But I wasn't all that surprised. I always wanted to be a baseball player, from the time I was in elementary school, out in San Dimas, California. It's hard to believe today, but at that time I wondered if I'd ever be big enough to play ball. When I was a sophomore in high school I was five feet five. In my junior year I went to six-three, and in my senior year to six-six. No, it wasn't so surprising; they seemed to run to height on my father's side of the family. They were all very tall men. I just took my time getting up there, that's all.

My dad encouraged me to play ball. He built a "control box" for me and hung it on the garage wall in the backyard. It was a frame of the strike zone. I'd stand out there about three hours a day and try to throw to spots in it, using old baseballs or a tennis ball, whatever was most handy. I always had pretty good control, and I think all that early throwing helped.

When I was a freshman in high school I went out for the football team, even though I was real small then. They had me playing guard, which I don't think was a very good idea. One day there was a play and some big guy landed on my shoulder and gave me a pretty sound shaking up. Now, I don't know if that accounted for it or not, but I never could get up and throw overhand with any real power. So I pitched sidearm. The so-called "Whip" delivery. I never thought too much about it. It was just my way of throwing, that's all. To me sidearm is more natural, anyway. There isn't as much strain on your arm as there is in throwing overhand.

Ewell Blackwell in 1947. "It was just my way of throwing, that's all."

That delivery was rough on righthanded batters. With the height I had, coming from way around with that ball, it was tough for them to pick up. Some of those righties would come up to me and swear it was the third baseman pitching to them. I've had many guys taking called strikes lying flat on their backs, thinking the ball was coming right at them. But, as I said, that delivery was very natural to me.

When I had my good stuff, before I hurt my arm, I never cared who was standing up there with the bat, righty or lefty. Stan Musial was a great hitter, but he never hit a home run off of me. Neither did Johnny Mize. He still can't understand that. John used to have a liquor store in Florida, you know, and he had the shelves lined with baseballs autographed by the pitchers he'd hit home runs off. I walked in there one day and stood gazing at all of those baseballs.

"John," I said, "where's my baseball?" He growled a little and said, "You don't have one."

Johnny had his laugh on me, though. This happened in the Polo Grounds, in 1946. It was two out in the bottom of the ninth and I had a big lead, and at the same time was working on a big old chaw of tobacco in my mouth. I threw a pitch to Mize and he hit a line drive. I never saw it, but I heard it—it whistled right by my ear. I was so startled I swallowed that whole plug. I thought I was going to die, right out there on the mound, in front of all those people. Somehow I got the next man out to end the game, then took off for the clubhouse. That was about five hundred feet away, if you remember. I just did make it, but when I got in there they told me I had more colors in my face than a rainbow.

I'll tell you about another hitter. The best I ever saw. A fellow I pitched against in a high school tournament. Ted Williams. That's right. I pitched for the high school in San Dimas and Ted for the one in San Diego. That's the first time I ever saw him. He was a pretty good-looking pitcher. But he looked even better with the bat.

I always loved to watch Ted hit. One spring, when I was with the Reds, we were heading north and played an exhibition game against the Red Sox in Birmingham, Alabama. The wind was blowing in from right field at about forty miles an hour. The guys on the bench were saying that you would need a cannon to get the ball through that wind.

Ted was leading off an inning late in the game and I called my catcher, Ray Mueller, out to the mound.

"Let's see how strong he really is," I said. "You tell him I'm going to throw a fastball belt-high right down the middle."

Mueller went back and gave Ted the message. The first pitch I threw was right there. Ted jumped on it and hit a line drive straight through that wind into the right-field seats. I wasn't at all surprised—he had the greatest eyes and wrists of any hitter I ever saw.

As I said, I was confident I was going to have a good year in '47 and I did. On May 10 I had a 2–2 record and started a game against the Cubs. I won that game and then didn't lose again until July 30. In between I won sixteen straight. Every one was a complete game, too, and five of them were shutouts.

The eighth game of the streak was a no-hitter against the Braves. That was a night game at Cincinnati, on June 18. The score was 6–0. Remember Babe Young, the first baseman? Well, we'd just bought him from the Giants and he had just reported that morning. He went right into the lineup. He came up in the first inning with two on and hit a home run. Then around the fifth or sixth inning he hit another home run with two men on. That was my six runs. His first day in town.

He walked up to me in the clubhouse after the game and said, "Blackie, here I am a 'pheenom' tonight, and you had to be a double 'pheenom.'" Here's a fellow joins a team and in his first game knocks in all six runs with two homers and after it's over nobody's paying him any attention. I paid him some attention though, you can be sure.

I had real good stuff that night. I think the closest anybody came to a hit was Bama Rowell. He hit a line drive in the fourth or fifth inning that Frankie Baumholtz caught against the right-field screen. Johnny Hopp tried to bunt his way on in the ninth inning, but Ray LaManno made a great play coming from behind the plate and threw him out.

You know, my third baseman, Grady Hatton, who was also my room-mate and good friend, didn't even know I had a no-hitter in the works. I had two men out in the ninth and was really taking my time on that last hitter. You come that far, you *want* it. All of a sudden I look up and here's Grady walking over to the mound, as casual as could be.

"For cryin' out loud, Blackie," he says, "I'm tired. Throw the ball down the middle and let him hit the damn thing. Let's go home."

I thought he'd gone out of his mind or something. I looked at him and there must have been homicide in my eyes, because he turned around and got out of there in a hurry. I can laugh now, but it wasn't so funny then. But I got the last man out and the fans went wild, and the team came running out to pound me around—and Grady still didn't know what was going on. He finally came up to me later in the club-house wearing the most sheepish grin you ever saw.

"Next time pay attention," I said.

Well, the next time *everybody* paid attention. It was four days later, on June 22, and I was starting against the Dodgers. I suppose you might say that's the most well-remembered game I ever pitched, more so even than the no-hitter. Were there any thoughts about a second con-secutive no-hitter? Yes, there were. I went on a talk show right after pitching the no-hitter and I told the guy I was going to pitch another one next time out. You're not supposed to say that, are you? What made me say it? I don't know. I just felt strong, felt I had real good stuff. Sure, that was a pretty nervy thing to say over the air, but I wasn't talking bigger than I could handle, because there should have been the second no-hitter. Didn't miss it by more than an eyeblink.

I had a good feeling from the moment I began warming up. Just never felt better. I walked out onto that mound with all the confidence in the world.

The way things developed, though, I had a tougher game on my hands than I bargained for. Joe Hatten started for the Dodgers and he seemed to have the same idea I did—through four innings neither one of us had given up a base hit. Eddie Miller finally got a double in the fifth. In the sixth Hatten walked four men and we took a 1–0 lead.

By the top of the ninth we were leading, 4–0, and I still had the no-hitter going. You know, looking back, it was interesting how many coincidences were at work. The only man in major-league history ever to pitch consecutive no-hitters also pitched for Cincinnati—Johnny Vander Meer. He'd pitched them in the same month that I was going after mine—June. And not only that, but he had pitched them against the same clubs and in the same order as I was hoping to do—the Braves and the Dodgers. And to cap it all off, Johnny Vander Meer was still with Cincinnati and was sitting on the top step of the dugout, waiting to come out and shake my hand.

First man up in the ninth was a pinch hitter, Gene Hermanski. He flied out to Augie Galan in left.

Eddie Stanky was next. He took a pitch for a ball.

Then on the next pitch he hit it back to me. I thought he had hit it harder than he actually had; when it's hit straight back at you it's sometimes hard to judge just how fast it's moving. But it wasn't hit as hard as I thought—in fact he'd broken his bat on it—and I made my move too quickly. I went down for it and came up thinking I had the ball. Well, I didn't have it. It went under my glove and right through my legs, rolled through the infield and died on the center-field grass, about twenty feet out.

I just stood there looking at that ball, that little white ball lying on the grass. How did I feel? Well, I figured about $100,000 had gone down the drain, and I felt accordingly.

I won the game, 4–0. That was the ninth win in the streak. I was going for my seventeenth, against the Giants, when I finally lost one. I was leading them, 4–3, with one out in the ninth, with a count of two strikes and no balls on Willard Marshall. I tried to brush him back, but that was one of the times the ball didn't go where I wanted it to; it went right down the middle of the plate, and it went where he wanted it to. He hit a home run and tied it up.

Then in the tenth they got a man in scoring position with two out

Ewell Blackwell in 1949.

and Buddy Kerr up. I got two strikes on him, then threw a pitch that, so help me, cut the middle of the plate belt-high. I swear I never threw a cleaner strike. But the umpire missed it. So I had to try it again, and this time Buddy looped it over short for a base hit and that beat me, 5–4.

No, I didn't take that home with me. I left it right there in the ball park. I wasn't the sort to brood over what happened on the field. As they say, it's a game of seconds and inches; it can't be played any other way. You could, if you wanted, brood over everything that happens in a game, it all happens so fast; but there's no sense in letting it get to you.

But while I hated to see the winning streak come to an end, in some ways it was a relief. That sort of thing can become a burden. It got so I felt like I was carrying a piano on my back every time I went to the mound.

You know, some people thought I might be putting too much strain on my elbow the way I whipped my arm around to deliver the ball. But the elbow never has bothered me in my life. When I did hurt my arm it was in the top of the shoulder. It happened in an exhibition game in Columbia, South Carolina. We'd been training in Tampa, in real fine weather, and then broke camp and began heading north. We played a game with the Boston Braves in Columbia. It was a week before opening day. I hadn't gone more than six innings in a game in Florida, but Luke Sewell, who was managing, said I had better try to go nine in that game. It was a miserable day, wet and cold and windy. In the eighth inning something just popped in my shoulder. I finished the game all right, but I had torn some kind of a nerve in my shoulder.

It became painful for me to throw a ball. I'd wind up and begin to deliver and halfway through my delivery it would suddenly feel like somebody was sinking his teeth into my shoulder. I tried to pitch out of it but couldn't. My wins dropped from twenty-two in 1947 to seven the next year. Then, in January of '49, I had a kidney out. I just couldn't throw right and won only five games. But in '50 I came back strong and won seventeen and in '51 I won sixteen. Then in '52 I had a bad year and went to the Yankees. I was just about through then.

I started one game at Ebbets Field early in 1952, I never will forget it. In the bottom of the first I walked a few and then gave up a few hits. Sewell came out.

"Blackie," he said, "it's not your night."

"I'm getting the same idea," I said.

Bud Byerly came in to relieve and I left. I went into the clubhouse, took a shower, then left the ball park and took a cab back to the Commodore Hotel over in Manhattan. I went into the bar and sat down for a drink. They had the game on television and when I looked up at it I heard the announcer say Brooklyn was still hitting in the bottom of the first inning. I thought he had to be mistaken, but he kept saying it over and over. The Dodgers were going around those bases like they were on a merry-go-round. They scored fifteen runs that inning. I couldn't believe that I was sitting in a bar in Manhattan looking at the bottom of the first inning of a game I'd started over an hour and a half ago in Brooklyn.

Then the next thing I know Bud Byerly comes in and sits down next to me.

"What inning they in?" he asks.

"Bottom of the first," I said.

He didn't say anything.

"Don't you want to know what the score is?" I asked.

"Frankly," he said, "no."

"Don't feel so bad," I said. "At least they can't blame it *all* on us."

But the pitching did tighten up a bit after the first inning and the final score was only something like 19–2.

I remember at the end of one season, it must have been around '49, we had the wildest train ride home. We ended the season in Pittsburgh and the club had arranged to have two Pullman cars to take the players who wanted to go, back to Cincinnati.

After the game we got on the train. They had those Sunday blue laws in Pennsylvania, which meant you couldn't buy beer or liquor or anything else to celebrate the end of a baseball season with. So we arranged with the railroad people to have the men's rooms in our private cars all filled with beer and about three cases of liquor.

We sat on the train for about an hour before it took off and by that time the beer and liquor were all gone. So when the train began rolling everybody was feeling real good. There was a lot of noise and some hi-jinks. About an hour later the conductor came back and said they were going to disconnect us from the train and put us on a siding because we were causing too much trouble. Just leave us there. Walker Cooper—he was just about the strongest man I've ever known—went up to him and said, "I don't know what your name is today, but it's going to be shit tomorrow if you try that." The conductor went away.

Then we stopped someplace in West Virginia. It was supposed to be a thirty-minute stop. Cooper and our trainer, Doc Bohm, got off to get some more beer. No sooner were they off than the train started up again. Well, we figured we'd see them again in the spring.

We cruised along for about thirty minutes and then all of a sudden came to a screeching halt, in the middle of nowhere. Pitch black outside. We looked out and couldn't believe it—here's Cooper and Doc Bohm walking up the tracks, each of them carrying two cases of beer.

What those guys had done was hailed a cab and told the driver he had to beat that train to the next crossing. When they got there they made the driver straddle the tracks with his cab, to make the train stop. So they got back on, the cab went away, and here we go again.

It was still quite a way to Cincinnati and things kept getting wilder. Soon nobody had any buttons left on his shirt. I didn't have any buttons or any sleeves either on mine. Then Cooper started going around and reaching back into your pants and ripping your underwear off. He'd take the top of your shorts in his hand and just rip them right off you. Grady Hatton tried to go to sleep and somebody poured a bucket of water on him. A good time was had by all.

When we pulled into Cincinnati we were in great shape. We came rolling off of that train without buttons, without underwear, half of us without shirts. We were the drunkest, happiest, noisiest baseball team that ever got off a train. But then all of a sudden you could have heard a pin drop. There wasn't a sound, because there they were—our wives, standing in a group waiting for us. I don't think we realized what we looked like until we saw the expressions on their faces. My wife said we were the sorriest-looking bunch of people she ever did see.

Very quietly we all shook hands, wished each other a good winter, promised to meet again in the spring, and then went home to face the music.

BUDDY HASSETT

JOHN ALOYSIUS HASSETT
Born: September 5, 1911, New York, New York
Major-league career: 1936–42, Brooklyn Dodgers, Boston
    Braves, New York Yankees
Lifetime average: .292

A first baseman in the Yankee farm system in the days of
Lou Gehrig, Buddy Hassett came to the big leagues with the
Brooklyn Dodgers. His career was marked by quiet consis-
tency; only once did his batting average slip under .284, and
three times it was better than .300. He entered the Navy after
the 1942 season and did not return to the big leagues when
the war was over.

I got started playing ball right on the sidewalks of New York, in the
1920's. Played a lot of semipro ball around the city. Semipro was a
big thing in those days. We'd pass the hat during the game and this was
how we helped the team going. If there was some rain during the game
the manager would hand me a megaphone and I'd sing "When Irish
Eyes Are Smiling" and other songs to the fans, to keep them enter-
tained until the rain passed. I always had a pretty good voice.

I was attending Manhattan College when Paul Krichell, the old Yankee scout, had a look and decided he liked what he saw. Upon gradua-
tion in 1933 I signed a contract with the Yankees, and they sent me
down to Wheeling in the Middle-Atlantic League. I had a good year,
then had a couple more good years, at Norfolk and Columbus, where I
played on option. I hit. 332, .360, and .337, but I wasn't any closer to
playing first base for the Yankees than I was on the day I started. They
had a roadblock up there named Lou Gehrig; so it didn't make much
difference how well you did. George McQuinn was in the organization
the same time I was, and we shared the problem.

So I asked to be traded and they accommodated me, selling me to

Buddy Hassett in 1937.

Brooklyn in '36. I went over there and that was my first exposure to Charles Dillon Stengel, who was managing the Dodgers then. He was a great person and a good baseball man. Playing for him was a memorable experience.

Stengel was a vivid character, but so were a lot of the fellows we had with the Dodgers in those years. Van Lingle Mungo was one. Gee, he was a great pitcher; but he could do some funny things too. Now and then he'd jump the ball club and get lost for a couple of days. Frenchy Bordagaray was another one. Good-natured guy. Always happy. He came to spring training in 1936 with a goatee and mustache. What a fuss it caused! Today it wouldn't mean anything, but in 1936 it was really something different.

I remember one day we were playing an exhibition game. A ball was hit over Frenchy's head; it wasn't a matter of him catching it, it was a matter of him running it down. He wheeled around and started running, and as he ran his cap flew off. Well, most people would run the ball down first, wouldn't they? But Frenchy wasn't most people. He went back, got his cap, and then went after the ball. Stengel stood in the dugout with his arms hanging and his mouth open. He couldn't believe what he was seeing. When Frenchy got back to the bench Stengel asked him what he thought he was doing out there. "The cap wasn't going anywhere, Bordagaray," Casey said, "but the ball was." "I forgot," Frenchy said.

Another time Frenchy got into an argument with an umpire and in the course of it spit in the umpire's face. Of course the umpire ran him out of there, even though Frenchy claimed he had simply been talking fast and that you can't help spraying a little when you do that. Then the league fined him fifty dollars and when he heard about it, Frenchy said, "That's more than I expectorated."

Once Frenchy was on second with two out and we're down a run. Stengel was coaching third and he kept yelling at Frenchy not to come over, to stay there. Sure enough, on the next pitch here he comes, stealing third, with two out. He slides in and makes it. Stengel walks over and looks down at him.

"I ought to fine you for that," Casey says.

"With the lead I had," Frenchy says, "you ought to fine yourself for not inviting me over."

But that was the way we did things in Brooklyn in those days. We had Max Butcher. I don't know if you recall Max or not. He was a pretty fair pitcher. Max's eyes were always blinking, and the guys used to say that he pitched between blinks. In 1937 Burleigh Grimes was managing the club. We were playing an exhibition game and Burleigh was coaching first base. The steal sign was when he winked at us. "When I wink, you go," he said. Then in the middle of the game he gets a long-distance phone call and has to leave the field. They put Max in to coach first base. Gibby Brack gets on. Gibby, Lord rest his soul, wasn't the brightest guy in the world. He looks at Max, Max's eyes are blinking away, and Gibby lights out for second. He's shot down by about fifteen feet, just as Grimes is coming back. Burleigh starts roaring. "Who gave that steal sign?" And somebody says, "Nobody gave it, but look who's coaching first base." And there's big Max Butcher standing there, blinking away.

We had Babe Phelps, too, in those years. Great hitter. Wonderful fellow. They tell a story about Babe—I don't know if it's true or not—that he built a home in Maryland and forgot to put a toilet in it. Then we had Freddy Frankhouse, the pitcher. Freddy was always looking out the window hoping it would rain. He loved rainy days. I asked him once what he did on rainy days. "Nothing," he said. He just liked having the day off.

We were always scrambling for players back then, signing anybody we thought might help, no matter how much mileage they had on them. We had big George Earnshaw for a while. Heinie Manush was with us for a year or so, too. He used to call me "The Red-necked Thrush." "You're always either singing or you're mad," he said. Great line-drive hitter. He came up under Cobb, and Cobb worked with him and taught him an awful lot. Now there, as far as I'm concerned, is probably the greatest of them all, Ty Cobb. When you look at that average of .367 over twenty-four years it's just phenomenal. They say he was a driving, slashing player. Never went out onto the field to make friends. I met Cobb only once. I was coming out of the Yankee Stadium after a World Series game with Paul Krichell and we bumped into Cobb. Paul introduced me and then they stepped aside to talk. Later, when we were driving out, Paul said, "Now there's a funny one."

"What's that?" I asked.

"What do you think he wanted to talk to me about?"

"I don't know, Paul," I said.

"He told me that he would give up all his money and just about everything he's got if the fellows he played with and against would only accept him and talk to him today."

That's a pretty sad commentary; but at the same time it gives you some idea what he must have been like out on that field.

We had Waite Hoyt and Kiki Cuyler, too, for a while. And Freddie Lindstrom was with us in '36. I saw Freddie play his last game. He was out in left field. We were playing the Giants in the Polo Grounds, it was the last of the ninth, the tying run was on second base, and I think Mel Ott was on first with the winning run. Somebody hit a pop fly into short left and Lindstrom came running in, the shortstop went running out, and it was "I got it, you take it, who's got it." The ball dropped in and both runs scored and we lose the game. Lindstrom came into the clubhouse and said, "I'm a son of a gun. I heard about these things that happen in Brooklyn. I never thought it would happen to me, and I'll tell you, it's never going to happen again." He took off his uniform and never put it on again.

In 1939 I was traded over to Boston. Stengel was managing up there then, so it was a reunion. We had a situation there one day which, to say the least, was highly unusual. There was a certain guy on the club whose ambition it was to drive in a hundred runs that year. That's very commendable, of course, and every hitter would like to do it; but with this guy it became an obsession. Every time he came up with a man in scoring position you'd see him grinding the sawdust out of the bat handle. Listen, I'd rather not mention his name; let's just call him "RBI."

We were playing the Phillies this day and beating them about 12–5. I always used to say thank the Lord for the Phillies, because they kept me out of eighth place just about every year I was in the National League. Frank Demaree led off with a single, and I'm the batter. Well, as I always said, the pitcher had good control and he hit my bat, and the ball fell over the third baseman's head for a double. Up comes RBI. You could see the gleam in his eye—men on second and third and nobody out.

The first pitch is right down the middle, and he pops it up. You never saw a guy so disgusted. He flung his bat away and went through the motions of running down to first. He gave the bag a kick, turned around and began walking back go the dugout, which was on the third-base side. He's got his head down and he's muttering to himself. While he's walking, the pitcher is beginning to work to the next hitter, who happened to be Paul Waner.

They liked to work inside to Paul in those years, figuring he'd have trouble getting around on those pitches. Well, the first pitch is way inside and off the catcher's glove and rolls right across RBI's path—he's still looking down and muttering. Frank Demaree's on third and he starts storming down the line. The catcher—it was Bennie Warren—for some reason never left the plate. RBI sees the ball, doesn't know what's happening, picks it up and flips it to Bennie Warren who then whirls around and tags out Demaree sliding into home plate. This actually happened.

I go over to third base on the play and say to Stengel, who's coaching there, "Casey, do you think they'll give him an assist on the play?" I don't think he heard me; he was fit to be tied.

The next pitch is another wild one and now I come in to score—successfully, what with no teammate hanging around the plate to throw me out. I go into the dugout and there's RBI, walking up and down, mortified and miserable; not only did he pop up with ducks on the pond, but now he's pulled this boner. He's walking up and down, still not paying attention. All of a sudden Waner fouls a screamer right into the dugout and hits RBI on the side of the head. He goes down like he was poleaxed. Naturally we ran to pick him up, but Casey comes running over from third base yelling, "Don't anybody touch the son of a bitch; let him lay there—it might drive some sense into him."

You know, I roomed with Paul Waner for a while. He could drink pretty good. That's no secret. But he could also sober himself up in a hurry. He would do backflips. He had remarkable agility, like an acrobat. Fifteen or twenty minutes of backflips and he was cold sober, ready to go out to the ball park and get his three hits.

Paul was a very serious-minded person. He studied the writings of Seneca. This is what he read. And he had his little sayings. We were playing a game of pepper one time and right out of the blue I hear Paul saying to me, "You know, they say money talks. But the only thing it ever says to me is 'Good-bye!'"

Jimmie Wilson, the old catcher, told me a story about Paul. They were playing against each other one day and each time Paul came to the plate he asked Jimmie where he wanted the ball hit. "I called the right and left-field lines four times," Jimmie said, "And he hit four doubles right where I said, and of course we're pitching him exactly opposite."

Paul and I would get to talking hitting. Of course when you're in close proximity to such a fine hitter you want to talk to him about it, hoping that somehow something might rub off. But he had no great theories. He said he just laid that bat on his shoulder and when he saw a pitch he liked he threw it off. That's all. Simple, isn't it? Lay the bat on your shoulder and then throw it off.

I'll tell you about a guy who was a great ballplayer and who should have been one of the greatest: Pete Reiser. He came out of nowhere in 1941 and in his first full season led the league in batting. He had everything—speed, power, good arm, good fielder. I always felt that he played *too* hard. He was a very intense kid. He suffered those injuries—running into walls, breaking bones—that he might otherwise have avoided. But it was his style of playing, I guess. He was an awful tough man to play against because he could be explosive in any situation, whether it was in the field, at bat, on the bases.

Now, let's talk about Arky Vaughan. This is one of my pet peeves. Why isn't he in the Hall of Fame? Here was another guy who could do it all. A .300 hitter, year in and year out, and he could run and field with

Arky Vaughan. "Why isn't he in the Hall of Fame?"

the best of them. You know, there was a time when I bore a slight facial resemblance to Arky. One day I was coming out of Ebbets Field after a game with the Pirates. When I hit the street a dirty-faced little kid came up to me and said, "Hey, Arky, will you give me your autograph?" I thought it over for a second, then took his scorecard and signed Arky Vaughan. It felt nice.

In the winter of '41 I was working as a plumber in upstate New York when I heard I'd been traded to the Yankees. It was a surprise, a very pleasant surprise. That year, 1942, was my last in the big leagues, and it's nice to say I went out a winner. After all those years in the second division in the National League I finally got into a World Series, against the Cardinals. I played in only three games because in that third game I was trying to bunt against Ernie White and the ball came in on me and broke my finger. That finished me for the Series, and as a matter of fact, I never played major league ball again, because I went into the Navy after the season. But the nice thing was that after having signed with the Yankees so many years before, and after having spent all of my career with the Dodgers and Braves, when I did get into a World Series it was with the Yankees. So it finally came full circle, you might say.

A few years ago I attended a B'nai B'rith gathering where a lot of the old Dodgers were being honored. It was a nice, nostalgic evening. When I came up to be introduced the band started playing "When Irish Eyes Are Smiling." So instead of saying thank you, I asked the band to strike it up again and I sang "When Irish Eyes Are Smiling." One more time.

GEORGE CASE

GEORGE WASHINGTON CASE
Born: November 11, 1915, Trenton, New Jersey
Major-league career: 1937–47, Washington Senators, Cleveland Indians
Lifetime average: .282

Although he was a fine outfielder and a steady hitter, George Case will always be remembered as one of the greatest base-stealers of all time, despite a career prematurely ended by injuries when he was thirty-one. Between 1921 and 1961, no major leaguer stole more bases in a single season than Case. He led the American League five consecutive years in stolen bases, between 1939 and 1943, a feat at that time unprecedented in major league history. His single season high was 61, in 1943.

I could always run. When I was in high school I ran against the track stars in my baseball uniform. It was always a challenge to me because I used to feel I could have been a track star if I'd wanted. And more times than not I did beat them. But I never did have a reputation for being that quick until my second year in the minors, when I led the league in stolen bases. From then on that was my reputation. Still is, I guess. I still meet people today who say to me, "Oh, yes, you're the fellow who stole all those bases."

During the war years I ran more match races than anybody that ever put on a uniform. One year I ran five races for purses, and the only guy that ever beat me was Jesse Owens. That actually was in '46, when I was with Cleveland. It was Bill Veeck's first promotion in the big leagues, matching me against Jesse Owens.

Sometime in July 1943, Clark Griffith got hold of me and said, "George, our publicity man has arranged for you to try and beat Hans Lobert's record for circling the bases. I'm going to give you a thousand dollars for doing it." He thought it would be a good gimmick and would draw some people, which we needed to do; we weren't drawing flies at that time.

Lobert's record for circling the bases was 13.8 seconds. Evar Swanson, an outfielder who played in the early thirties, had done it in 13.2, but while that was considered the official time it really shouldn't have been, because they held only one watch on him. A lot of people considered Lobert's mark to be the official one, and that was the one I was trying to better.

The ball club made a big thing of it, the newspapers played it up, and sure enough we pulled a good crowd that day. When it was time to make that run all the players left the field and I went up to home plate. There were three AAU officials there as timers; in the event I set a record it would be official.

Well, I beat Lobert's record, circling the bases in 13.5. Now, Swanson's record is still regarded as official, but it really shouldn't be. I feel I hold the record and ought to be given credit for it because I had three AAU people holding the clock on me.

Remember Gil Coan? He came up from the minor leagues with the reputation of being tremendously fast. After I was sold to Cleveland in 1946 some of the Washington writers seemed to think he could take me. One day I got a phone call from one of them.

"George," he said, "next time you come to Washington I can get you a thousand dollars if you'll run against Gil Coan. We think it'll draw a lot of people, and Mr. Griffith's all for it. What do you say?"

"Hell, yes," I said. A thousand bucks was a lot of money in those days.

So the race was announced and the next trip into Washington I ran against Coan. Just before the race was to start somebody came over to me and said, "George, step over to the boxes for a minute, somebody there wants to shake hands with you."

I was concentrating so intensely on what I was going to have to do that I didn't look up until I reached the box-seat railing. Well, I'll be darned if it wasn't General Eisenhower, standing up with that big grin and his hand stretched out.

"Hello, George," he said, and we shook hands,. "I want to wish you luck. I've come a long way to see this."

I found out later he'd come up from Virginia especially for the race. Well, we gave him a good one. Gil Coan was very fast, but I beat him. It was a darn good promotion and pulled a lot of people into the ball park—including General Eisenhower.

You know, you don't see that sort of thing anymore in baseball—no field days, no match races, no attempts to circle the bases. They're all afraid today that a ballplayer will pull up lame. I think that's nonsense;

hell, a ballplayer is used to running, it's his living. It's too bad they've done away with those things, because the fans love that sort of competition. There's always some question in everybody's mind about who is the fastest man in baseball. Everybody has their candidate, whether it be Bobby Bonds or Lou Brock or whoever. Why not have that as an added attraction at the all-star game? Pick your three fastest from each league and let them run it out, for a purse. The fans would love it.

I never ran from signs; I ran on my own. Any good base runner has to be on his own. Of course you have to earn the privilege. The manager will watch you for a while and then pull you aside and tell you, "Look, you have the speed, you know when your timing is right, and you know the pitchers better than I do. Just use good judgment. Don't run us out of an inning." They play it differently today, but back then if you ever tried to steal third base with two out or second base when you were three or four runs behind, you'd get the hell chewed out of you. I remember one time I'd stolen twenty-one bases in a row. We were playing the Browns in St. Louis and were down by three runs in the middle of the game. I led off an inning with a base hit and then decided to steal second. I stumbled breaking away and was thrown out. And before I'd even gotten back to the dugout Bucky Harris had already told somebody else to get ready to go out and replace me; he was taking me out of the game.

I went into the clubhouse, took a shower and sat around. Harris came in after the game and never said a word to me. But that night I was sitting in the lobby of the Chase Hotel, and he came up to me. I can still see him standing there. He had a rolled-up newspaper in his hand and he hit the paper lightly in the palm of his hand a few times, then said, "You got a pretty good idea why I took you out of there today?"

"Obviously because I ran at the wrong time," I said.

"That's right," he said. "And as long as I'm managing the ball club, don't you ever run like that when we're down."

And I never did. But that took away from my stolen bases.

So you can see how they played it then—a bit more conservative. Nevertheless, I still stole 61 bases one year and 51 another. If I was running today, the way they're playing it, there's no doubt in my mind I'd be stealing a hundred bases, too. No doubt at all. One year I stole 44 bases and was caught only six times, and three of those times I was thrown out of the game for arguing the decision. Were they that close? Hell, no, they weren't close—that's why I was arguing. They were bad calls; I had the damned base stolen, and I told the umpire so, which was why I was run out of there.

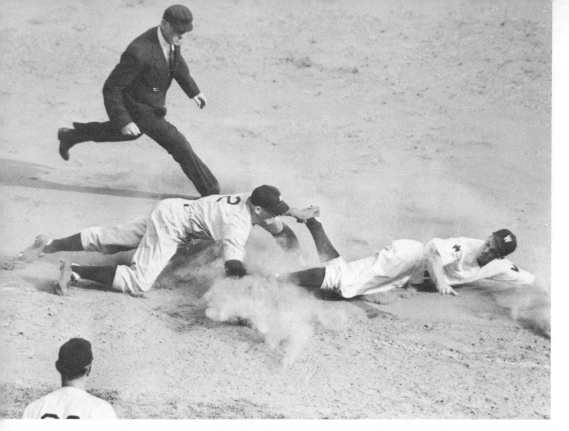

George Case stealing third, beating the tag by Yankee third baseman Red Rolfe in 1939.

You know, sometimes I was able to steal a catcher's pitch-out sign. The pitch-out, of course, is the one thing a base runner has to fear more than anything else, because in that situation you're running against a ball thrown to a catcher who's trying to throw you out. But I came to realize that most catchers signaled for a pitch-out by either wiggling their fingers or making a fist. Well, when I got on first base I would watch their arms. If a guy made a fist you could see the muscles tighten in his forearm, or if he was wiggling his fingers you could see that action by his arm, too.

The toughest catcher for me to steal on was Paul Richards. I had a hell of a time running against him. He always seemed to be guessing right along with me. Now I'll tell you something funny about that, just to give you some idea what goes on inside of a ball game. I had a bad left shoulder, it bothered me for about four or five years until I had it operated on. One spring during the war, when we were training at the University of Maryland, Bill Dickey stopped by to visit. Bill was in the Navy then. He sat down next to me on the bench.

"You don't have too much luck running against Richards, do you?" he said.

"Tell you the truth, Bill," I said, "he gives me a fit."

"Well, I'll give you a tip," he said. "Whenever you're about to run you tuck your left arm into yourself. Richards has spotted that."

Well, I'll be a son of a gun, I thought to myself. Dickey was right. Whenever I knew I was going to run I became conscious of that bad shoulder and protective of it; so I used to bring that arm in against myself. And Paul Richards, being a very shrewd man, picked it up.

In 1939 I stole 51 bases, which was quite a few steals for those years. That winter, just before I was going to leave for spring training, I get a call from Tampa, from a guy I'd never heard of. He's the representative of the Camel cigarette people, through an advertising agency in New York. "I understand you smoke Camels," he said.

Well, it so happened I did.

"Would you be interested in endorsing them?" he asked.

"Sure," I said. "What's in it?"

"When are you going to be in Florida?" he asked.

"I'll be down in Orlando in a week," I said.

So we arranged to meet down there and talk further about it. I arrived in Orlando a week later, and this fellow meets me in the hotel lobby.

"This is the deal," he said. "If you'll endorse Camels for one year I'll give you a thousand dollars and a carton of cigarettes every week for fifty-two weeks."

Now, this was only my second year in the big leagues, remember. I was flattered, but curious.

"Why me?" I asked.

"Listen," he said, "you don't know it, but I followed you around the league last year. I went into every town that you played in on the road and was impressed with the fan reaction to you. You're the kind of person we want to advertise our product because the fans come out to see you play. Your style of play excites them."

Frankly, I was surprised. A ballplayer doesn't really know how the crowd is reacting to him; he's so busy concentrating on his game he just can't pay attention. But apparently the base-stealing had caught the fans' imagination and this fellow was aware of it and wanted to capitalize on it.

So they chartered a DC-3 and brought down a whole production crew to shoot the pictures. They trucked in three tons of sand, spread it out around second base, set up platforms for angle shots, and were otherwise very thorough in their preparations. I spent a whole afternoon being photographed sliding through that sand into second base.

The advertising campaign was keyed to the opening of the season. I was on the back of *Liberty* magazine, *Saturday Evening Post*, and other publications. "George Washington Case. I smoke Camels." That's what it said. It was quite a campaign. But then do you know what happened? One week after it was launched I started to get very indignant letters from parents all over the country, saying I was a bad influence on American youth. What's more, Will Harridge, the president of the league, was getting the same kind of mail. So he called me on the phone and asked me to stop in and see him the next time I was in Chicago.

First trip into Chicago I went up to his office. He opened up a desk drawer and it was stuffed with mail. I read a few of them and they were awful.

"Mr. Harridge," I said, "I've been getting the same thing."

"Well," he said, "we can't have this."

So he called the advertising agency and told them that no American League ballplayer was ever to be photographed endorsing a cigarette in their baseball uniform. The advertising people called me.

"Look," they said, "we've got a lot of money invested in this and we don't want to drop it."

A compromise was reached—I would pose for a new series of photographs in street clothes. That's what happened. I think I was the last baseball player ever to endorse tobacco in a baseball uniform. There had been a few before me, but they had mostly been pitchers. I think it was because my name was associated with running speed that upset so many people. Kids were probably saying to their parents, "Hey, George Case smokes cigarettes and he can run like the devil."

But that wasn't the end of it. As a result of that Camel advertisement these three guys used to get on me whenever we came to Fenway Park. They'd parade around the stands during batting practice yelling, "George Washington Case. I smoke Camels. *You stink!*" Over and over. Every time we went to Boston. Finally I couldn't stand it any longer and went up into the stands after them. You're damned right I did. And I went in swinging, in full uniform. The cops came over right away and broke it up; but I was ready to take on all three of them.

That was some deal I made with Camels.

You know, I almost went with the Philadelphia Athletics instead of the Senators. After I graduated from prep school in New Jersey I was invited to Shibe Park to work out with the A's. Connie Mack liked me but said he didn't have an opening for me in his organization. But he did help get me placed in the New York-Penn League. This was in 1936. In '37 I led the league in batting and that fall went up to the big leagues with the Washington Senators.

The Senators were a chronic second-division team, but at the same time their lineup was chock-full of .300 hitters. They had Buddy Myer, who was always a good hitter, and one of the most rugged competitors I ever saw. Off the field he was the nicest, most placid guy in the world; but the moment he put on his baseball uniform his personality changed; he became aggressive and pugnacious. It was the most amazing thing; you wouldn't think it was the same person. And they had Cecil Travis, who was certainly one of the best hitters I ever saw. And Buddy Lewis was a good one, too.

The ball club also had a lot of old and established players. Let's see, in addition to Myer, there was Goose Goslin, Rick and Wes Ferrell, Sammy West, Al Simmons.

When I joined the team in the fall of '37 those old guys didn't want to know that I existed. The only ones on the club who came up to me and introduced themselves were Buddy Lewis and Cecil Travis. The next spring when I went south with the team Al Simmons didn't remember me from the previous fall; he didn't even know I was on the ball club. I had to reintroduce myself to him.

At that time Al was on his way out; still a good hitter but no longer the devastating one he had been. They'd play him a couple of days, then rest him a couple of days. He was at that point in his career.

One evening in Boston I was sitting in the lobby of the Copley Plaza after the ball game. Simmons came in at about nine-thirty with a newspaper under his arm. He stopped, looked around, then looked at me. He was never particularly friendly to me, but I was the only ballplayer sitting there, so he came up to me.

"Young fellow," he said, "come on and have a drink with me."

Here's the great Al Simmons asking me to have a drink with him, and all I could get out was, "Al, I don't drink."

"Hell, you drink ginger ale, don't you?"

"Sure," I said.

"Then come on in," he said.

They had a merry-go-round bar in the Copley Plaza; you know, one of those bars that go around and make a full circle every sixty minutes. We had an off-day the next day and I sat at that bar with him until two-thirty A.M. drinking ginger ale until it was coming out of my ears, while he was drinking Scotch and water. For some reason, he told me the story of his life, practically from the day he was born. One of the things he said was, "You know, I've got a reputation for being coarse and a little bit ornery, but believe me, enough things have happened to me in my lifetime to account for that."

He told me about his boyhood, about what a rough time he'd had, how poor his family was, how hard he had to work when he was a boy.

George Case in 1940.

It was all very interesting and sad, and I got to know Al Simmons that night.

After that, he was my closest friend on the ball club. He took me under his wing, gave me an awful lot of good advice and encouragement. I considered it a privilege to be on the same team with Al Simmons. He turned out to be, under that gruff exterior, a very kindly and thoughtful man. Of course he was one of the greatest right-hand hitters that ever lived, a man of tremendous achievement and tremendous pride. Bearing that in mind now, you can imagine what it was like one day when Bucky Harris took him out for a pinch hitter.

Al was having some difficulty making contact and we were in the late innings of a game, with a chance to win. We had a couple of men on base and Al's turn was coming up. He picked up his bat and headed for the on-deck circle. All of a sudden Harris called him back. Frankly, I was stunned, and not because I thought Harris was making the wrong move, but because it was happening. We all looked at one another on the bench, but nobody said anything. Those few seconds were highly charged; the moment Bucky called out to him we knew what it was, and when Al turned around there was a look of puzzlement on his face; he couldn't believe it. It was the first time he had ever been hit for. He stared at Harris for a few seconds, then took that bat and threw it up into the air about fifteen feet, let it drop, and walked back to the bench, right on through the dugout and into the clubhouse without saying a word.

Hank Greenberg is another guy I always think of when they talk about the great right-handed hitters. Hank was a very fine person, and I can tell you a little story to illustrate what I mean. We were playing Detroit one time, and I was on first base. I guess my mind must have been wandering a bit because I'd lost track of how many outs there were. Somebody hit a long fly ball and Hank said, "Two out, get going." I took off. Well, there was only one out and I was doubled off the base. Boy, was I mad! I was in the league just about a year or so and I was a pretty hot-tempered kid. When I realized what had happened I yelled at Greenberg, "You big so-and-so, I'm going to cut your leg off next time I come down there." That was me, rookie George Case, talking to Hank Greenberg that way.

Next time up I pushed a ball between first and the pitcher. The pitcher had to field it and shovel it over to first. It was going to be a close play and Hank was stretched way out to pull it in, and there was his leg, right where I could get at it. I hit him on the heel and tore his spike off. Fortunately it was nothing more than that. When I turned around I saw him standing there looking at his shoe. As I walked back past the base—I'd been thrown out—Hank said, "Well, young fellow, I hope you're satisfied." That's all he said. Just that and nothing more. Well, that sank in. Taught me a lesson. Something like that impresses you more than a guy coming at you. He let me know in a quiet way that I'd done something foolish and I never forgot it.

By the time I came into the league Lefty Grove was strictly a one-day-a-week pitcher. His fast ball was pretty much gone, but that crusty personality I'd heard so much about hadn't mellowed one bit. On the day he was going to pitch his teammates on the Red Sox wouldn't talk to him and he wouldn't talk to them. He would come into the clubhouse and lay down on the trainer's table and take a nap. If you wanted a rubdown you were out of luck—Lefty was snoozing there. Then he'd get up, take a shot of whiskey and get ready to pitch. This was his ritual.

Lefty was along in years then and he had a hard time fielding bunts. As a matter of fact, he couldn't field a bunt worth a damn. He never shut me out in his life, because if I went up a couple of times without a base hit all I had to do was bunt and I was home free. And of course he hated when you bunted on him. One particular ball game I pushed one up along the first-base line and Lefty came after it. I was really flying down there, outrunning the ball and Lefty both. When he saw he couldn't get me, he got mad as hell and out of frustration kicked the ball over to first base. Then he stood there jawing at me a mile a minute, calling me a "bush bastard" and giving me an awful going over. Lefty Grove was all by himself as a character. But when you talk about colorful characters I think you have to put Bobo Newsom on top of the list. If he were living today and pitching today, on television, he would have to be one of the greatest attractions in the game. There was only one Bobo Newsom and there will never be another one. Some people might say amen to that but not me; I thought he was great.

He was with the Washington ball club on four or five different occasions—he was always being traded. On one of those occasions, in 1942, we got him from Detroit. Well, on our first trip into Detroit he went to his bank to draw out his money. He showed up later in the lobby of the hotel, where a few of us were sitting. He spotted Bob Repass, who was his roommate, and went up to him and said, "Bob, you got change for ten?"

Repass went into his pocket and pulled out a couple of fives. Bobo handed him a ten, but it wasn't a ten-dollar bill, it was a ten-*thousand*-dollar bill. In typical Newsom fashion, instead of getting his money in a bank draft, he got it in cash, and then walks up to Repass and asks for change. We all just stood around with our mouths open, looking at that piece of paper. I'd never seen one before and I've never seen one since. I don't think they even circulate them anymore.

Newsom was one of the best natural comedians I ever saw. Once in a while on those long train rides he'd suddenly get up and begin preaching a sermon. He would stand on a suitcase in the club car, holding one of those Gideon Bibles in his hand, with a pair of glasses pushed all the way down the end of his nose, and preach a hellfire sermon in the style of a Southern Baptist minister. He'd have us rolling in the aisles. Just about everything he did or said was funny; he was a natural.

Ted Lyons was another veteran in the league when I came up. He was just as tough and unforgiving a competitor as Grove. I'll never forget the time I pulled something on him—I was just a rookie at the time—which I don't think has been done since: I got two bases on a base on balls. He walked me on a three-and-two pitch and I trotted down to first base. When I got there I glanced at second; Luke Appling wasn't paying attention, he had his back to the infield; and Jackie Hayes, the second baseman, was away from the bag. So I lit out for second, and I don't think there was even a play on me.

Lyons, being the competitor that he was, didn't like that one bit. He stood on the mound growling at me, calling me every name in the book. Then he turned around and took off his glove and began to rub up the baseball, I guess trying to work off some of his steam. When he turned his back I lit out for third—Marv Owen, the third baseman, was away from the bag. They yelled at Lyons and he whirled around and fired the ball and Owen made a great play on it, catching the ball and making a diving tag on me. Just did get me.

In the process of sliding I threw my shoulder out. So there I am, lying on the ground in great pain and all of a sudden there's Ted Lyons standing over me, chewing me out again. Oh, he was steaming! Called me a busher and a show-off and a lot of other things, none of them complimentary. Even while they were helping me off the field, Ted was following me, still yelling at me. But I damn near wound up on third base on a base on balls. Ted Lyons and I became good friends later on, and he'd often remind me of that base on balls and we'd laugh about it; but he wasn't laughing that day.

Right after Pearl Harbor the country was in a turmoil. Nobody knew what was going to happen. But the owner of the ball club, Clark Griffith, who was a friend of President Roosevelt, kept telling us that baseball was going to continue because the country needed it as recreation and diversion.

Nevertheless, ballplayers were no different from anyone else and whoever was eligible was soon drafted. Little by little guys began being called into service. The personnel changes during the war went on all the time, almost from week to week. And I'll say one thing—everybody that played during those war years were legitimate rejects from the service. Most of them were either color blind, or had bad cartilages, bad shoulders, bad stomachs. Our center fielder, George Binks, was hard of hearing in one ear; as a matter of fact, I ran into him a half dozen times one year because he couldn't hear me calling for the ball.

In my own case, because I was a professional baseball player, I was examined three times in one year to see if I was eligible for the service, but I was a reject because I'd had a serious shoulder operation and had limited movement in my arm.

A lot of people won't remember this, and most will find it hard to believe today, but during the war years the fans used to throw balls that were hit into the stands back onto the field, because it was announced that those balls would be sent to service bases. Anybody who didn't throw a ball back was looked upon as unpatriotic, which was no light accusation to have made against you in those days.

Baseballs were scarce as hell, and after a while we began running out of bats. Louisville was having a difficult time manufacturing bats, and believe it or not, we used some bats that were designed by the Glenn Martin Company, the aircraft manufacturers in Baltimore. Glenn Martin was an avid Washington Senator fan and when he read in the papers that we were having bat problems he had his engineers design a bat for us that looked liked an airplane wing. It was tapered at the hitting end, and actually the principle of it was very sound. The swing weight was excellent. I don't know why none of the bat manufacturers ever followed up on that. Martin made us ten or twelve dozen of those bats and we used them. They did break easily, which was one of the problems.

There were shortages of everything in those days, and rationing. We had trouble getting gasoline, sugar, meat, and a whole lot of other things. Dutch Leonard was on our ball club at the time and he was a shrewd fellow. He seemed to know of every service station in the Washington area that had gasoline, and he seemed to know what meat markets were getting deliveries. Naturally, in order to be able to receive this information, Dutch had to give something in return, and what he gave were autographed baseballs. He was always swiping them from the ball bag. There's a certain magic about an autographed baseball, isn't there?

Buddy Lewis was one of the first to go into the service. He joined the Air Corps and became a pilot, stationed in Georgia. One of his first assignments after he got his wings was to fly some VIP's up to Washington. He happened to come into town on a Sunday, when we had a double-header scheduled, and as soon as he could he came out to the ball park. Just before he had to leave, he said, "It's been great seeing you guys. I'll be leaving before the double-header is over, but I'll tell you

"Little by little, guys began being called into service." Ted Williams on his way to take examinations for naval flight training, 1942.

something—I'm going to split this ball park in two with that airplane when I leave Washington. I'm going to come right down center field."

Well, right after the second ball game started here comes a low-flying airplane over the top of the stands, heading straight for the flagpole in center field. As it so happened, I was just getting ready to hit when it came roaring over. It was Buddy, flying at a ridiculously low altitude, breaking God knows how many laws and regulations. I got so excited I threw my bat up in the air as if to say, "Hi, Buddy, we know it's you." He wiggled his wings a little and went soaring over the center-field bleachers and off into the blue sky. We didn't see him again until the war was over.

We finished second in 1945, a game and a half out. Detroit beat us out on the last day of the season. I think that was one of the most unusual pennant races there ever was. You see, we had finished our season a week before everybody else. So we had to sit around and watch it happen, to see if we were going to win it, or get a tie, or whatever. The Tigers were playing the Browns a double-header in St. Louis that last day, and if the Browns won we were going to have to go to Detroit for a play-off. We were sitting in the clubhouse in Griffith Stadium with our bags packed, listening to the radio. It was a tie game until the ninth inning, when Hank Greenberg hit a grand-slam home run for the Tigers that won it for them. So instead of going to Detroit for a play-off we all said good-bye to each other and went home for the winter.

The reason we had finished our schedule a week earlier was because George Marshall, who owned the Washington Redskins, had made arrangements with Mr. Griffith to have the ball park for the football team a week before the baseball season ended. Well, we had finished seventh the year before and nobody expected us to rise up and get in a close pennant race. But we did, and almost won it, and that was as close as I ever came to a World Series.

I was fortunate enough to play on the same team with Bob Feller after he came back from the service. I was in left field when he threw that no-hitter against the Yankees in April of '46. That was the greatest game that I've ever seen pitched. After it was over I said to one of the Yankees, "Bob had pretty good stuff today, didn't he?" And the guy said, "He was all right. But I think if we'd gone another eight or nine innings we might have got a hit off of him."

I'd batted against Bob before the war, of course. He was just a big, rawboned kid then, in 1937 and '38. He'd scare you throwing that ball, he'd scare the hell out of you. He had a little nervous twitch in his eyes and he'd stand out there on that mound with those eyes twitching and you'd be up there saying to yourself, "I hope the son of a gun sees me all right."

You talk about a ballplayer having magnetism, Bob Feller had it, with plenty to spare. He was continually hounded by the press, by well-wishers, by fans, by people wanting something from him. There were times when you simply couldn't get out of the ball park after a game because there were so many people waiting to see Bob. But I'll say this, with it all, he kept a pretty level head. There weren't many ballplayers who had that kind of magnetism. Williams had it, of course, and sometimes it worked against him, because the fans could react very violently to him. He had some people who used to sit out in left field in Fenway Park for no other reason, it seemed, except to boo the hell out of him.

Ted was an incredibly endowed athlete. I remember one time we went out to Fenway Park early, even before the Red Sox got there. We got outside of the ball park and we hear Bang! Bang! Bang! Bang! Shooting. We couldn't imagine what was going on in there. We walk into the ball park and there's Ted Williams in the bull pen with a case of shotgun shells, shooting pigeons. Shooting the hell out of them; they were lying all over the outfield. It seems the pigeons were a health menace in Fenway Park, because of their droppings. So Tom Yawkey gave Ted permission to shoot them, and that's what he was doing.

Along those same lines, Ted was certainly one of the best trap shots I've ever seen; also he's probably one of the best fly fishermen in the world. When it comes to anything that involves coordination between the hand and the eye, Ted is in a class by himself.

To all of us who played back in the thirties and forties it's a new era in baseball. You've got new ball parks, a different kind of playing field, a new set of standards. And of course the money is so much bigger today in baseball, it makes us look like we were playing in a stone age. I can vividly remember coming back from a western trip on the same train with the Red Sox; this was around 1939. About a half dozen players from each team were sitting in the club car that night and the talk got around to salaries.

"You know," somebody said, "I'd like to know how many guys in the American League are making more than ten thousand dollars."

We started naming some names and wound up with about eight or ten guys who were making more than ten thousand dollars, as far as we could determine. There might have been more, but not many. Can you imagine that? And this was during an era of some mighty good players.

One picture stands out in my mind which illustrates to me how different it was then. We had a kid pitcher join the ball club in the late thirties. He walked into the clubhouse one day and I swear, he looked like something out of a painting by Norman Rockwell. He was from a farming community in the deep South, and he was carrying a cardboard suitcase with a belt wrapped around it.

A day or two later we put him in a game to relieve. He walked out there—I wish I could remember his name—and the first thing he did before he began to warm up was take off his cap and put it down alongside the mound. Of course that's not permitted—you have to play in full uniform. The umpire came out and said, "What the hell's going on?"

"I can't pitch with my hat on," the kid said.

"Listen," the umpire said, "You've got to pitch with your hat on. You're in the big leagues."

A grand place to be, too.

DICK WAKEFIELD

RICHARD CUMMINGS WAKEFIELD
Born: May 6, 1921, Chicago, Illinois
Major-league career: 1941–52, Detroit Tigers, New York
  Yankees, New York Giants
Lifetime average: .293

Dick Wakefield was baseball's first big bonus recipient. He paid immediate dividends for the Tigers, hitting .316 and .355 his first two seasons. In 1943 he led the American League with 200 hits and 38 doubles. Returning to the big leagues in 1946 after serving in the armed forces, Wakefield hit well for several years, but never quite fulfilled the prom-ise implied by his first two seasons.

I stepped up to the plate on opening day in 1949 and fifty thousand people booed the hell out of me. Why? It was the press. I had a bad press in Detroit. It was brutal. I couldn't get away from it. Part of it started with the bonus. Some of those writers were making $8,000 a year and they resented an untried kid getting a $52,000 bonus. Who the hell is he to get so much money? they asked. Greenberg—the star of the team—was only making around $40,000 a year. Who the hell is Wake-field? But *Greenberg* didn't care how much money I'd gotten. Hank didn't give a damn. More power to you, kid—that's the way he felt about it.

They said I had the wrong attitude. They figured because a guy could smile when things went bad he had the wrong attitude. Hell, everybody isn't built the same, you know. But once you get a bad press in baseball, no matter how unjustified, it lives with you. I can give you a good example of how these things sometimes happen.

I had a tryout with the Giants in the spring of 1952. The day after I joined them in Phoenix one of the writers filed a story back to New York that cut me up and down. Now, I didn't know anything about it at

79

the time—in fact, I'd never even met the guy before. Meanwhile, I'm out there every day breaking my back trying to make the club.

Then we break camp and start heading East. We arrive in Evansville, Indiana, before jumping off to New York. By this time this particular writer and myself have become inseparable. Now, I still don't know about that story, and he's starting to behave strangely. He knows sooner or later I'm going to find out about what he wrote. He's getting morose.

He got loaded in a bar in Evansville just before we're supposed to leave. Nobody could get him out of there. Finally they send me in to get him—because we're such good pals, right? I find him in there, loaded, stiff, and he's crying. I don't know why, and he's in no shape to tell me. But I induce him to leave and get him on the bus and we begin heading for New York. The morning after we arrived in New York, he calls me. "I've got to talk to you," he says. We get together and he shows me the story. God, it was the most derogatory thing, about my attitude, and a lot of things like that.

"How the hell could you write that?" I asked. "We'd never even met."

"I know, I know," he said. He felt miserable.

"Who gave you that information?" I asked.

"One of the Cleveland writers," he said, and told me the guy's name. It was somebody who had never liked me.

"And you took his word on it?"

He nodded his head. Not only did he feel guilty and embarrassed, but his pride was hurt, too. "Now that I know you," he said, "I see that there's not one word of truth in that story. If that ever happens to me again I ought to get out of the business."

Well, it was too late then, wasn't it? It was already in print, people had read it and formed their judgments. I've always felt that if you hear something negative about a person you ought to first think about who you're hearing it from. What's the source? How well informed is the person, and what might *his* prejudices be? Too often it turns out that your worst enemy is some other son of a bitch's best friend.

When people talk today about the astronomical salaries in baseball they sometimes point back to me as the cause of it all. I was the original bonus baby. But that was an economic development which had to come sooner or later, and I happened to be there at the time.

As always in human nature, there was a certain amount of envy, which is I guess a natural thing, and I had to overcome that. But you can do it as you become one of the guys. They recognize the fact that you're doing the best you can and if things work out, fine; if not, you're gone. It's all cut and dried.

But most of the resentment came from the newspapers. Fifty-two thousand was a sockful of money in 1941 and the papers made a big deal out of it. They were writing about me every day. Today a kid receiving that kind of money barely rates a mention. But I got all the attention because I was the first. The first in anything gets the attention and is remembered, whether it's the first man on the moon or the first kid to get a big bonus.

The scouts started taking notice of me when I was in high school in Chicago. I was a big skinny kid who could hit. I heard later that some of the scouts were talking to my father about me when I was a junior in high school, but he never mentioned it to me because he wanted me to go on to college.

My father had been a major-league ballplayer, too, you know; he caught for the Washington Senators just after the turn of the century. The fact that my father had played big-league ball was an important factor in my life. His contribution to my development as a ballplayer was enormous.

Once I got into college at Michigan State the scouts started coming around in earnest. I went to Brooklyn, Chicago, Cincinnati, Cleveland, Detroit. There was a lot of interest. My criterion was the highest offer; they were all great organizations and great people and I had no particular preference.

Wish Egan, the Detroit scout, convinced Mr. Briggs, who owned the Tigers, to sign me, that I was worth the money. So they signed me, giving me a bonus of $52,000 and a brand-new car.

The first thing I did after signing was to go out to a place on Woodward Avenue that sold Lincoln Zephyrs. I'd made up my mind that was the car I wanted. I walked into that place wearing a pair of corduroys and an old shirt, just like any average university kid. A bunch of salesmen were sitting around talking; they glanced at me and went right on talking. Not one of them got up. I stood around for a while admiring my car—as I said, I knew just which one I was buying. Finally I spotted a kid about eighteen years old sitting at a desk. I called him over.

"Say," I said, "can you sell me a car?"

"You'd better get one of the salesmen," he said.

"I don't want one of the salesmen," I said. "I want you."

"Just a minute."

He brought out the general manager, who walked toward me looking kind of skeptical.

"I want to buy this car," I said, "but I want this young fellow to sell it to me and get the commission."

"Whatever you say," he said.

So I bought myself that Lincoln Zephyr and paid $1,400 for it. When I signed the papers the general manager looked at my signature and said, "Well, by God, you're Dick Wakefield."

"That's right," I said.

"Been reading about you," he said.

Then all the salesmen came over and shook hands and made a big fuss. When that was all over with, I said, "Now I'd like somebody to take me down to the Leland Hotel, because I don't know how to drive."

One of the guys drove me to the hotel and I watched carefully everything he did. By the time we got there I knew how to drive.

"You sure you can handle her?" he asked.

"Are you kidding?" I said.

Then I drove out to the ball park. Wish Egan spotted me as I was pulling in. He came running over looking like he was going to have a heart attack.

"Dick, for God's sake," he said, "what have you done?"

"What's the matter?" I asked.

"Do you know what kind of car you've got there?"

"Sure," I said. "A Lincoln."

"Well," he said, "*Ford* makes that. Don't you know that Mr. Briggs makes Chryslers and Packards?"

"So what?" I asked.

"Mr. Briggs and Henry Ford are having a feud," he said. "They hate each other."

Well, how was I supposed to know that? Welcome to Detroit.

I stayed with the Tigers for a while in '41, not playing much, but getting a chance to rub shoulders with guys like Rudy York, Charlie Gehringer, Barney McCosky, Pinky Higgins, Schoolboy Rowe, Bobo Newsom. Then I went down to Winston-Salem and played there a half year.

The next season, 1942. I played at Beaumont in the Texas League and was voted the Most Valuable Player there. I came up to Detroit in '43 and hit .316. In '44 I hit .355 and then went into the service.

I was in Hawaii for a while and played some ball there. I met Ted Williams in Hawaii. Did you ever hear about the bet I made with him? That was the craziest thing. After hitting my .355 in 1944 I guess I was feeling kind of cocky. So I told Ted that when we got out of the service and back to baseball, I'd outhit him in several offensive categories. I was some kid, huh?—telling that to Ted Williams. We bet a thousand dollars each on RBI's, home runs, and batting average. But I wasn't altogether crazy, because I also told him what I thought I was going to be getting by way of salary.

"You'll never get it," he said.

"All right," I said, "then let's bet on that, too."

What we did was split the bet in two—half on the batting departments, half on the salary. The total bet added up to something like five thousand dollars.

Well, when we got back in 1946, the first thing that happened to me was Joe Page broke my wrist with a pitch in April. Then a few weeks later I broke my arm running against the wall in Boston. I had one of my worst years. Williams hit .342 and had a great year all around. But I made the money I'd told him I would, so I didn't have to pay off. We broke even on it.

Toward the end of my career I got into a row with baseball. I had always felt that the relationship I had at Detroit was good, but when I needed the old man—Mr. Briggs—he wasn't there. The net result was that in the final run baseball beat me down.

Left to right: Doc Cramer, Pinky Higgins, Dick Wakefield, Rudy York in 1943.

What happened was, the Tigers traded me to the Yankees and then the Yankees traded me to the White Sox, for a pitcher named Joe Ostrowski and $100,000. Well, I refused to report to the White Sox without an adjustment in salary. When that happened, the White Sox said I belonged to the Yankees and the Yankees said I belonged to the White Sox. So I sat back and belonged to myself while I waited for them to settle it.

About a month later, after a lot of hand-wringing about who owned me, I was waived to Oakland in the Pacific Coast League, *waived,* by both leagues, for the price of $7,500. Which meant that Chicago could have gotten me on waivers for $7,500 and saved $92,500 and a pitcher. But you see what was happening—they were trying to ease me out, simply because I had asked for what I believed to be equitable treatment. I wanted them to be fair with me, that's all. Well, they weren't.

I went back to my home in Ann Arbor thinking about suing. I did in fact go to a very prominent attorney and told him the story.

"Dick," he said, "do you still want to play baseball?"

"Yes," I said.

"Then forget about the suit. Go to Oakland."

"What if I wanted to sue?" I asked.

"If you want to sue," he said, "I'll give you my services free of charge."

In other words, I had a pretty strong case against baseball. But I went to Oakland. Probably it was the worst mistake I ever made; but at the time I didn't want to hurt a game that was so good to me for a few years.

I played in Oakland in 1950 and came back again in 1951. Mel Ott was managing the team then and he wasn't playing me. One day he put a second baseman in the outfield, while I was sitting on the bench. I saw that, got up and walked into the clubhouse, packed up and left.

In the spring of 1952 Monte Irvin broke his ankle and the Giants were hurting for an outfielder. I was home in Ann Arbor at the time, just sitting around. So my landlord, completely on his own, mind you, picked up the phone and got hold of Durocher.

"Mr. Durocher," he said, "I've got a fellow here who's as good or better than what you've lost." This is my landlord talking, remember.

"Who?" Durocher said.

"Wakefield."

"Wakefield. What's he doing?"

"He's waiting for a chance," my landlord said.

"All right," Durocher said. "Don't let him leave the house. I'll call you back."

Meanwhile, I get up and go downstairs to have coffee. The phone rings and my landlord says, "That's for you."

"What have you got, ESP?" I asked.

I pick up the phone and it's Durocher.

"Get the first plane out here," he says.

So I joined the Giants in Phoenix. We played Cleveland all the way to New York. By the time we got to New York my batting average was .556. But I still hadn't signed a contract.

I was sitting in Toots Shor's with Bob Elliott. Toots came over and said that Chub Feeney was looking for me. I went upstairs to a room and a few minutes later Feeny came in. He was Mr. Stoneham's nephew. I knew he had to sign me. He had to. You can't release a guy who's hitting .556—especially not when one of your big guns is laid up for the year with a broken ankle.

He told me they'd give me $15,000 salary and that if things worked out they'd adjust it later. Now, I'd just been through a lot of grief, with the Yankees, the White Sox, Oakland, that whole thing. I wanted to get back in baseball. I knew I'd been barred. You know those things. You can sense them.

"Chub," I said, "do me a favor. The salary is fifteen thousand. What's the minimum?"

"Six thousand," he said.

"I'll tell you what," I said. "Give me six thousand in salary and a nine-thousand-dollar bonus."

I figured if they had that much money invested in me I might get a chance. He refused. Wouldn't do it. So I knew I was gone. I had two at bats for the New York Giants. I was released in May. They asked me to fill in at Minneapolis for a while. I did that, and then I quit.

Things like that probably happen today. I don't know. But if they do, if this kind of thing is still around, I think the answer to individual problems in any professional sport has to be in the hands of a very compassionate, intelligent, and shrewd commissioner who will not show favoritism to anybody but see that there is equal justice in all situations.

Money was only part of my problem with baseball. There were other things. I was one of the original founders of the baseball player's pension fund. A lot of strife and effort went into that thing. I guess a lot of the owners didn't like what I was doing, didn't like the way I thought about things. The idea of a pension fund was anathema to them. Why? Because it involved dollars. You see, every dollar we put in, they put in. They didn't like that.

I suppose in the owners' estimation I was something of a radical, although everything we started out to do in those days is part of the baseball structure today and nobody thinks twice about it. Baseball has always been kind of conservative when it comes to new ideas. I think one of the reasons is they're on very thin ice when it comes to contrac-

Dick Wakefield in 1950.

tual involvement. You have no freedom to sell your services where you want to. I think the owners have a right to protect what they've developed, but at the same time they have an obligation to be fair and equitable with the people with whom they do business. In too many cases they haven't been. And what can you do in those cases? Who are you going to talk to? In a tight-knit organization a powerful voice is inordinately strong.

I remember one time, when I was with the Yankees, I'd had it up to here with George Weiss. It was over contract negotiations, his inflexible attitude, and one thing and another. I just couldn't take it anymore and I called him up and gave him my thoughts over the phone. I'm sorry now that I did, but I really told him off. I told him what I thought of him and people like him. I told him where he should be rather than where he was. And later on I think that he, being one of the major-domos, got the word out at their little meetings and I was done. In those days there were only eight teams in the league. Eight owners. A very tight little group. All thinking alike to protect what they had. If a little bug comes into the ointment, get rid of it.

But there were some laughs along the way, too. One night in Seattle I faked a catch. I went back to the fence on a drive, leaped up and pretended I caught it for the third out. The ball went out for a home run, but I came trotting in very nonchalantly, pretending I had the ball. Artie Wilson, the shortstop, came out to get it while the pitcher and the rest of the team all headed for the dugout.

"Give me the ball," Artie said.

"Artie," I said, "I don't have it."

He flicked his glove around in the air and said, "Come on. Throw it."

Now we were standing next to one another at the edge of the outfield grass.

"Give me the ball," he said.

"Artie, I don't have it."

The umpire walked over.

"How about getting off the field, boys?" he said. The other team was out on the field now.

"Just a minute," I said. "That last batter is out, isn't he? He left the field of play, so he's out. Isn't that right?"

"Sure he's out," the umpire said. "Let's go. Come on, get the ball in play."

"I haven't got a ball," I said.

"What are you talking about?" the umpire asked.

Artie looked in my glove and then looked at the umpire.

"It's true," Artie said.

There followed one of the longest arguments I think there ever was

on a baseball field. Was the guy out for leaving the field, or was he entitled to a home run? All over the field there were little knots of guys trying to explain the rules to each other. Well, they finally gave the guy the
home run.

That was one of those goofy things I did for no reason other than cu-
riosity. I'd always wondered what would happen if something like that
occurred. So I tried it out and now I know. Why didn't I simply read
the rule book? Well, I could have, I suppose; but I felt that my way of
doing it was more interesting.

I find now at this stage of the game that if I had my life to live over
again, I'm inclined to think that I'd have to try and do something that's
more fundamental for humanity than a professional athletic career.
That probably sounds like middle-aged wistfulness, doesn't it? I don't
say I feel I've wasted my life, because I've had a wonderful time of it.
But I think a man ought to try and contribute more than just an athletic
career. I twice ran for Congress, you know, but without success. I wish
I could have been elected. I'd like to go to my grave thinking I passed
just one law that helped a whole segment of society. To think that you
might have had the ability to have done something, and never done it,
can be rather frustrating.

KIRBY HIGBE

WALTER KIRBY HIGBE
Born: Columbia, South Carolina, April 8, 1915
Major-league career: 1937–50, Chicago Cubs, Philadelphia
    Phillies, Brooklyn Dodgers, Pittsburgh Pirates, New York
    Giants
Lifetime record: 118 wins, 101 losses

One of the fine fastball pitchers and colorful personalities of his day, Kirby Higbe was a 22-game winner with the pennant-winning 1941 Dodgers. That same year, starting and relieving, the rubber-armed Higbe led National League pitchers in appearances. In 1940 he led the league in strikeouts.

I've had a lot of people say to me over the years, "Hig, why aren't you coaching somewhere, with all you know about the game?" Well, I had a reputation for doing what I wanted to do, if it was drinking or whatever it was. I did it and never tried to hide it. I'd say that ninety percent of them in my day did the same things I did, but they hid it. They were discreet. That's the way I ought to have been, I reckon. But that was my attitude and it was wrong, I can see that now. There are fellows who became managers, coaches, batting instructors—some still around today—who did as much as I did, or more, but were always on the sly about it. So that's the difference.

I came up with the Cubs in 1938 and the first man I ever roomed with in the big leagues was Dizzy Dean. One of the greatest guys that ever lived. A lot of people say he bragged, but as far as I'm concerned he didn't brag, he just told you what he was going to do and then went out and did it. If he said he was going to shut them out, he shut them out. I don't call that bragging, not when you can back it up.

I don't know if it's true or not, but my guess would be that there's nobody out there on that field with as much confidence as the pitcher who can throw the real good fastball. You know that when you're right you can just overpower those hitters and that's all there is to it. Greatest feeling in the world, to rock back out there and fire that thing in, especially with those big sluggers, those guys who swing from the heels.

I knew that feeling, and Dean knew it, too, until he hurt his arm. Then he pitched on heart alone, and he had plenty of that, buddy. You know what happened: Earl Averill hit a line shot off of Diz's toe in the 1937 All-Star game. When Diz went back to St. Louis he told Branch Rickey he couldn't pitch for a while, until that toe healed up. But Rickey told him they'd been advertising Dizzy was going to pitch, that there was going to be a full house, and that Dizzy was going to pitch, bad toe or not. So he went out and worked six or seven innings, favoring his toe, throwing off stride, and his arm just snapped on him. Right then and there he lost it all.

Do you remember Burgess Whitehead? Well, he and Dean roomed together in the minors. Later on Whitehead was traded to the Giants. Diz, being the kind of guy he was, would let Whitehead get a few hits off of him whenever he pitched against the Giants. He would say, "Hey, little bitty buddy, I'm throwin' it right over, so you get your hits. You got to get your hits off of Ol' Diz." One day in St. Louis he did that and Whitehead whacked a line drive, it hit Diz right between the eyes. Diz got up and looked over at Whitehead and said, "Little bitty buddy, you got to start pullin' that ball."

But that's the way Dean was. He could afford to let you get a hit off of him, because when it came right down to it and he had to get somebody out, there was no way you were going to hit him. He was colorful and unpredictable and a hell of a pitcher.

But there were a lot of good old boys back in those days. The Dodgers in particular had a reputation for employing characters. I used to hear stories about them from some of the old-timers. At one time there in the early thirties they had Babe Herman. Now there was a real buster. They were playing a game down in Florida one spring and Boom-Boom Beck was pitching, trying to make the club, but not doing too well this particular afternoon. He was throwing a lot of line drives, and back in those days there weren't any fences in the outfield down there. Every time a ball went between the outfielders it would go way on out and, hellfire, those guys had to run it down. After Babe had chased about five of those balls, Boom-Boom threw another one and Babe took off after it again. This time he picked up the ball and carried it all the way back to the mound.

"Boom-Boom," he said, "do us a favor, will you, and walk a couple of men while we catch our breath?"

But I'll tell you the best Babe Herman story. Babe, you know, had made a name for having unusual things happen to him on a ball field, like getting hit in the head with a fly ball and doubling into a triple play. Well, he actually was a good ballplayer and a hell of a hitter, and he finally got sensitive about what they were saying about him. So, the way I heard it, one day he walked up to one of the Brooklyn sportswriters.

"Listen," Babe said, "this is my livelihood and you know I'm pretty good at it. So I'm asking you to do me a favor: Lay off of me. Don't ride me about those oddball things, because you know darn well I'm not really that sort of a guy. I'm a serious-minded ballplayer."

The sportswriter was sympathetic to this, and said, "Okay, Babe. I'll tell you what, buddy, I'm not going to write anything belittling about you again."

They shook hands on it and then talked a few minutes more. Then Babe reached into his jacket pocket, pulled out a cigar stub, put it in his mouth and began puffing on it. The sportswriter took one look at that and said, "Forget what I just said. It's all off."

"What's the matter?" Babe asked.

"By God, you're walking around with a lit cigar in your pocket, that's what's the matter."

I think overall there was more color in baseball back in those days. We played for the love of the game. It had to be that, since there wasn't much money in it then, was there? I remember something Paul Waner told me once. "Kirby," he said, "I used to hold out every year, but if they'd known the truth of it, I would have played for nothing."

But it sure as hell could be frustrating sometimes. You can believe that, buddy. I was traded over to the Phillies early in 1939 in a deal for Claude Passeau, who at that time was an established pitcher. I guess we had one of the worst ball clubs that was ever in the history of baseball. Gerry Nugent, who owned the team, didn't have any money; whenever they had themselves a good ballplayer they had to sell him just to break even.

Doc Prothro was the manager. He was a good guy and a good baseball man, but there wasn't much he could do with that team. We won 45 games one year and 50 the next. That's 95 wins in two years, and I won 24 of them myself. I lost a few, too, but that was no trick with that team. I lost two games in one day in the Polo Grounds, the first one, 1–0 in eleven innings when Harry Danning plunked one down the right-field line for a home run. Then midway through the second game Doc said, "Kirby, let's try and win a game today. How about relieving if I need you?" I told him I'd be glad to.

Sure enough, we go into the bottom of the ninth and the score is tied. I come in. First guy hits one to short, the shortstop fields it cleanly and throws it into the lap of Mayor LaGuardia, who's sitting over there in the box seats. The runner goes to second and I walk the next guy on purpose. Next man bunts them over, so I have to walk another guy to load the bases. Force at any base now, right? Next guy flies to Joe Marty in short center. Joe's got a great arm, and the runner isn't even tagging up. But Joe decides to uncork one anyway, and he throws it up on the screen and I'm beat again.

There was a time in the 1940 season when we hit a real bad streak, even for us. We'd lost eight or nine in a row, and I mean losing them, not even coming close. "We've got to win a ball game," Doc says. He was all wrung out from losing and was getting desperate. We went up to the Polo Grounds and I pitched a good game against the Giants, but lost it, 3–1. That made it about ten in a row. The next day Doc is in the clubhouse. "We've got to win this one," he says. I've been in close pennant races and never saw a manager more determined. Well, the Giants tore us up that day.

After the ball game Doc says, "I want all you sons of bitches to go out tonight and get drunk. You can't be any the worse for it." So everybody took him at his word. But I didn't go out and get drunk; I had a friend out on Long Island and I went there and spent the night. I got back to the hotel the next morning at ten o'clock, and goddamn, Prothro is sitting in my room. His eyes are red from not sleeping and he's got miles and miles of wear and tear in his face.

"Oh, God, Kirby," he says, "am I glad to see you. I thought you'd jumped the ball club." He shook his head. "Wouldn't have blamed you either," he said. Man, he was glum.

Remember Hugh Mulcahy? Well, old Hugh was with us and he was a good pitcher. But there was a stretch in there when he lost about ten in a row. Every four days, there it was in the box score: "Losing pitcher: Mulcahy." It finally got to the point where that became his nickname and people started in calling him Losing Pitcher Mulcahy. And Hugh was a damned fine pitcher. But that's the way it was. Giving up two or three runs was just as good as a forfeit.

I think whatever money old Prothro earned in salary he spent up buying aspirin. I remember one time the Cardinals were in town. I beat them on Friday, and then we beat them on Saturday. Then up comes the Sunday double-header and we've got fifteen thousand people in the stands. That was a hell of a crowd in Philadelphia in those days, buddy. There used to be days when I could've whipped everybody in the stands. So here's this big crowd out to see us and Doc says, "Kirby, you've got to be ready to relieve in both games. I don't want to look bad today." "Good God, Doc," I said, "*both* games?" "Do it for me, Kirby," he says. So I said okay.

Well, so help me, in the first game they had scored seven runs before I could get to the bull pen. Doc said, "Okay, I won't use you; I'll save

Doc Prothro. "I want all you sons of bitches to go out tonight and get drunk."
(The "Frank" in the inscription is Frankie Frisch.)

you for the second game." The second game starts and it's the same
thing—the Cardinals are rattling the walls with line drives in the first
inning. Doc looks at me and says, "Get down there, Kirby. But this
time *run*, don't walk." So I ran down there, but by the time I got
warmed up it was too late again. We were massacred in both games.
Those fifteen thousand people got a hell of an impression of the Phillies that day, though I can't honestly say it was the wrong one.

In the winter of 1940 I went up to Philadelphia to talk contract with
Mr. Nugent. He told me he was going to give me $7,500.

"You'll be the highest-paid man on the team, Kirby," he said. I must
have looked skeptical about it because he showed me everybody else's
contract, just to prove it to me.

"See that," he said. "You're making more than any of them."

"Okay," I said. "I'll sign. But there's one stipulation—I won't be
traded or sold." The reason I said that was I wanted to have the opportunity to negotiate a contract with the new ball club.

"Kirby," he said, "if I sell you I don't have any pitching."

So I signed the contract. I left Philadelphia and started driving back
home. Around midnight I put on the radio in the car and heard the
news that Kirby Higbe had been sold to Brooklyn for $100,000 and
three ballplayers. When I got home I called Mr. Nugent.

"Say, Mr. Nugent," I said, "you ought to give me at least ten thousand of that money anyway."

"Kirby," he said, "it was all spent before I ever got here." Which it
probably was; they were always in debt in Philly in those days.

So I went to Brooklyn in 1941. You couldn't have picked a better ball
club to be with in those days than the Dodgers. I thought Brooklyn was
the best place in the world to play baseball. And the team was just
right, too. It was a rough-and-tumble club, getting set to win that pennant. We had the right manager, too: Durocher. He was a gambling
man on that field; he wasn't afraid to take chances. Leo hated to lose as
much as anybody I've ever seen. He was strictly right for Brooklyn. He
fit perfectly into that situation and became the best manager in baseball, in my opinion.

MacPhail had asked Leo that winter, "What do you need to win it?"
And Leo said, "Owen and Higbe." So MacPhail went out and got
Owen from the Cardinals and me from the Phillies. That gave Leo his
team and we knew in spring training that we had a shot at it. Hellfire,
look at the ball club we had: Mickey Owen, Dixie Walker, Joe Medwick, Pee Wee Reese, Dolph Camilli, Cookie Lavagetto, Pete Reiser,
and then right after the season started we traded for Billy Herman.
Pitching, besides myself, we had Whitlow Wyatt, Curt Davis, Freddie
Fitzsimmons, and Hugh Casey.

Hugh Casey was just about the best friend I ever had in baseball. He was some pitcher, buddy. And I'll tell you another thing about old Hugh: he could drink more liquor and look better the next day than any man I ever saw. He'd go back to his hotel after a game—it was practically all day ball in those years—and start drinking and not stop until he fell asleep. Next morning he'd get up at six A.M., take a shower, light that big cigar and you'd never know he'd had a drop. And he wouldn't take another drink again until after the game. Then he'd go back to the hotel and start over again. Late in the season in '41, when we were fighting for the pennant, MacPhail said to him, "Hugh, are you going to last the season out?" And Hugh said, "If you buy me two cases of Canadian Club I'll finish up in grand style." MacPhail, being a hell of a man himself, sent him two cases of Canadian and Hugh finished up in grand style, just like he promised.

That Reiser was a ballplayer to remember, too. If he hadn't had those injuries he might have been one of the greatest that ever lived. There wasn't a thing that boy couldn't do on a ball field, and do it better than most anybody else. He had speed, power, could field, throw, and he had it inside, too. You know, in those days they'd throw at you. Well, Pete never cared. Didn't bother him at all. They'd knock him down and he'd get up and bang a line drive somewhere.

You just can't believe what a difference there was in playing for the 1940 Phillies and then for the 1941 Dodgers. One of the most memorable games I ever pitched in was against the Cubs that year, at Ebbets Field. Hooked up with Johnny Schmitz. Remember him? Good left-handed pitcher. We each had a two-hitter going into the last of the ninth and there was no score. Mickey Owen leads off with a triple. He's batting seventh. Next hitter pops up. I'm next. Leo comes in to pinch-hit for me. He was a great bunter, and he squeezed the run in and we win, 1–0. Boy, Leo was proud of that. Next day he says, "You see the importance of being able to do that," and tells us we're going to have a little bunting practice. He gets in the cage and lays down four or five perfect bunts. The next few guys don't do too well, and Leo says, "Christ, you guys don't know how to bunt." And Herman says, "Hell, Leo, you ought to know how to bunt—that's all you did for fifteen years."

We fought all year for the pennant, against the Cardinals. Half game ahead, half game behind. That's the way it seemed to go, week after week. And everybody hated the Dodgers, on account of Durocher. He stirred them up. One year Cincinnati had a chance to break the double-play record. Well, Durocher stole every time somebody got on. He said, "Nobody's going to break any records at my expense." That was Leo, all the way. So as a result they were always lined up waiting for us. Go to Cincinnati, there's Walters, Derringer, Vander Meer. Go to Chicago, Passeau and Bill Lee. Everybody wanted to beat us. Brother, if anybody ever won a pennant, the Dodgers won it in '41. Nobody gave us anything.

Durocher liked to play hunches, you know. More times than not they'd pay out for him. Sometimes they didn't. One time we're in the bottom of the ninth at the Polo Grounds, up one run, they have a man on and Johnny Mize is up. I'm pitching. I hear something from the bench, look over and Leo's giving me the curve-ball sign. I shake my head. He gives it to me again—emphatically. I shake my head again. Man, he comes flying out of there to the mound.

"I told you to throw the big son of a bitch a curve and I mean throw him a curve," he says.

"Leo," I said, "he's the best goddamned low-ball hitter in baseball and you want me to throw him the curve, right?"

"Right," he says.

"Okay," I said. "Good enough."

Leo goes back to the bench. I throw Johnny the curve and he hits it over those right-field stands clean out of the ball park. Back in the clubhouse Leo come up to me.

"Hig," he says, "I lost this one, not you."

"Oh, yeah?" I said. "You look in the papers tomorrow and see who's the losing pitcher, Durocher or Higbe."

You don't get cute with guys like Mize up there. I'll tell you what my philosophy was when I was pitching: I never tried to outsmart a hitter; I always tried to out-dummy them.

I'll give you another example of the way Leo thought. We were in Chicago. This was in '42. Around the fifth inning we were up, 5–0. They'd loosened up a few of our hitters, but nothing serious. The Cubs had just got Jimmie Foxx, and he was leading off the inning. I did a dumb thing and threw him a change-up—you shouldn't throw a guy as old as Jimmie Foxx was then a change of pace. He hit it by my ear, it sounded like a bee going by. It ended up in the center-field seats. I mean, he branded that ball. Then up comes Lou Novikoff. He hits one in the same spot. Leo comes charging out to the mound.

"What the hell are you going to do?" he asks. "You going to let them take the bread and butter out of your mouth?"

"Don't worry," I said. "I'll take care of it." I knew what he meant. So I flattened a few of them.

Next inning they bring in Paul Erickson. He could throw hard, buddy. Real hard. Old Paul went out on that mound and flattens Mickey Owen four times. I'm the next hitter. I hear Claude Passeau yelling, "Knock this cocky son of a bitch down." I yelled back, "He doesn't

Kirby Higbe in 1941.

have the guts." Smart thing to say, right? The next pitch was right on target. I went down so fast the ball passed between my hat and my head. When I got up I looked out at Erickson and he's standing there staring at me. He's not finished with me, I could tell. He knocked me down three more times. Then Reese comes up, and down he goes four times. Bases loaded now. Billy Herman comes up and cleans them. It was just beautiful to see.

We went into the bottom of the sixth inning leading, 9–2. I'm so damned mad I can't see. I figure I'm going to straighten them out now. Leo says to me, "You throw at one man it'll cost you five hundred."

"What the hell are you talking about?" I asked.

"We got what we wanted," he says.

And, by God, he was right. They'd handed us four runs. For the rest of that game they came up with their tails in the dugout, waiting to be knocked down. But I just kept throwing that ball right over the plate, and I don't think they got a base hit the rest of the way. Later on, when it was over, Leo comes up to me and says, "See how easy it is when you know how to play this game?"

Remember George Magerkurth the umpire? He was a character. Mage used to chew tobacco during a game, and he had this gap between his front teeth and when he got excited he'd just shower you with tobacco juice. One time there's a close play against us and everybody knew it had been called wrong. Everybody except Mage. Leo comes barreling out and they start yammering away at each other. Every word Mage says is soaked with tobacco juice. Finally Leo starts spitting back at him. "That'll cost you five hundred," Mage says. Leo wipes some of that juice off his face and says, "What the hell do you call this—snow?" It cost Leo fifty. That's the time the fans in Brooklyn collected five thousand pennies in a sack and put it on home plate to pay the fine for Durocher. Those were some fans in Brooklyn; they were just about on the roster.

Charley Dressen was a hell of a guy, too, in those days. He was our third-base coach. Smart baseball man, old Charley. One day I was pitching in Cincinnati, and they were hitting some line drives off of me which they had no business hitting. Charley comes up to me and says, "They're getting the catcher's signs."

"I don't believe it," I said.

"Well, they are."

"Let's see about it," I said.

Frank McCormick led off the next inning for them. I told the catcher to signal for a curve on the first pitch but that I'd throw the fastball. He did that and I fired the fastball at McCormick's head. Well, damn if he didn't stride into it, thinking that ball was going to break. Hit him right in the ear. So Dressen was right—they *were* getting the catcher's signs.

I went to the hospital that night to apologize to McCormick.

Cincinnati had another guy in the lineup in those days—Ernie Lombardi. I guess Lombardi is the greatest hitter I've ever seen. How he hasn't made the Hall of Fame is beyond me. He couldn't run—I could outrun him with an elephant on my back—and the infielders played him back on the grass. But he still hit. You'd see the infielders' lips moving in silent prayer when old Ernie came up. He's got one of the highest lifetime batting averages of any catcher. Look it up and see if it isn't so. And a great receiver, too. Biggest hands I ever saw on a man. The umpire would give him a new ball to put into play and Ernie would rub it up with one hand. You ever see anybody do *that*, buddy?

We took part of our spring training in 1942 in Havana. I think that was probably the wildest spring training any ball club ever had. Unbeknownst to all of us, MacPhail had private detectives following us around. I guess he had an idea there'd be some monkey business and he wanted to know about it. That was a different Havana from what you've got today, you know; it was wide open then.

Everybody had one of these damned Cuban detectives assigned to him. They didn't know our names, we were numbers to them, the numbers corresponding to our uniforms, you see. You'd walk out the front door and they'd start following you. But Casey sniffed them out right off. So we had that advantage. What we did, Hugh and me, we used to climb out the window at night and go our merry way. Nobody ever saw us. Then at about three or four in the morning we'd come back and climb back through the window. This goes on the whole time we're there.

Where was everybody going? To a place at 258 Colon. You never saw anything like this place at 258 Colon. The most beautiful girls in Havana. They had music, soft lights, drinks, and about fifteen rooms. Guys would come back from the ball park, have a drink at the hotel, and head straight for 258 Colon. Some of them just about had their laundry sent out from there. They'd stay till four or five o'clock in the morning and then go back to the hotel, with those Cuban detectives tailing them every step of the way.

Then it's over and we fly back to Miami. We land there and the damnedest thing happens—they don't want to let us through customs. You see, the war had just broke out a few months before and everybody was a little touchy, I guess. What happened was, when they started going through everybody's luggage they found the detectives' reports in the traveling secretary's bag, with all those numbers and information about mysterious moving around. "Number so-and-so: Returned to the hotel, had a few drinks, and went to a house of ill-repute at 258 Colon."

Pee Wee Reese (left) and Leo Durocher (right).

All these reports, one after the other. The Customs people must've thought we were spies or something, and they held us up there for quite a while. Finally they realized we were the Brooklyn Dodgers and let us back into the country.

The real thunder and lightning came the next day, though, when Leo started reading those things. He was slapping fines everywhere. Johnny Allen got hit for a thousand bucks. Johnny said if he would have known it was going to cost him that much he would have killed the detective. And if you knew Johnny Allen, he wasn't just a-tootin' his horn.

Then Leo comes to the reports on Casey and me. "Numbers so-and-so: Returned to the hotel, went to their room, and never left." Night after night. Leo crumpled those pages in his hand and looked at us. "You two guys," he said. "I don't understand it and I never will." We never told him we were going in and out of the window.

I went into the service after the 1943 season. I was in the 342nd Infantry, part of the 86th Division, the Blackhawk Division. Went through all the hell and thunder in France and Germany. No, I didn't play any ball over there; kept my arm in shape throwing hand grenades.

After the war was over in Europe they brought us home for thirty days and then shipped us out to the Pacific. We were halfway across when we heard the war with Japan was over. "Well," I told my colonel, "that's it. I'm not mad at anybody anymore." He said that was fine, but that we still had to go to the Philippines and tell the Japs there the good news that it was over.

We landed in the Philippines and sure enough, the Japs were still shooting at us. They were holed up in those hills and caves, popping away. I thought it would be a hell of a thing to get killed after the war was over. I finally ended up in Manila coaching an Olympic team. I was the only PFC in the army who had a sergeant driving him.

I came out of the service and had a good year in '46. Then in the early part of the year in '47 I was traded over to the Pirates. Billy Herman was managing the Pirates then and he wanted me. As far as being a student of the game is concerned, I'd say he was just about the smartest man I ever knew. But I think he made one mistake when he took over the team. He told them, "Fellows, there aren't going to be any rules, because rules are made to be broken." Well, there are some ballplayers who can handle that and some who can't. We had a lot of "can'ts" on that ball club.

We were playing the Dodgers in Ebbets Field one day and one of our guys had the shakes so bad his teeth were rattling. He hid out down in the bull pen the whole game so Herman wouldn't see him. After the

Ebbets Field.

game he grabbed me and said, "Kirby, I got to have a drink." I had to help him out of the ball park to a bar across the street. He ordered himself a triple shot, but he was shaking so bad he had to reach down and pick up the glass with his teeth and drink it that way. He did that twice and then was steady as a tree.

The next year we had the ball club they called "the casino on wheels." Ernie Bonham was with us that season. You remember Ernie Bonham, the old Yankee pitcher. One of the greatest guys I ever knew. Of course Ernie had come from a pretty straitlaced and businesslike organization and he wasn't prepared for what he found on the Pirates. After the train pulled out of California, where we'd gone for spring training, Ernie came up to me and said, "Hig, this is the damnedest ball club I've ever been on. You get on the train and the next thing you know the girls come back into the club car and the fellows start pairing off with them. And then it's not long before they start going back to the Pullman. And then the rest of the team begins playing high-stake poker and hearts. And when we pull into Las Vegas nobody gets off because there's more action on the train."

Ernie used to say that the ball had a rabbit in it. "Hig," he'd tell me, "it's just got to have a rabbit in it, the way it travels." One day he brought a stethoscope into the clubhouse, fixed it in his ears and put it on a ball. "Hig," he said, "I can hear the rabbit breathing in there." Then one night we were playing an exhibition game somewhere out in the boondocks. They'd roped off the outfield because it was standing-room-only out there. Somebody hit one into the crowd and goddamn if a rabbit doesn't come running out. You should've seen old Ernie jump and yell, "I told you, Hig! Told you there was a rabbit in the son of a bitch. They've knocked him right out."

Looking back, it seemed like it was all good times. Some people don't like to look back, but I don't find the view all that bad. One night in the winter of '41 I was in a nightclub in Camden, South Carolina, drinking with a good friend of mine. There was a little combo playing on the bandstand. One of the drums was resting on the floor, facing in my direction.

"Tell you what, Hig," my friend says. "I'll bet you fifty dollars you can't throw a glass through that drum."

I don't know how far it was, maybe forty feet. I picked up a shot glass and threw it right straight through that drum. So never mind those stories about Old Hig not having control. Anyway, a guy walks up and says, "That drum cost a hundred dollars, buddy." I collected my bet, added another fifty of my own and paid the guy. So I lost half a hundred on the deal, but what the hell, it gave everybody a laugh.

RALPH KINER

RALPH MCPHERRAN KINER
Born: October 27, 1922, Santa Rita, New Mexico
Major-league career: 1946–55, Pittsburgh Pirates, Chicago
  Cubs, Cleveland Indians
Lifetime average: .279

One of the greatest home run hitters of all time, Ralph
Kiner led, or was tied for the lead, in home runs his first sev-
en years in the major leagues, which is an all-time record.
Twice he hit over 50 in a season, reaching a high of 54 in
1949. Holder, or co-holder, of numerous home run records,
Kiner also had six seasons of over 100 runs batted in. In percentage of home runs per at bats, only Babe Ruth and Har-
mon Killebrew top him.

Kiner was elected to the Hall of Fame in 1975.

I've always been given credit for the line, "Home run hitters drive
Cadillacs, singles hitters drive Fords." Well, I never said it, although it was said about me, by Fritz Ostermueller, who was a pitcher
on our ball club. And I think there's probably a certain amount of in-
sight in what Fritz said. People enjoy the big pass play in football, the
heavy punchers in boxing, and the home run in baseball, but not simply the home run—they want to see that ball go a long, long distance.

When people talk about home run hitters the landmark names are
Babe Ruth, Jimmie Foxx, Mickey Mantle, Ted Williams—the men who
could put that ball out there a long way. Ironically, you don't often
hear mentioned the name of Hank Aaron, and the reason for that is simple: Hank as a rule does not hit for tremendous distance; he hits steadi-
ly and well, but it's that long ball, that 500-foot clout, which seems to
capture the imagination of the fans.

I guess I was always a power hitter, to the extent that I was always
able to hit the ball further than anyone of comparable age, going all the

way back to when I was eleven or twelve years old. It just so happened that I always set myself up to go for the long ball; this was my style, what I was capable of doing, and what the game is all about anyway—putting solid wood on the ball, scoring runs, and winning games. I was always a fellow who hit tremendously high, long fly balls. I don't know why I sent them that way; it was just a natural part of my swing.

No, I didn't consciously go for home runs. Not after my first year in the big leagues anyway. When I first came up I would swing with one hundred percent of my velocity. But that wasn't the answer. I soon learned that you set yourself up to cover the strike zone, give yourself the best possible opportunity of meeting the ball, and that if you hit it correctly with about eighty percent of the velocity you need, that was enough to send it out of the ball park. So I stayed well within myself. The secret of home run hitting is not the distance the ball goes. Sure, it was great for the ego to rock it 500 feet, which I was fortunate to do on occasion; but Johnny Mize used to say that a home run was a home run whether the ball went a mile or whether it scraped the back of the wall going over.

I was raised in Alhambra, in Southern California. I moved there from my birthplace, Santa Rita, New Mexico, with my mother after my father died. The weather being what it is in Southern California, we were able to play ball all year round, which was great. I think I must have averaged around 190 or 200 games a year when I was a kid, counting the pick-up games.

I loved all sports. Going back to when I was seven or eight years old, I wanted to be whatever the sport in season was. When the football season started I wanted to be a football player; same thing with basketball. During the Olympic Games of 1932 I wanted to be an Olympic track star. I went with the tide, and I think it was standard behavior for the average kid growing up. You like to identify with what's going on.

It wasn't until high school that I started to get seriously interested in baseball, and I think from around the time I was thirteen there was no question in my mind that I was going to be a professional baseball player.

The scouts were watching me play ball all through high school. Although the scouting system was not as elaborate and sophisticated then as it is today, there seemed to be a lot of them in the Southern California area. I had a very good offer from the Yankees, but finally decided to sign with Pittsburgh. Their offer was three thousand dollars to sign, another five thousand if I made it to the major leagues, and that they would sign me to a Class A minor league contract.

That Class A contract probably put the clincher on the deal, as far as I was concerned. That meant something in those days, because this was back when they had the sprawling minor-league organizations, and it was not unusual for it to take six or seven years to get to the major leagues. Because of the legalities involved in baseball contracts at that time, signing a Class A contract assured me of getting a chance at the major leagues in no less than four years.

The scout who signed me was Hollis Thurston, an old-time pitcher. They called him "Sloppy." The reason they called him that was because he was always impeccably dressed and indeed was a high-class man. The fact that he was the scout involved played a very influential part in my decision to sign with Pittsburgh. But I can tell you, when I saw the Pittsburgh ball park for the first time I wanted to wring Hollis Thurston's neck. It was probably the biggest ball park in the major leagues. It was 365 feet down the left field line and 457 in left center. When I saw that I was really downhearted.

I went to spring training with the Pirates in 1941 and in my very first game, against the White Sox, I hit two home runs, one off of Bill Dietrich and the other off of Thornton Lee. Later in the spring they shipped me to Albany, New York, in the Eastern League. I played there for two years, in '41 and '42. I started the 1943 season with Toronto in the International League, but after five weeks went into the Navy.

I was discharged in December, 1945. As soon as I got home I began working out. I worked out every day for two months before spring training started, so when I joined the ball club in San Bernardino I was in great shape. I was ready. I'd heard that I was slated to go to the Pacific Coast League and play with the Hollywood Stars, which was then a Pirate farm club; but I was confident I could make the big team and had made up my mind that I just wasn't going to let them send me back to the minors.

Well, I had such a tremendous spring that I think I even surprised myself a little. I hit at least a dozen home runs, some of them for real distance, knocked in a ton of runs, and won a job that nobody ever expected me to win. I opened the 1946 season in center field for the Pirates and that was the start of my major-league career.

Just to prove that that good spring I had wasn't a fluke, I went on to lead the National League in home runs that year, and I don't think any rookie, before or since, has ever done that. So it was a good beginning—but the next year I almost ended up back in the minor leagues, which tells you something about how quickly fortunes can change in baseball.

Hank Greenberg joined the ball club in 1947. Hank had been one of my first idols in baseball. The year before, 1946, he had led the American League in home runs and runs batted in. One of the great right-handed power hitters of all time. During spring training he used to spend a lot of time taking extra batting practice, after the day's session was over. I was impressed by the fact that this great star, who certainly didn't have to prove anything to anybody, was working that hard. I asked him if I could join him, and I ended up shagging balls for him and he'd shag balls for me. Later on we became roommates, and to quote Yogi Berra on Bill Dickey, Hank "learned me his experience." I got some very sound advice from him. You see, even though I'd led the league in home runs, I'd also led in strikeouts and hit only .247. So I still had some distance to go.

Hank got me in a better position in the batter's box, right on top of the plate, which enabled me to start pulling outside pitches for home runs. I changed my stance and my whole approach to hitting. Those were the right changes for me to make but they were also very tough to adapt to.

I got off to a horrendous start in 1947 and for a month and a half I was really struggling. By the end of May my record was still dismal. I was confident I'd straighten out in due time, but the ball club was beginning to have its doubts. I hit rock bottom in a game against the Cubs when Hank Borowy struck me out four times. That was the low point of my career, and I was right on the verge of being sent out to the minors.

Hank Greenberg (left) and Ralph Kiner (right) in 1947.

But Hank Greenberg went to Frank McKinney, who owned the Pirates, to speak up for me.

"Don't send this boy out," Hank said. "He's going to make it. He's got a great swing, he's very determined, and he's going to make it."

Well, they didn't send me out, but it was a close call. At the end of May I started to put it together and the turnaround came. At that point I had hit only three home runs, but starting June 1 I hit forty-eight and ended up the season with fifty-one home runs, tying Johnny Mize for the league lead.

Well when you hit fifty-one home runs in the big leagues, you get your name in the newspapers, to say the least. And it had all happened very quickly. But one thing that made it tolerable was that I don't think we had the pressures then that ballplayers have now, because there was no television. Because of the nature of the medium, television can make you very conspicuous and bring an awful lot of pressure to bear.

So while I don't think the pressures were anything like they would be today, I did get what was probably the maximum amount of exposure at the time. Frankly, I kind of liked it. I'm sort of a gregarious type person anyway. I wasn't like a country boy suddenly hitting it big in the city. Bing Crosby had bought into the Pirates in 1946 and through Bing's interest in the club and in baseball I had gotten to meet a lot of Hollyood celebrities, played golf with Bing and Bob Hope and people like that; so when I made my own way into the limelight I wasn't a total stranger to it and that helped a lot.

The Pirates in those years had a reputation for being a pretty loose and freewheeling ball club, and I guess there was some justification for that. One incident always stands out in mind. Vinnie Smith, who was one of our catchers, got married. The wedding took place on the afternoon of a day when we had a night game scheduled. Some of the ballplayers served as ushers, and after the wedding they all came out to the ball park still wearing their tuxedos, their pockets filled with cigars. When the door opened and they walked in we knew right away they'd been in champagne about as deep as you can get.

"Who we playing tonight?" they asked.

"Cincinnati," somebody said.

"Who's pitching for them?" they asked.

"Blackwell."

Their faces dropped. Ewell Blackwell was at that time just about the toughest pitcher in the league; it was bad enough to go up against him when you were sober; in the condition they were in, it could be frightening. So they marched over to the Cincinnati clubhouse, still in their tuxedos, and gave Blackwell all of the cigars and asked him not to throw too close. I don't think Blackwell had too much trouble beating us that night.

Another time, one of our pitchers got into the sauce pretty good before a game at Ebbets Field. When he got to the ball park he had the good sense to stay out of the way. During batting practice he went down the foul line and crawled into the big cylinder that held the tarpaulin which they used to cover the field with when it rained. That would have been perfect for him, he could have slept in there all day, except for one thing—it rained. The ground crew came running out and began rolling the tarpaulin out into the field and in so doing they rolled him right out of the cylinder. He was the most surprised man you ever saw, and you can be sure it sobered him up in a hurry.

I had a reputation for hitting home runs in streaks, but I think every long-ball hitter is that way. You just don't consistently get the good pitches; but then suddenly you find yourself in a groove when you are getting them, and if your timing happens to be exceptionally good on those occasions you're going to fatten up. I connected for eight home runs in four games and twice had four home runs in four consecutive times at bat, and those were both instances when I suddenly found myself getting just the right pitches to swing at. You've got to have those streaks, because it's nearly impossible to hit home runs consistently.

There's no question that the toughest pitcher for me was Ewell Blackwell. I wouldn't rate him as the fastest I ever saw, but his delivery was the toughest to fight. The fastest might have been Rex Barney, but he never had the success he might have had because he always had problems with his control. Probably the best fastball I ever saw was Robin Roberts'. Robin didn't throw as hard as Barney, but his ball would rise around six or eight inches, and with plenty on it. And he had great control, which made him very difficult to hit.

When I joined the Pirates Honus Wagner was still there as a coach. The greatest ballplayer of them all, some people say, and really a fantastic character. You know, he was one of the few old-timers who didn't knock modern-day ballplayers. He was quick to admit that the game was played better in the 1940's and 50's than it was when he played.

He used to carry an old silver dollar and after a game he would go to a saloon and throw that big coin on the bar so it made a loud ringing noise. People naturally looked around to see who it was and invariably they'd recognize him—everybody in Pittsburgh knew and loved Honus Wagner. So somebody would buy him a beer, Honus would drink it, thank the fellow, pick up the silver dollar and go to the next place and do it all over again.

We always enjoyed sitting around and listening to Honus tell stories, and he seemed to have an inexhaustible supply of them. One time he was playing shortstop, he said, and it was the top of the ninth, two out,

Honus Wagner, circa 1910.

and the tying and go-ahead runs on base. It had been a long game and it was quite dark out—this of course was long before the ball parks had lights. Somebody hit a hard smash at him and it went right through his legs. This was very embarrassing for the great Honus Wagner, but fortunately, he said, at that moment a rabbit ran by and he picked it up and threw it to first base and got the runner by a hare.

He could go on for hours with those stories. Another time there was a fight on the field, he said, and somebody got a lucky punch in against him and knocked him kind of dizzy. He was the first batter up in the bottom of the ninth and the score was tied. He hit one out of the ball park, but he said he was so dazed from the blow he'd taken that he ran the bases backwards. When he touched home plate they subtracted a run from the scoreboard and the Pirates lost the ball game.

He was a marvelous old man, and it was always a pleasure to be around him.

When Branch Rickey took over the ball club in 1952 I knew I was gone. He had a reputation for not having high-salaried ballplayers; he also had a reputation for trading players whom he felt had reached their peak and might begin to decline. I fit into both categories, so it seemed a foregone conclusion that I would be traded.

Rickey was extremely difficult to deal with when it came to signing a contract. One year I hit thirty-seven home runs and took a twenty-five percent cut. But that wasn't unusual in those days. You can't compare today's salary structure to what it was back then. But I was very fortunate in that salaries did begin increasing after the war. Before the war most of the stars made nothing compared to what we were getting. Fellows like Medwick and Dean were lucky to be getting $15,000 in their heydays. I was the highest-paid player in the National League at one time, so when Rickey took over I knew my Pittsburgh days were numbered.

Throughout most of my years with the Pirates we were a second-division club, and there's no question about it, the hardest thing in the world is to play on a losing team. The mistakes and the failures are all the more glaring and frustrating. It's an altogether different game when you're winning; it's easier to play and, obviously, more enjoyable. I always had a strong competitive drive and I hated to lose. I took an awful lot of pride out on that field with me. As far as I'm concerned, that's an important element in the makeup of a big-league ballplayer. It has to be, if you're going to get the maximum out of your ability. I could have played a few years longer than I did, but I had a bad back, and when I couldn't reach the performance level I was used to, the high standards I always set for myself, I didn't feel it was right to continue. So I quit.

MICKEY VERNON

JAMES BARTON VERNON
Born: April 22, 1918, Marcus Hook, Pennsylvania
Major-league career: 1939–60, Washington Senators, Cleve-
    land Indians, Boston Red Sox, Milwaukee Braves, Pitts-
    burgh Pirates
Lifetime average: .286

One of the most durable first basemen in big league history, Mickey Vernon was also a two-time batting champion,
leading the American League in 1946 and 1953 with averages of .353 and .337. He also led the league three times in
doubles. He holds lifetime records for most games by an
American League first baseman, as well as most putouts, as-
sists, chances accepted, and the major-league record for double plays.

Yes, I guess it's true that I was President Eisenhower's favorite ballplayer. He was quoted in the papers as having said that. The year
after I'd led the American League in batting for the second time, he
came out to the ball park to present the Silver Bat to me. I don't think
any President ever did that, before or since. Naturally I was pleased
and highly honored.

I'll never forget what happened one opening day, I think it was 1954.
The President was there, having thrown out the first ball. We were
playing the Yankees and the game went into extra innings. Allie Reynolds was pitching. I came up and hit one over the right-field fence to
win the ball game. As I rounded third I saw some of the players waiting at the plate to congratulate me, and there was one civilian there. As
I crossed the plate he grabbed my arm. I figured he was just an overly
enthusiastic fan and kind of pulled away from him.

"It's okay," he said. "I'm a Secret Service man. The President wants
to see you over at his box."

Mickey Vernon in 1940.

So I went over there and Mr. Eisenhower was standing up with a big grin on his face and his hand outstretched.

"Nice going," he said.

That was a great thrill, hitting the home run to win on opening day and then being congratulated by the President. I met him on a few other occasions and was always impressed by how much he knew about the game; he was a real fan.

I grew up in Marcus Hook, Pennsylvania. It was an industrial town. Sun Oil has one of their largest refineries there—my dad worked for the company for over forty years—and there's also a British properties refinery, a rug mill, and a lot of other industry. When all this talk about pollution started, it wasn't anything new to me; I'd grown up in it.

I always wanted to be a ballplayer. Living near Philadelphia, I used to go to Shibe Park and watch those great Athletic teams that Connie Mack had. Some of my idols back then were Lefty Grove, Mickey Cochrane, Jimmie Foxx. I used to wait outside the ball park hoping to get Grove's autograph, but I never did get it. He'd come storming out and brush right past you. Seemed like he was always mad..Of course, later on I played against some of those men. The first time I hit against Grove my knees were shaking so bad they wouldn't stop. As luck would have it, I singled to center and when I got to first base I just couldn't believe it. Here was a guy who was already a legend, whom I'd watched pitch so many times from the bleachers. It's a peculiar experience to suddenly be in there against somebody like that, who was always bigger than life. I guess once you've been a fan a little of the awe and wonder stays with you forever.

I went to Villanova for a year, where I played freshman ball, but then I had a chance to play pro ball in the Eastern Shore League and I jumped at it. The club had a working agreement with the St. Louis Browns. Bill DeWitt was running the Browns at the time and he came down to look the team over, decided there were no prospects, and didn't pick up my option or anyone else's. So I was sold to the Washington club. That's how I got to the Washington Senators.

You've heard the old saying, "Washington, first in war, first in peace, and last in the American League." Well, it wasn't true during the period I played there. We always had the Browns and the Athletics underneath us. As a matter of fact, when I first joined the Senators they had a pretty good ball club, with guys like Cecil Travis, Buddy Lewis, Taft Wright, Buddy Myer, George Case. They were all good hitters. We were a bit thin on pitching; that was our problem.

Cecil Travis was a really outstanding hitter. You know, the year Ted Williams hit .406, Cecil hit .359, but nobody noticed it. He hit .300 as steady as clockwork, until he went into the service. He went through

Left to right: Ossie Bluege, Joe Kuhel, Buddy Lewis, John Mihalic, Buddy Myer, Cecil Travis during 1937 spring training in Orlando, Florida.

the Battle of the Bulge, where he had his feet frozen, and when he came back after the war he was never the same again.

I went into the Navy after the '43 season. I spent the summer of '44 at Norfolk, playing ball. After the season they rounded up a bunch of ballplayers, put us on a ship in San Francisco and sent us over to Honolulu. That's when I found out I shouldn't have gone into the Navy. I got seasick even before the Golden Gate Bridge was out of sight. I think it must have been one of the most monumental cases of seasickness anyone ever had. It was supposed to be a ten-day trip to Honolulu but it took us eleven because of a submarine threat that cost us a day stalling around. That was around the fifth day of the trip and I'll tell you, by that time I was so sick I was almost hoping that baby would come around and sink us.

On about the third day out I was lying in my bunk absolutely dead to the world. Big Mike Budnick, who pitched for the Giants, picked me up and threw me over his shoulder and carried me to sick bay where they kept me for a day or so, giving me pills and trying to cheer me up. Then they turned me out and I spent the rest of the trip up on the deck, which helped a little but not enough to make much difference.

I was too weak to shave, and by the time we got to Honolulu my beard had grown, and I had become so gaunt in my misery that the other players started calling me "Abe" — they said I looked like Abraham Lincoln. For years after the war anytime I met any of the guys who were on that trip they called me Abe. We had Elbie Fletcher, Johnny Lucadello, Pee Wee Reese, Pinky May, Johnny Mize, Barney McCosky, Tom Ferrick, Virgil Trucks, Johnny Rigney, Johnny Vander Meer, Gene Woodling, and some others.

Del Ennis was with us too out in the Pacific. Del had played just one year of minor-league ball, but he did very well against the big-league ballplayers. He was really impressive. There was a story to the effect that Dan Topping, who had recently bought the Yankees and who was in the service himself, saw Del playing in Hawaii and offered him a twenty-five-thousand-dollar bonus if he would sign with the Yankees.

"I'm already signed," Del said.

"With who?" Topping asked.

"The Phillies."

"You get a bonus?" Topping asked.

Del smiled and said, "Fifty dollars."

After about five months in Honolulu they got us together and sent us out to the islands to play ball for the guys stationed out there. The deal was we were supposed to come back to Honolulu when the tour was completed; but when we got to Guam they separated us and assigned us to different islands for duty. Elbie Fletcher, I remember, went to Peleliu and I went to Ulithi, while the rest of the guys stayed on the three big islands, Guam, Saipan, and Tinian. Fletcher and I always wondered how in the heck they decided to ship us out. As far as we could tell, Peleliu and Ulithi really didn't need left-handed hitting first basemen. I ended up on an atoll about a mile long by a quarter mile wide. I stayed there about ten months and by then I had the thousand-yard stare.

We organized a softball league on Ulithi and two of the young fellows we had in the league were Larry Doby and Billy Goodman. Doby was a great athlete. We got to be good friends. Many a night he'd come by my tent and we'd spend hours and hours talking. He was planning to go back and play for the Newark Eagles in the Negro League after the war. This was before the color barrier had been broken, of course. He never talked about that, though I'm sure he was hoping the situation would change. I remember I wrote a letter home to my father saying that if they ever did accept Negro players that here was a fellow I was sure would be in the big leagues someday. And sure enough, he was the first one in the American League, and he had a great career.

I guess a lot of people were surprised when I led the league in 1946. And I'll confess, I was one of them. I hadn't had a .300 year before the war and suddenly I come out and hit .353. I don't think you can explain what the difference was. Luck was part of it. Most every time I hit a ball well it went in. Sometimes you can have a year like that, when you just stay sharp and healthy and lucky all the time.

When I tell you a lot of people were surprised, I'm not kidding. At the All-Star game in Boston that year Bob Feller was going around talking to fellows to see if they were interested in going on a barnstorming trip after the season. He was guaranteeing them so much a game. I was leading the league at the time, and I don't think he thought I would still be on top at the end of the season, because when he made his offer to me he said, "I'll give you so much extra if you lead the league." Now, Bob can be pretty conservative with a buck, so I'm sure he never expected me to finish up on top. When I was traded over to Cleveland in '49 we talked about that and he laughed and said, "You got one on me, didn't you?" But it was a wonderful trip. Bob let me bring my wife along and he couldn't have been nicer.

Bucky Harris used to have a saying every time Feller would pitch against us: "Go up and hit what you see, and if you don't see it come on back." That first half year I was up, in '39, I faced Feller about fifteen times and I think he struck me out nine of those times. He was tough, the toughest pitcher I ever faced. He didn't just have the best fastball, he also had the best curve I ever saw.

Ted Lyons was still going strong when I broke in, and he was another tough pitcher to hit. He had a good knuckleball, and he was quick, and had an outstanding change-up. I used to hear stories about how physically strong he was. I didn't see this, but I heard about it: The A's and the White Sox were on the same train going somewhere. Ted was walking through one of the cars and Jimmie Foxx was standing in the aisle. Jimmie was a playful guy and he wouldn't move out of the way. So Lyons just took hold of him, lifted him up and sat him in an upper berth and then walked on.

Satchel Paige was on the club with me in Cleveland. I remember one day in spring training in Arizona some of the guys were kidding him about his control. "I'll show you some control," he said. He took a chewing gum wrapper and put it down in front of the catcher and threw about eight out of ten right across it. And he wasn't lobbing them in either, he was putting some zip on them.

I had a bad year in '48 and so did Early Wynn, and we were both traded to Cleveland. I did all right in '49, but at the same time they had Luke Easter having a great year in Triple-A. Luke was ready to come

Larry Doby.

up and become the first baseman in 1950. So Hank Greenberg, who was general manager at the time, asked me during contract negotiations if I would like trying to play the outfield.

"Well," I said, "if I try it I'm going to have to have more money on my contract."

"I can't do that," he said.

"Why not?"

"It just isn't done," he said.

"Well," I said, "I remember a first baseman with Detroit in the thirties who moved from first to the outfield and got x number of dollars for doing it."

I was talking about Hank himself, of course. He kind of grinned, but he didn't give me the money.

They tried Easter in the outfield for a while, but that didn't pan out, and they put him back on first. That made me expendable, and I was traded back to Washington in June, 1950. It would have been nice to have gone to a contender, but I really couldn't complain too much. You had to look at it this way: there were only eight first basemen in the American League at that time, and you were one of them.

Early Wynn and I sort of grew up together in the Washington organization. When he was with Washington he was still pretty much of a thrower, a guy with a good arm and a good fastball. But when he went to Cleveland in that deal Mel Harder began working with him and Early developed some good breaking stuff and became a great pitcher, a 300-game winner.

He was a tough competitor and wasn't shy about bearing in on you. When we were together with Cleveland we were roommates and good friends. After I was traded back to Washington I got four hits off of him the first time I faced him, the last one knocking the glove off his hand. He hated when anybody hit back through the middle. When I got to first base I turned around and I could tell he was steaming. He looked over at me and said, "Roommate or not, you've got to go in the dirt next time I see you." Sure enough, next time I faced him the first pitch was up over my head — not at my head — to let me know he hadn't forgotten.

In 1953 I got lucky all over again and won the batting crown for a second time, with an average of .337. Beat out Al Rosen by one point. Al is a very good friend of mine and I would have liked to have seen him win it because it would have given him the Triple Crown; but naturally I wanted to win it, too. I was leading the league most of the year, but then coming down the stretch he got hot, getting two or three hits a game. I think if the season had been just a few games longer he might have passed me.

I had a few points cushion that last game, which it turned out I needed, because Al got three hits and still didn't catch me. I heard that he missed another hit when he grounded to third and beat the throw but then ran over the bag at first without touching it and was called out. That sometimes happens, you know, when the runner thinks he's an easy out; but in this case the third baseman was a little slow coming up with it and Al just didn't step on the bag. I guess that made the difference, since I beat him out by just a point, even though I had a bad game.

I could have won the batting crown by sitting down that last game, but I just couldn't do it. I wanted to win it swinging, or lose it swinging.

You know, in my first full year in the big leagues we came into New York to end the season against the Yankees and I was hitting .302. This was my rookie season and I would loved to have hit .300. Before the series Bucky Harris said to me, "You want to hit three hundred?"

"Sure I do," I said.

"Okay," he said. "I'll sit you down."

"No," I said. "I want to play." I thought he might be testing me, to see what kind of guy I was.

By the last game, on Sunday, I was down to .299. In those days the visiting club came onto the field through the Yankee dugout. I was coming along the runway and Red Rolfe stopped me.

"I see you need a few hits to get three hundred," he said. The New York papers printed both teams' batting averages in the box scores and I guess that's where he'd seen it.

"That's right," I said.

"Well," he said, "if you drop a bunt or two I'll be back on my heels." The Yankees had long since clinched the pennant, of course, so this game didn't mean anything.

The first three times up we had men on base, so I didn't have a chance to bunt. But I did get one hit. I came up for the last time, needing one more hit for .300. There was nobody on base. I looked down at Rolfe and he was playing way back. Okay, I thought, here's my .300. I dropped one down and Rolfe barely moved. But I'll be a son of a gun if Dickey doesn't come charging out, pick up the ball and throw me out. We'd forgotten about him. And I ended the season with an average of .299.

I've heard about guys sitting down on the last day of the season to clinch a batting title or freeze an average. Well, I don't like to criticize anybody, but I would think that that standard was set once and for all by Ted Williams in 1941. He came into the last day of the season hitting .400 on the button and had a double-header scheduled. Ted could

Griffith Stadium, Washington, D.C.

very easily have sat down and taken it. But he wouldn't think of it. He played both games and rapped out enough hits to end up with .406. Now *that's* the way to do it.

I was on the Rex Sox when Ted hit .388. That was in 1957, when he was thirty-eight years old. Was I surprised at what he was doing? Not in the least. I'd been watching him for more than fifteen years by that time, so I was never surprised at anything he did with the bat.

I was hitting right behind him that year. You know, if he was leading off an inning he couldn't wait to grab his bat and get up to the plate to watch the pitcher take his warm-up throws. Or if he was the hitter and they were changing pitchers he would move up to watch the new pitcher warm up, to see what the ball was doing. He was always studying. Well, one day we've got the bases loaded against the Yankees and they're making a pitching change, Ted's the hitter, and I'm on deck.

The Yankees bring in Tommy Byrne, a good left-hander. Tommy was something of a character; a well-educated guy, but he would do some quirky things now and then. When Tommy reaches the mound Ted turns around and calls me over. "Have a look at this guy," he says. "See what his ball is doing." So I walk over and we're standing together about seven or eight feet from the plate, watching Byrne get ready. Tommy didn't like that. He winds up, watching us out of the corner of his eye, and the first pitch is right at us, with something on it. We ducked under it, and Williams says, "Flaky left-handed bastard. If that ball had hit us I would have gone out there and pinched his head off." And then Ted stepped in and hit one right back through the middle for a base hit.

When I first came into the league in 1939 the Red Sox had Williams and Foxx in the lineup. That was a one-two punch to match anybody's. I can remember, when I was a rookie, whenever somebody would hit a real long ball and there was some comment about it on the bench, one of the older players would say, "You think that was long? Well, there's where Foxx hit one," and they'd point much further, much deeper. And that was in every park.

I'd put Mantle right there, though. He hit some of the longest balls I ever saw. He hit one off of Chuck Stobbs that went over the bleachers in Griffith Stadium. That was one time when nobody stood up and said, "You should have seen the one Foxx hit." That was a blast all by itself. They said it went around 560 feet and I can believe it.

My all-star team? Well, that's not as easy to answer as it seems. I'll try, but I think we'd better confine it to the American League, to the era I played in. Dickey was just finishing up, so I won't put him on, even though everybody knows how great he was. So my catcher would have to be Berra. I didn't see that much of Foxx, so I'll pick George

McQuinn for first base. The rest of my infield would be Joe Gordon, Luke Appling and Brooks Robinson. The outfielders are Williams, Di-Maggio, Mantle. My right-handed pitcher is Feller and my left-hander is Whitey Ford. That's my team. And when people read this I'll probably get some letters, right?

JOHNNY VANDER MEER

JOHN SAMUEL VANDER MEER
Born: November 2, 1914, Prospect Park, New Jersey
Major-league career: 1937–51, Cincinnati Reds, Chicago
    Cubs, Cleveland Indians
Lifetime record: 119 wins, 121 losses

Johnny Vander Meer will, of course, be remembered primarily as the only man in major-league history to pitch two
consecutive no-hit games. However, for many years after
that unprecedented and unequaled feat, Vander Meer
reigned as one of the National League's premier left-handers. He led the league in strikeouts in 1941, '42, and '43.

I do a lot of traveling today in my work and I'd say that at least once a
day I hear about my no-hitters. Somebody will hear the name—my
name isn't all that common — and ask me if I'm *that* Johnny Vander
Meer. Nobody else, before or since, has ever pitched consecutive
no-hitters and I guess it's just something that's caught the public's imagination. Some of the people who talk to me about it weren't even born
when I pitched those games back in 1938; but that doesn't seem to
make any difference, they still like to ask me about them. No, I don't
mind. It's no burden when they remember you for something you're
proud of having done.

Did I want to play big-league ball? Well, kids always have had their
dreams, haven't they? I played ball all the time, in the streets, in the
fields, at school; that's all I did. Ate it, drank it, slept it. I think most of
the boys at that time wanted to be big leaguers. What do they want to
be today? Astronauts maybe. I don't know. But the thinking is the
same.

I grew up in Midland Park, New Jersey. That's not too far out of New
York City. Carl Hubbell was my idol in those days. Whenever I could
scrape together the money I'd make the trip into New York and go up to
the Polo Grounds to watch him pitch. He was the greatest left-hander

of his day, so naturally I tried to imitate him. Of course we were direct opposites in our pitching styles. He relied on that marvelous screwball and a great curve, and sharp control—when Hubbell was wild he threw the ball over the heart of the plate. I was a power pitcher, trying to get the ball over the plate, and when I did I was all right.

Ironically enough, my first big-league start was against Hubbell at the Polo Grounds. I pitched the first nine innings of an extra-inning game and wasn't involved in the decision. But there I was, pitching at the Polo Grounds against Carl Hubbell. So when you hear about kids chasing rainbows, don't laugh, because we live in the kind of world where they can catch them. It happened to me.

You know, I was originally signed by the Brooklyn Dodgers. I was pitching semipro ball in New Jersey at the time. This was in 1932. We had our own team, our own little organization. You got thirty cents an inning when you pitched. That's right, paid by the inning. You never heard of that, huh? If you didn't go nine you got paid only for the innings you pitched. There was always a guy down in the bull pen waiting for you to get knocked out. This was back in the Depression, remember, and everybody was scrambling for whatever they could get.

The Dodgers sent me out to Dayton, Ohio, in 1933. I was supposed to be getting $125 a month, which wasn't bad money in 1933. But things were a little tough. When payday came around they'd say, "How much do you need to get by?" They might give you a third of your money, or two-thirds. At the end of the season they owed me $250. Everybody was at the bottom of the barrel in those days.

The next year I was assigned back to Dayton. I went, but I wouldn't sign a contract until they paid me what they owed me from the previous year. Halfway through spring training the Dayton club made a deal for me with Scranton, in the New York-Penn League. So I was now the property of the Scranton Miners, and the deal there was if I was sold they were going to split the money with the Dodgers. Then the Dodgers stepped in and wanted to know what I was doing at Scranton; they claimed they still owned me. In those days there was a lot of manipulating of minor-league players, contrary to existing baseball law.

I finally wound up in front of Judge Landis. He held a hearing and awarded me to Scranton. He also got me my back money. The following year the Boston Braves bought me from Scranton. Then they traded me to Nashville and Nashville sent me to Durham. That's where I pitched in 1936 and I had a good year. I won *The Sporting News* Minor League Player of the Year Award for 1936. The Reds had a working agreement with Durham and they bought me. That's how I ended up with Cincinnati.

In 1937 I went to spring training with the Reds and split that year between Cincinnati and Syracuse.

Carl Hubbell in 1933. "Carl Hubbell was my idol in those days."

Bill McKechnie was managing the Reds at that time. I can sincerely say that I was proud to play for him. He was one of the greatest individuals I ever met in my life, either on the field or off. Ballplayers never feared McKechnie; they respected him. He had a remarkable ability for evoking respect; a great handler of men. He was the most outstanding defensive manager I ever saw. We were not noted as a heavy hitting team, so all of his skills and insights were directed toward defense, from handling his pitchers to positioning his men in the field. He was so skillful at doing these things that we never had to score too many runs to win. McKechnie knew how to hold onto a one- or two-run lead better than any other manager.

If you're willing to listen and learn in baseball you'll find there's an awful lot of experience around you all the time. One spring, it was either '37 or '38, we traveled north with the Red Sox. Grove was on that ball club, near the end of his career now, but still the greatest mechanical throwing pitcher I've ever seen. He threw easily, with a tremendous amount of rhythm, which probably is one reason he was able to pitch for so many years. When I wasn't in the game I'd go and sit in the Red Sox bull pen with Grove and just listen to him. He alway had that great will to win and he helped fix that in my mind. I absorbed as much as I possibly could and became a real Lefty Grove fan.

I always had a tendency to walk a lot of men, but at the same time I always struck out a lot—I led the league in strikeouts three years in a row. You can minimize the disadvantages of wildness if you can strike them out. If you can pitch yourself out of trouble after you've pitched yourself in, the manager will leave you in there. I always had the ability to strike somebody out in a jam. So wildness never bothered me mentally. Neither did three-and-two pitches. I followed Grove's philosophy in that. He always said that if you had good stuff, then on a three-and-two pitch the batter was hurting more than you were.

You see, you have to understand your abilities in relation to the job you're being asked to do. I knew I was wild, that I was going to throw more pitches in a game than the average pitcher. So I trained harder, worked harder to stay in condition. As far as I was concerned, I was going out there to pitch eleven innings, because my nine innings were equivalent to somebody else's eleven.

On Saturday, June 11, 1938, I started against the Boston Braves. I had pretty good control that particular ball game, though I wasn't real fast. But I had good stuff and my ball was tailing. I was hitting that low and outside spot consistently all day and a lot of balls were hit on the ground. Harry Craft made a nice catch in center field during the game to rob somebody of a base hit, otherwise it was pretty much a routine ball game. I was in control all the way; never in trouble at any time. I shut them out without a hit, 3–0.

That was the first no-hitter, the one that nobody remembers. But without that one there wouldn't have been a second. The second one was an entirely different type of ball game. First of all, the game was a festive occasion even before it started. It was June 15, 1938, the first night game ever in Ebbets Field. Larry MacPhail made a big thing out of it. The ball park was jammed. The game was held up for about twenty-five minutes, as a matter of fact, because they were still selling tickets. People were sitting in the aisles and were standing all over the place. The fire department had to come and remove some people from the park because of overcrowding, and naturally they didn't want to go, and this took some time. So it was quite a background for what was going to happen.

And on top of all that, I figured I was going to be jinxed that night. You see, a whole contingent of friends and relatives from New Jersey came out for the game. Around seven hundred of them. There was a little ceremony prior to the game and they gave me a watch. According to baseball tradition, anytime you're honored like that by your friends you're supposed to have a bad game. I was sure I'd be out of there by the third inning.

I started the ball game and I was quick. I was real quick that night. I don't think I threw more than five curveballs over the first seven innings. The curve was hanging; for some reason, when I had the exceptionally good fastball I didn't have the real sharp curve. But the fastball was moving and I wasn't having any trouble. Along about the seventh inning the fastball was easing up a little and I began throwing more curves. The curve started to work for me and that was a break because everybody was looking for the fastball and that made me a little more effective.

In the last of the eighth I put them down in order. I got Woody English, Kiki Cuyler, and Johnny Hudson. So you can imagine what that ninth inning was like. The Brooklyn fans were pulling for me by that time; they wanted to see it happen. We were winning the game 6–0, so that wasn't a factor. Frank McCormick had hit a big three-run homer in the third inning, and that lead made things a whole lot easier.

Now, in neither game did I consciously go for a no-hitter until the last inning. By that I mean I just pitched along as I would have under ordinary circumstances. I'd been involved in too many ball games with no hits for six or seven innings. You've got to wait for the big inning, the ninth. So in the ninth inning I started pressing.

Buddy Hassett was the first man up. He hit a little grounder along the first-base line and I fielded it and tagged him out myself.

One out.

Then I got wild. I walked the bases full—Babe Phelps, Cookie Lavagetto, Dolph Camilli. Three pretty good hitters. Maybe it was a good thing I walked them. What I was doing was forcing myself, trying to throw the ball harder than I could. I wasn't holding anything back.

McKechnie called time and came out to the mound.

"You're trying too hard, John," he said.

I knew exactly what he meant. And he was right.

"Just get it over the plate," he said. "For all you know somebody will hit it right back to you and you'll get a double play out of it."

Then he went back and I was alone out there again.

So I concentrated on throwing strikes. Ernie Koy was the batter. I ran the count on him to one and one and then he hit a ball down to Lew Riggs at third base. Lew had the option of going for the double play, but it was a long double play, and Ernie Koy was one of the better runners in the league. So Lew went home with it, to Lombardi. Lom took the throw and wheeled around to try and get Koy at first. But Koy was a smart baserunner and he was running inside the line, blocking Lombardi's line of vision, and there was no throw.

But that was two out and now Leo Durocher was up. I got two strikes on him and then something happened that I'll never forget as long as I live. The umpire was Bill Stewart, and incidentally, he was a good one. But Stewart was kind of short and occasionally had trouble seeing over big Lombardi. Well, I hit that outside corner with about two inches to spare, and he missed it. He called it a ball. Lombardi gave him a little blast, but I didn't say anything. There was no sense in upsetting myself, not in that spot.

On the next pitch Durocher lifted an easy fly ball to Harry Craft in center field, and that was it. And do you know who was the first guy out to the mound? Bill Stewart. He came running out and he said, "John, I blew that pitch. If you hadn't got him out I was the guy to blame for it." That was real nice of Bill to say that; but I'm just wondering: If Durocher had got a base hit, would he have come out and said it anyway?

Of course there was chaos after it was over. The fans spotted my dad in the stands and mobbed him to congratulate him. The police had to take him through the dugout to get him away. The funny thing was, Dad didn't know very much about baseball and was probably the only person in the ball park who didn't know I'd set a record. He was wondering what all the fuss was about.

Four days later I started again, up in Boston. Casey Stengel was managing the Boston club then. Well, I started off with three more hitless innings. That was 21⅓ straight no-hit innings. You could just feel what everybody in the ball park was thinking: *What gives with this guy?* To tell you the truth, I was beginning to wonder myself.

In the bottom of the fourth Stengel switched from coaching third and went over to first. Of course, Casey is Casey, and I think he tried to

Bob Feller (left) and Johnny Vander Meer (right) at the 1938 All-Star Game.

psyche me a little. As he was crossing over to first he made sure he passed in front of me as I was beginning to loosen up. He looked down so nobody could see he was talking to me, and said, "John, we're not trying to beat you, we're just trying to get a base hit." And they did, that inning. Debs Garms got it; he hit a three-and-two pitch right back through the box. To be honest about it, I was relieved; the pressure had become too much and I was glad to get out from under it. Enough was enough.

In 1939 I was going along pretty good. Then one day I was pitching a ball game in Pittsburgh. There was a rain delay for about an hour, and then we started up again. I went back out to the mound, and as I was throwing a ball my foot slipped as I came down on it, and I heard something in my shoulder make a noise. I finished the ball game all right, but the next day the pain set in. I had torn all the muscles underneath my shoulder blades into my back.

I had to go down to Indianapolis in 1940 to work it out and finally came back to Cincinnati at the end of August. That was in time for the September drive. We'd won the pennant in '39 and were about to win it again. We were in Philadelphia and needed one more win to clinch it. McKechnie gave me the ball and told me to go out and win us a pennant.

The Phillies were not a very strong club in those days, but they had a first-rate pitcher going for them that day, Hugh Mulcahy. This was an important game for me, very important. Not only was I anxious to nail it down for the club, but it was going to be a good test to see how far I'd come back from that injury.

In the seventh inning the score was 2–2. It went into the tenth inning. We scored a run in the top of the tenth, but darn if I didn't let them tie it up. So we kept going, into the thirteenth. I led off the inning and got hold of one and whacked it for a double. They sacrificed me to third, and then Ival Goodman brought me home with a fly ball. McKechnie brought in Joe Beggs to pitch the last of the thirteenth and Joe held them. That gave us the pennant.

That was a tremendous game for me. I had pitched twelve strong innings without tiring. It gave me back all my confidence. I knew I hadn't done any permanent damage to my arm and was going to be able to continue playing ball.

What's the greatest game I ever pitched? That was in Brooklyn. No, it wasn't the second no-hitter. It was in September of '46. The Dodgers were deadlocked at the time with the Cardinals, fighting for the pennant. The game meant an awful lot to them. It went nineteen innings and ended in a 0–0 tie. They finally had to call it because of darkness because at that time you weren't allowed to turn the lights on to complete a game.

I went the first fifteen innings and gave up only seven hits. I struck out fifteen and walked only two. I was still going strong, too, and probably could have kept pitching, but I was thrown out at the plate trying to score in the top of the fifteenth and McKechnie was afraid I might have tired myself out. Harry Gumbert came in and finished it. I don't think I made a bad pitch that whole game. Branch Rickey said later it was the greatest game he ever saw pitched. I thought it was pretty fine myself, but I wish I could have won it.

BILL WERBER

WILLIAM MURRAY WERBER
Born: June 20, 1908, Berwyn, Maryland
Major-league career: 1930, 1933–42, New York Yankees,
    Boston Red Sox, Philadelphia Athletics, Cincinnati Reds,
    New York Giants
Lifetime average: .271

A scrappy, aggressive player, Billy Werber was one of the game's most consistent third basemen during his ten years in the big leagues. Three times he led the American League in stolen bases, and in 1934 hit .321 for the Red Sox, his finest season. In 1939–40 he anchored third base for two pennant-winning Cincinnati teams.

I signed a contract with the New York Yankees after graduating from Duke University and I joined them at the Chase Hotel in St. Louis. I made the tour of the western cities with them and we came back to Yankee Stadium. This was in early July, 1930. Then Lyn Lary, the regular shortstop, was hurt in a ball game, and George Wuestling, the utility man, played the first game of a double-header and became ill. So they put me in at short for the second game. That was my introduction to professional baseball.

No, I wasn't awed by it at all, even though I was out on the field with some remarkably gifted ballplayers. The Yankees had a tremendous ball club. They had Bill Dickey, Lou Gehrig, Ben Chapman, Tony Lazzeri, Earle Combs, Babe Ruth. All of those fellows hit over .300 that year. In fact, the low man among the regulars that year was Lyn Lary, and he hit around .290. But I was a very confident young man and I expected to go out there and take over the shortstop job. I really did. After all, I'd hit .450 at Duke, hadn't I?

But you live and learn. I soon realized that I really didn't have enough experience as yet to go right in and play major-league baseball. There are a lot of tricks you think you know when you're a collegiate star, but it's a far cry from the major leagues.

The coach at Duke when I got there was an old-time major-league ballplayer named George Whitted. I think George saw in me a good major-league prospect and the possibility of his earning some additional money if he could sell me to a big-league club. So there were a lot of scouts that looked at me in my freshman year at Duke. At the end of that year I had made a verbal agreement with Paul Krichell to play with the New York Yankees when I was through at Duke. There were certain sums of money to be paid for my education the remaining three years at the university, plus a certain bonus amount to be paid when I graduated.

I had always been interested in baseball and I worked awfully hard at it, but that was primarily for personal success and satisfaction and not necessarily to make a career. I went to Duke with the idea ultimately of going into law; I had taken a prelegal course and intended to practice law. The Yankees finally asked me whether I meant to go on with my educational pursuits or play ball. By that time I was married and had a young child and had to go to work for a living. So I got into baseball, was reasonably successful at it and began earning pretty good money.

As I said, that was a tremendous Yankee ball club I joined in 1930. And right at the heart of it was Babe Ruth. Babe was a loud, gregarious person. I played a lot of bridge, with Dickey as a partner, against Ruth and Gehrig. Babe used to drink quite a bit on the trains, and he was a good bridge player until he had put away some of that liquor, and then he'd begin giving Gehrig bad bids, at which point the game usually broke up.

Ruth never knew who you were. He called everybody "Keed." One day at Back Bay Station in Boston Tony Lazzeri brought Myles Thomas up and introduced him to Babe as a new pitcher who had just joined the ball club from Yale. Babe stuck out his big mitt and said, "Hi, Keed. Glad to have you on the club." The fact was, Myles Thomas had been a relief pitcher on the Yankees for three or four years.

Ruth was a friendly man, always kindly toward strangers. He would sign autographs by the hour. He was much more responsive to people than Gehrig was. Lou didn't like to stop and sign autographs when leaving the ball park. He was a loner, never had much to say to anybody. But on the other hand, unlike Ruth, he was a clean-living fellow, didn't smoke, didn't drink. He seemed to have a great deal of tolerance for pain. I saw him play a whole series of ball games with a broken finger on his glove hand. This was before his consecutive-game streak had reached unique proportions and there was no special reason for him to be in there, except that he was that kind of man and that kind of ballplayer. He was a tremendously powerful man physically, extremely muscular, very determined, a great hustler.

Billy Werber in 1940.

Babe and Lou were total opposites in personality, and they didn't hit it off too well, actually. Babe would needle Lou a great deal. Ruth didn't have too much regard for anybody that had gone to college, and he would call Lou a kink-head college kid, and things like that. Gehrig ignored it. I guess he considered the source.

Well, the Yankees farmed me out to get that experience. I was out for two years and came back in the spring of 1933. I had a very fine spring and under ordinary circumstances would have been the Yankee short-stop. But at that time the Yankees were well stocked at short; they also had Lyn Lary and Frank Crosetti. So I was sold to the Red Sox.

I was disappointed about leaving the Yankees, but at the same time I was glad to have the opportunity to go to Boston and play regularly. I had heard good things about Tom Yawkey, that he was determined to build a winning club in Boston. And he did go out and buy a lot of good ballplayers over the next few years. The same year I joined them they got Rick Ferrell from the Browns, and later on they got fellows like Jimmie Foxx, Lefty Grove, Rube Walberg, Doc Cramer.

We had both Ferrells there for a while with the Red Sox. Wes came over from Cleveland in 1934. He was a good pitcher and possessed a world of confidence. For example, in spring training in 1935 every-body was hitting him. He just couldn't get anybody out. But each time he was knocked out of the box he'd go to Cronin and say, "Joe, don't worry about it. I'm going to be just fine. I want opening day. I want to pitch against Gomez at the Stadium. I'll be ready." And Cronin would say to me, "How in the world can I start that guy on opening day? He hasn't gotten anybody out in spring training."

Well, he started Wes on opening day in Yankee Stadium, against Gomez. Wes walked the first man that faced him on four pitches. And then he tore the mound up with his spikes, pulled his cap down tight on his head, and went ahead and pitched a whale of a ball game. He beat Gomez, 1–0.

Wes was a marvelous character. I've seen him, after being removed from a ball game, hit himself in the jaw with both fists and nearly knock himself out. I've seen him jump in the air and crush the face out of an expensive watch. I've seen him tear card deck after card deck to pieces because he wasn't getting good hands. He hated to lose, at any-thing. He was a very determined competitor, the kind you like to have on your side.

Jimmie Foxx joined us in '36. Jim could hit a ball so far that it's just a pity they weren't putting tape measures on them in those days. I saw him hit one in Cleveland one day I never will forget it. It went beyond the left-field bleachers, which was 417 feet. The bleachers ran up to a big Lux soap sign and beyond the sign was a very tall white oak tree.

Foxx hit the ball through the top of that tree. We all jumped up in the dugout the moment he hit it to see where it was going. Dusty Cooke stood on the top step of the dugout gazing out toward left field for a few moments, then turned to me and said, "It's a damned lie." That ball must have gone close to 600 feet.

Jimmie was a very pleasant fellow. Happy-go-lucky, always smiling. Never saw him mad. And as strong as he was, it was a good thing he had that sort of disposition. He could wrap his hands around my ankles and lift me straight up off the floor—and I weighed 178 pounds. We called him "The Beast." Amazing calves, forearms, biceps, shoulders. Unbelievable strength. And he showed it the way he hit those long balls. There wasn't a ball park in the league that could hold Jimmie.

I played for Bucky Harris my second year at Boston. Harris was a great practical joker, you know. One time on a long train ride to St. Louis he decided to liven things up. He had a cigar and I got some bluehead matches and we pushed them into the cigar. There was a very intense poker game going on around a table in the men's room. We went in there and Harris lit the cigar. The moment those matches began to flare up he threw the cigar onto the table. Well, those guys thought it was a giant firecracker and they jumped up and went barreling out of there so fast that the table flew up and the cards and the money all went flying into spittoons and wash basins and all over the floor . . . while that cigar just lay there smoking harmlessly away.

You always had practical jokers on ball clubs in those days. We had another fellow, Tom Daley, who could knock your eye out with a bamboo toothpick and a BB. He'd take a BB shot and press it down hard between his teeth and with a flick of this hard tensile bamboo sliver shoot that BB with great velocity and uncanny accuracy. He would go into a movie theater and always find himself a baldheaded man and drive him crazy, sitting there in the dark quietly bouncing BB's off of that man's bald head.

One year down in spring training they found out that Oscar Melillo had a fear of animals. So somebody went and got a baby alligator and put it in Melillo's locker and covered it with a shirt. When Oscar came in to dress after the game and picked up the shirt he uncovered the alligator. He took one look at it, whirled around and, in an advanced state of undress, shot out of that clubhouse and wouldn't come back until somebody had got rid of the alligator.

Another time Melillo went to the movies with Heinie Manush. As they were going through the lobby Manush spotted a cat sitting there and picked it up, without Melillo knowing it. When they got inside and were going down the aisle through the dark, Manush suddenly threw the cat onto Melillo's back. Well, Oscar didn't know what it was; all he knew was that something furry and alive was digging its claws into

him. He started running down the aisle and screaming, making such a
racket that they stopped the movie and put the lights on to see what
was happening.

One day Rollie Hemsley went out and got himself a bullfrog. He put
it inside his shirt and went up to the batting cage where Melillo was
standing. Rollie put one arm around Melillo's shoulder and started
talking, and while he was doing that he reached into his shirt and
pulled out the bullfrog and sat it on Melillo's other shoulder and took
his hand away. So there was the frog, sitting on Oscar's shoulder, about
two inches from his face. He didn't notice it right away—he probably
thought the pressure he felt was still Hemsley's hand—but then he
turned his head and looked the frog right in the eye. Boy, he took off;
ran right out from under that thing.

One spring in Sarasota Wesley Ferrell rented a car. Well, the car was
sitting outside of the hotel one afternoon. Some of the guys went
around to the back of the hotel where the garbage was put out and got a
pile of crab guts and fish heads. Then they went to the car and lifted
out the seat and dropped this filthy, foul-smelling stuff in there and replaced the seat. And of course that car stayed out there in a broiling
Florida sun, all that day and the next day too.

The following night Roy Johnson had a date and asked Wes if he
could use the car. Wes, always the good fellow, said sure. When Roy
opened the door the stench almost blew him over. There were some old
clothes lying in the back that Wes used to wear when he fished, and
Roy thought they were the cause of it. So he got rid of them and went
along. He drove past the hotel later that evening with his date and she
had her head stuck out the window on one side of the car and Roy had
his head stuck out the window on the other side. When we asked him
about it the next day, he said, "It was the most horrible experience I've
ever had. She thought it was me and I thought it was her."

The next day in the clubhouse before we went out on the field Wes
got up on a stool and called everybody to order. "If the man who put
those fish leavin's in my car will come forward I'll whup him right here
and now. And if it was three or four of you, then I'll whup all of you."
But of course nobody knew anything about it. Wes was talking to a
room full of innocent men.

That same year we had a fellow by the name of Dib Williams. He
was a country boy from Arkansas. One night we were coming back
from the movies and an opossum was going across the street. Dib
picked it up and took it back to the hotel. We took it up to the room of
Johnny Orlando, the clubhouse boy, and put it under the washbasin in
his bathroom. Then we unscrewed the bulb in the bathroom and
closed the door.

We asked the front desk to dial a certain room and let us know when

Orlando came in. When the phone rang and the clerk told us Johnny was back, we went out into the corridor and watched him go into his room. Then Dusty Cooke went to the door and took hold of the door-knob and held onto it. Meanwhile, Orlando undressed and got ready for bed. When he opened the bathroom door and the light from the bedroom hit that opossum's eyes they lit up like fire and the opossum hissed.

Well, we were out in the corridor and we heard the yell. The next thing we heard was John hitting the door, but Cooke was holding the knob. There was a lot of yelling and scrambling and then we saw John up at the transom, glaring out in horror and screaming that there was a sewer rat in his room. Then Cooke opened the door and we went in to try and calm him, but that wasn't going to be so easy. As soon as the door opened, John dropped from the transom and pushed through us and took off down the corridor, stark naked. We went after him to bring him back, but you know what a naked man does in public—he runs, fast. There was a good deal of yelling and excitement and I guess a certain amount of misunderstanding on the part of some of the other guests until we caught John and calmed him down.

In 1937 I was traded to the Athletics for Pinky Higgins and there I had the opportunity to get to know Connie Mack. I was very fond of him. He was a wonderful gentleman. He was over seventy years old when I got there, but he was still an extremely perceptive and intelligent baseball man. I enjoyed talking to him and, whenever I could, would sit down and have dinner with him when he was eating alone. He would reminisce quite a bit. His favorite ballplayer, of all the stars who played for him, was Rube Waddell, the great left-hander who pitched for Mr. Mack around the turn of the century.

He would sit there and chuckle away while telling stories about all the problems he had had with Rube Waddell. Rube, it seemed, would disappear for three or four days at a time and Mr. Mack would have to hire detectives to go out and find him. The detectives would fan out and go to all the firehouses in and around Philadelphia, because firehouses had a fascination for Rube. And ultimately that's where they would find him, sitting in a firehouse, and bring him back. Mr. Mack said that if Rube was sitting on the bench during a game and a fire engine went past, Rube was apt to run out of the ball park and follow it. But that was Mr. Mack's favorite ballplayer of all time—Rube Waddell.

In 1939 I was traded to Cincinnati and walked into two pennants. I recognized immediately in spring training that we had an exceptionally good ball club. I felt we could win it and we did win it. It was a beautifully balanced team. We had fine pitching, good defense, and pretty good power. We had Ernie Lombardi, who could hit with any-

Ernie Lombardi. "Enormous hands. . . ."

body; if he hadn't been so slow afoot I don't think he ever would have hit much under .400. Frank McCormick was another strong hitter, and so was Ival Goodman. Then we had Wally Berger, Lonny Frey, Billy Myers, Harry Craft. And a good bench.

We were particularly strong on the mound. Bucky Walters and Paul Derringer won fifty-two games between them that year, and in addition we had Whitey Moore, Junior Thompson, Lee Grissom. We beat out a good Cardinal ball club by four and a half games.

But that Ernie Lombardi was something special. He wasn't just a hitter, he was a great catcher, too. Enormous hands; he could wrap his fingers completely around a baseball so that you couldn't see it. Twice I saw him do something I never saw another catcher do, or even try to do. Once it was with Vander Meer pitching, the other time I think it was Derringer. They threw balls outside that were going to be wild pitches. Lombardi couldn't get his glove across in time, so he just stuck out that big hand and plucked the ball right out of the air as easily as you'd pluck an apple off of a tree.

We didn't have much success in the Series against the Yankees in 1939; they took us four straight. The 1940 Series was a better one, for the ball club and for me personally. We won a tough, well-played seven-game Series and I hit .370.

We came down to a seventh game that was a classic pitching duel between Paul Derringer and Bobo Newsom. Going into the bottom of the seventh inning we were losing, 1–0. Then Frank McCormick doubled. Jimmy Ripple came up and hit a drive to right field that Bruce Campbell had a chance to catch. But Campbell didn't catch it. McCormick, however, had to hold up and when he saw the ball falling safe he got a late start. When the relay came in from the outfield to Dick Bartell at short I don't think McCormick was halfway home yet. Bartell, with his back to the plate, had made the assumption that McCormick would score easily. The place was in an uproar; it was a hometown crowd, remember, and they were up on their feet yelling—I'll never forget that uproar. We were all on the top step of the dugout yelling, "Run, run, run!" to McCormick. If Bartell had turned around Frank would have been a dead duck. Charlie Gehringer was yelling to him to throw it home, but Bartell couldn't hear him above all the noise. By the time he turned around McCormick had scored.

That tied the game. Ripple was sacrificed over to third and then Bill Myers hit a fly ball to center that scored Ripple. Derringer shut them out over the last two innings and we were World Champions. And that was a great feeling.

We had Al Simmons with us at Cincinnati as a utility outfielder in 1939. Al was near the end of his career and he didn't play much. He was an entirely different fellow than he was when he was hitting .380 and .390 in his heyday with the Athletics. He hardly spoke to you then; he was a swashbuckling pirate of a man. But over at Cincinnati he was going the other way and he was extremely pleased if you invited him to go to a movie with you. He had become a very decent, quiet, humble guy. When I joined the Yankees out of college, Herb Pennock told me in a conversation, "Bill, in this business be awful nice to people on your way up, because you're going to meet a lot of them on your way back down." Well, you've probably heard that before; it's a shopworn piece of wisdom but nonetheless valid for that. You know the day you begin that inevitably you're going to start losing that stamina and resilience, that your talent is going to fade. So you don't want to be overly impressed by it.

Werber caught in a rundown against the Giants in 1941. Harry Danning is the catcher; pitcher Bill Lohrman is covering third. With a teammate already occupying the base, Werber's predicament seems serious.

Did I look ahead when I was playing? I'll say I did. I quit baseball twice before I left it for keeps. I quit after the 1939 World Series. I didn't want to play baseball any longer. But Mr. Giles, who was general manager of the Reds, persuaded me to play another season. I quit again after the '41 season, but Mr. Giles called me and told me he had the opportunity to sell me to the Cubs, the Giants, or the Pirates.

"They'd all like to have you," he said. "I'll sell you to whichever club you prefer and I'll pay you ten percent of the purchase price."

I chose the Giants, and he sold me there for $35,000. So I played for the Giants in 1942. After that season I retired and this time made it stick. You see, I was making as much money in the insurance business as I was playing baseball. I felt that if I devoted full time to my business I could do even better.

I still had some good years ahead of me, but I never had any regrets about retiring when I did, just as I never had any regrets about playing. I'll always be a strong advocate of baseball and am very appreciative of what it did for me. But I had realized as far back as 1934 that baseball was not going to be part of my future and so I worked to get out of it.

I can tell you exactly when and why I determined that I would get out of baseball just as soon as I was able to. We were playing the Yankees in Boston and I hit a low line drive out to Babe Ruth. He came in for it but couldn't make the play and the ball went through his legs to the wall for a triple. Babe had a bad game generally and the people that day in Boston booed that man unmercifully. Babe was nearly forty years old then and obviously near the end of his career, and I said to myself, "If this game can be so unkind to a man who's done so much for it, maybe it's not for me."

But I enjoyed my years in baseball and, as I said, I have no regrets. There was always a great deal of enthusiasm on the part of the players. I can remember sitting in the dugout one day and Rick Ferrell turning to me and saying, "Can you imagine getting paid for doing this?" There were an awful lot of fellows back then who would have played for nothing, because they loved the game.

Of course, you've got a different breed of player today. I don't know them, I don't profess to understand them, so I can't fairly criticize them. But when I read in the newspapers about a .210 hitter asking for a raise, I can't help but to wonder. In my day a ballplayer who hit .210 would pray all winter that he was going to be invited to spring training the next year, much less demand an increase. Why, back then if you hit .210 you would have been ashamed to go back to your home town after the season.

BOBBY SHANTZ

ROBERT CLAYTON SHANTZ
Born: September 26, 1925, Pottstown, Pennsylvania
Major-league career: 1949–64. Philadelphia and Kansas City
   Athletics, New York Yankees, Pittsburgh Pirates, Houston
   Astros, St. Louis Cardinals, Chicago Cubs, Philadelphia
   Phillies
Lifetime record: 119 wins, 99 defeats

Bobby Shantz put together his finest year in 1952, when he won 24 games and lost only 7 and was voted Most Valuable Player in the American League. In spite of an injury suffered the next spring, Shantz remained in the big leagues for many more years, leading the American League in earned-run average in 1957. Often described as a "fifth infielder," Shantz was considered by many to be the greatest fielding pitcher of his era.

I was playing in a semipro league on the sandlots around Philadelphia and a few scouts from the Phillies were looking at me. Not saying anything; just looking. They'd show up, watch, then go away. I was getting curious about what they were thinking. Then one day I found out. After a game one of them walked up to me and shook hands.

"We've been watching you," he said.

Well, that much I knew.

"You've got a good arm," he said. "You've got a hell of a good arm. But I don't know if you could make it in pro ball."

"Why not?" I asked. I knew what he was going to say.

"You're too small," he said.

That was in 1947. Five years later, after I'd won the Most Valuable Player Award in the American League, I met him and he laughed and said he'd made a big mistake.

To tell you the truth, at the time I was half convinced he was right; I really thought I was too small to ever get anyplace in baseball. I was only five feet six and a half.

But then after that season in '47 a scout from the A's, Harry O'Donnell, came around and asked me if I'd be interested in going away. I didn't know what to do. I was working in a sawmill, making seventy-three cents an hour, which was decent money at that time. You know the saws they use to cut the wood with? Well, my job was to glaze them. I was called a handsaw glazer. I'd put emery dust on them and put them through a machine and all this black dirt would come out in my face. I had to wear a mask and goggles all day. It was a terrible job, but I had to make a living somehow.

But as much as I disliked the job, still I hated to quit it. I kept remembering what the Philly scout had said and couldn't help wondering if maybe he was right, that I was too small for pro ball. My parents saw I couldn't make up my mind, so my father talked to me.

"Do you want to stay in that sawmill for the rest of your life?" he asked.

"No," I said.

"So, why don't you sign that contract?"

"I don't know if I can make the big leagues," I said.

"Why not?"

"I'm too small," I said.

"How do you know?" he asked.

Well, that was the point: I *didn't* know. Whenever, wherever, and whatever I played, the competition was always taller, and I'd always done all right. My parents were all for me taking advantage of the opportunity, for getting out of the sawmill; and the Athletics certainly didn't think I was too small. So I quit my job, signed the contract and went away. Best thing I ever did in my life.

The A's started me off in Class-A ball, in Lincoln, Nebraska. I had a pretty good year there, winning 18 ball games. The next year, 1949, I went to spring training with the Athletics. I had a good spring and it looked to me like I'd made the team. They brought me back to Philadelphia with them and I'd no sooner unpacked my bags than they told me they were sending me to Buffalo.

A little disappointed, I packed up again, got in a car with another guy and took off for Buffalo. Well, a few hours after we left I was recalled. But I didn't know that. I was driving to Buffalo, bemoaning my luck all the way. The Athletics called the state troopers and the local police and asked them to try and head us off, but they missed us. We just kept going. That's a long, long drive, especially after you thought you'd made the ball club.

Bobby Shantz.

When we arrived in Buffalo word was waiting for me: Get on a train and go to Detroit—that's where the A's were playing. I thought somebody was kidding.

"Why'd I drive all the way up here?" I asked.

"To get the good news," they told me.

They handed me a train ticket and I was on my way to Detroit. You know that song, "Shuffle Off to Buffalo"? Well, don't sing it around me.

So it was all kind of roundabout, but I got there, and once I did I stayed for sixteen years.

A day or two after joining the club I relieved Carl Schieb in a game. I came in with nobody out in the third inning and pitched nine consecutive innings of no-hit ball. I think I must have been half unconscious out there. Honestly. I mean, this was my first big-league game and I'm pitching the equivalent of a no-hitter. We finally scored in the top of the thirteenth. In the last of the thirteenth I gave up a hit, but it didn't mean anything. George Kell got the hit. He was the first big leaguer to get a hit off of me.

When I walked off the mound after that game I don't think my spikes touched the grass. I was really floating. I think that game was what kept me in the big leagues that year. I finished up 6 and 8.

Connie Mack was still managing the A's at that time. He had been managing them for a long time when I was born, and he was still at it when I joined them. He was around eighty-five years old and the years were beginning to tell on him. He wasn't able to handle the ball club very well. His son Earle sat on the bench with him and helped him out. Mr. Mack still moved the outfielders around with his scorecard, but he had difficulty staying with the ball game. Sometimes you'd have to wait and wait for a sign to come.

He managed the first two years I was there, '49 and '50. He was very nice, but didn't say too much; tell you the truth, I don't think he even knew my name. All the same, I think I was very fortunate to have played for him. I grew up in the Philadelphia area and of course he was a legend there, and it's nice today to be able to say that I played for Connie Mack.

You know, I never really followed the big leagues all that closely when I was a kid. I loved baseball and now and then my dad used to take me down from where we lived in Pottstown to Philadelphia to see a game, but I didn't keep up with it that much. I sure never expected to be there myself. Naturally I knew about Ted Williams and Joe DiMaggio, that they were supposed to be the greatest, and they were. And then all of a sudden, holy mackerel, I'm competing against them.

Did they tell me how to pitch to Williams? Sure they did. It was great

Connie Mack in 1940. ". . . it's nice today to be able to say that I played for Connie Mack."

advice, very encouraging. They said he has no weakness, won't swing at a bad ball, has the best eyes in the business, and can kill you with one swing; he won't hit at anything bad, but don't give him anything good. Good luck. Man, I threw him some wicked curveballs that didn't miss by more than a fraction, and he'd just stand there and look at them, and that bat would stay right back, not budging an inch. You'd just do the best you could with him and hope your number wasn't up when he swung.

In 1951 I won 18 games and I think that really built up my confidence. I began to move that year; I got the feeling I could start getting them out consistently. I remember, one of our catchers, Joe Tipton, pulled me aside one day and said, "You've got a hell of a curveball, but you're going to have to learn to change speeds on that fastball. You learn to do that and I think you can win some ball games." That sank in. I began practicing taking something off the fastball. I finally learned how to throw that darn thing without slowing up on my arm motion, and, boy, I started winning. Wow, did I start to win!

I figured I'd have a good year in 1952, but never expected it to be that good. I was 24 and 7. I was surprised. You'd better believe I was surprised. I kept asking myself, "What the hell is going on here?" I couldn't lose a game. But, say, don't forget, I had some pretty good guys behind me, and that really helped. We had guys like Ferris Fain, Pete Suder, Eddie Joost, Dave Philley, Gus Zernial, Elmer Valo.

I got to a point where I could do just about anything I wanted to out there on the mound. Everything seemed to go right. I was changing speeds when I was behind the batter and throwing the ball right on the corner. You sometimes get into ruts where everything goes wrong, but this was the opposite—everything was going right. And of course the confidence keeps building.

I pitched an inning in the All-Star game that year, which turned out to be the last inning. The game was called after five because of rain. It was played in Philadelphia, in front of the hometown crowd. Boy, I was nervous as the devil out there. The first man I faced was Whitey Lockman, and I struck him out. Next was Jackie Robinson, and I struck him out. Then came Stan Musial, and I struck him out. Then the rain started to fall and it washed away the rest of the game. It was too bad, because I felt good and would liked to have kept going.

After the game the writers crowded around me in the clubhouse.

"Do you think you might have broken Carl Hubbell's record if it hadn't rained?" they asked.

"What record?" I asked. I wasn't too sharp on baseball history.

"What he did in the '34 All-Star game."

"What'd he do?" I asked.

"Struck out five in a row—Ruth, Gehrig, Foxx, Simmons and Cronin."

Well, I'd never known that. And I guess I'll never know, either, how far I could have gone in that game. But I'll settle for the three.

Jimmy Dykes was managing the A's that year. He'd been after me to switch from batting right-handed to left-handed, because he didn't like the idea of my left arm being exposed to the pitcher when I stood at the plate. I tried switching but it didn't work out, so I went back to hitting righty. I loved to hit.

Toward the end of the season, with still a couple of weeks to go, I was batting against Walter Masterson. A pitch got away from him and sailed in at my head. I threw up my hand to protect myself and the ball hit me in the wrist and broke two bones. That's my left wrist I'm talking about. The pitching one. I was through for the year.

I went to spring training the next year and felt pretty good. My wrist didn't bother me. Then the season started and I was making my first start, against the Red Sox in Fenway park. I threw a ball and felt something pull in my shoulder. It felt just like somebody had stuck a knife in there. I'd really torn up that shoulder muscle. The doctor said I might have been favoring the wrist. I don't know if that's true or not. I know, though, that I never did seem to have the good snappy curve that I used to have. Something was gone.

I wasn't worth a damn all year. Won only five games. I just couldn't throw. Frustrating? I'll say it was. You talk about a roller coaster ride from the top to the bottom in a hurry, that's what that was. I'd received a pretty good raise, from $12,000 to $25,000. I hated even to take the money.

The following year I did the same damn thing, in the very first game of the season. Tore something back in there again. I didn't pitch another game for the rest of the season.

It was depressing. It looked like baseball was all over for me, and I didn't know what else I could do. I didn't have a real good education and didn't see many opportunities for myself away from baseball. You're just not prepared for an injury like that early in your career. So I kept hanging in there, taking shots of cortisone, taking pills, all kinds of treatment.

Baseball can be a lot of fun, but, boy, you never know what can happen all of a sudden, do you? Look what happened to Herb Score. I was there when he got hit in the eye with that line drive. Man, did he get belted. You heard the crack of the bat and he was down, just like that. Never had a chance to protect himself.

Before he had that injury Herb could fog that ball. But you know, as fast as he was, I don't think he was quite as fast as Koufax. It's hard to tell, really, but I'd say Koufax was just a little quicker. I pitched against Koufax when I was in the National League. He was in his heyday then, and he was tough. Exceptionally tough. Best pitcher I ever saw. I never saw anybody throw harder, and he had a great curveball, too. He threw everything straight overhand, right out of the same motion. That fastball used to rise. You'd think it was going to be low and all of a sudden it just shot up at you. And the way he came over the top with that curve, it broke straight down, with tremendous speed. Even if you got your bat on it, where were you going to hit it?

In the winter of '56, after a couple of mediocre seasons, I was traded to the Yankees. How did I feel about that? Are you kidding? To go with that ball club? I was delighted. My only concern was if I could win for them. And I did have a pretty good year in '57; won 11 and lost 5 and led the league in ERA.

You know, I never thought I'd ever get into a World Series, but with the Yankees in those years that's about all I did. Winning pennants was part of their routine. I was with them four years and we won it three times. The White Sox beat us out in '59. I still don't know how that happened.

You remember that Series against Pittsburgh in 1960, don't you? That was something. We did all the hitting but they came out on top. I can't figure out how we lost it. We hit .338 as a team for the Series. But the whole thing turned around in the seventh game because of a damned pebble or something.

Everybody remembers the ball that hit Kubek in the throat. But do you know who was pitching for the Yankees when it happened? Yours truly. I came in in the third inning and was really mowing them down. Shut them out for five innings while we caught up and went ahead. We were winning, 7–4, going into the bottom of the eighth. Gino Cimoli came up to pinch-hit and he got a single. Still nothing to worry about, right?

Bill Virdon was the next hitter. I threw him a good pitch and got him to hit it on the ground to Kubek at short. A sure double-play ball. Richardson was running over to cover second. I turned around and could just see that double play being executed. But it never happened. The ball hit a pebble or a clod of dirt or something, took a wild bounce and got Tony right in the throat. He went down and lay there gagging. I'll never forget it. He had to leave the game.

Boy, that was a lousy break if there ever was one. Instead of two out and nobody on, they had two on and nobody out. I left the game at that point and Jim Coates came in. He gave up a base hit to Dick Groat, but got the next two guys out. Then Clemente hit a little roller down the first base line and beat it out when Coates didn't cover the bag. Skowron fielded the ball okay but Coates just didn't get over there. Skowron was mad as hell. That should have been the third out. Instead, Hal Smith came up and he hit a home run and we were down, 9–7.

We came back and tied it in the ninth, but all that did was set the stage for Bill Mazeroski. He was a fastball hitter and Ralph Terry, who was in there then, threw one right up his alley and he really tagged it. I felt sorry for Ralph. I felt sorry for me, too. As soon as I saw Mazeroski hit that ball I knew it was going to be a long winter.

ENOS SLAUGHTER

ENOS BRADSHER SLAUGHTER
Born: April 27, 1916, Roxboro, North Carolina
Major-league career: 1938–59, St. Louis Cardinals, New
    York Yankees, Kansas City Athletics, Milwaukee Braves
Lifetime average: .300

Despite the loss of three prime years in the Air Corps during World War II, Enos Slaughter still compiled a hit total of nearly 2,400. A nonstop hustler, the remarkable Slaughter hit .304 as a part-time player at the age of 42. His finest year was 1949, when he hit .336. He led the National League in hits once, doubles once, and triples twice.

I think the game of baseball is just like any other sport, in that you've got to keep your legs in shape. I was able to play for so many years because I took care of my legs. I've always been fond of hunting, and every winter I tried to do as much of it as I could, to get in all that walking. Even though I was living in St. Louis then, I'd still come back to North Carolina in the spring of the year and get out on a farm for two or three weeks and cut wood and maul wood and get shaped up that way, because, boy, I loved that farm life.

We used to have these good old wood choppin' contests; get up on the log with that ax and chop away. I can see the danger in that now—I could've cut off my foot as easy as not. One glance of that ax would have been enough. But nobody thought of that. We had a lot of fun cutting wood in those days.

You see, we used wood at that time to cure tobacco with. That was before your oil burners and gas burners came in to cure the tobacco. We'd cut the wood to about six- or eight-foot lengths and then take maul wedges and bust it open and stack it to dry. Later we'd put it in these big concrete and brick flues to cure our tobacco with. You could run that heat up to two hundred degrees in the barns, just throwing those good old logs into the fire. I tell you, that kind of work kept me in shape. I played ball until I was forty-three years old and was still doing a capable job.

I was born in Roxboro, North Carolina. I guess it was what you'd call a textile town, though there was also quite a bit of farming done around there, too.

My father owned a farm and we raised a little corn, some wheat, and tobacco, of course; tobacco was our money crop. There were five boys in our family and we took turns milking cows. I used to walk to and from school, and when it was my turn to milk the cows I'd come home and get my pails and go down to low ground where we kept the cows, and milk them until it got dark. Next morning I'd get up early and do my milking and then head for school. I was doing that until I got out of high school. You know the old saying: "You can take the boy out of the country, but you can't take the country out of the boy." I guess that's how you'd have to describe me. In fact, you know the nickname I had all through my baseball years—Country. Country Slaughter. I was strictly a country boy, and still am.

I was playing semipro ball with a team sponsored by one of the textile mills when I was recommended to a sportswriter for the Durham *Morning Herald.* He in turn contacted somebody in the Cardinal organization. Soon after, I got a letter from the Cardinals inviting me to Greensboro for a tryout that September. They said if I made good and they signed me up they would pay my expenses; otherwise I'd have to pay my own. That was all right with me; I just wanted the chance, because I was confident I could make good. So I went to Greensboro and was hitting the ball real well, but they said I was too slow and too clumsy to be a second baseman, which I fancied myself at that time. So they moved me to the outfield and I was signed up as an outfielder. This was in 1934.

Money? Never crossed my mind. I just wanted to play baseball. I signed a contract calling for $75 a month that first year. Coming off the farm, that looked like great money. Remember, this was during the Depression and there wasn't too much money stirring. The important thing to me was that I was getting the opportunity to play professional baseball.

I played at Martinsville, Virginia, in 1935. I had a little trouble with the strike zone—I struck out over a hundred times. I hit .273, but almost half of my hits were for extra bases. Mr. Rickey, who was general manager for the Cardinals then, noticed that. He noticed everything, that son of a gun. So he sent me to Columbus, Georgia, the next year, which was Class-B ball. Eddie Dyer was the manager there.

I got off to a poor start that year. I was hitting something like .220 for

Enos Slaughter as a Cardinal rookie in 1938.

the first half of the season. Still having a tough time keeping my bat in the strike zone. I'll never forget one night, we were losing by a run and I was up with the bases loaded and the count was three and two. I swung at a pitch around my ankles and struck out. Eddie Dyer came up to me later.

"Kid," he said, "if you can learn where the strike zone is you've got a chance to go to the major leagues."

Well, hearing that must have done something for me. I found myself laying off the bad balls after that and wound up the season hitting .320. Another thing happened that year. You know, I always had this reputation for running on and off the field. In fact, it flatters me no end when I hear a young kid described as being an "Enos Slaughter type" because of his hustle. Well, that came about in 1936, at Columbus, Georgia. I used to come running in from right field and when I reached the third-base line I'd stop and walk the rest of the way to the dugout. One day Eddie Dyer said to me, "Son, if you're tired I'll get you some help." Don't ask me why, but those words made a tremendous impression on me, and from 1936 until I finished my career in 1961, I never walked on a ball field. I left the dugout running and I hit the top step running coming back. And I always ran out everything I hit; I put on the same speed whether I was running out a triple or a one-hopper to the pitcher. Didn't know any other way to play. And I trace it all back to that one remark Eddie Dyer made to me.

In 1937 they promoted me to Columbus, Ohio, in the American Association. That was Triple-A ball, one slice away from the top. I got off to a good start there and kept going. Ended up leading the league with .382. I was making all of $150 a month then. Branch Rickey, you know, was probably the most knowledgeable man that was ever in baseball, when it came to spotting talent. But he didn't like to pay out money. He'd go into the vault to get you a nickel change.

They had a big party for us at the end of the season, and I eased up to Mr. Rickey and asked him for a little bonus. He stared at me from out under those big bushy eyebrows, chewed his cigar a little, and said, "The older boys have been talking to you, haven't they, Slaughter?" So I didn't get a bonus.

I went up to the Cardinals the next year and wasn't exactly overpaid there either—$400 a month. This is the big leagues now. Around mid-season they raised me to $600 a month, because I was hitting. In 1939 I hit .300 and led the league with 52 doubles and they were paying me $750 a month. That's not much more than they get in meal money today, I reckon.

When I joined the Cardinals in 1938 Frankie Frisch was still managing—it was his last year there—and he was a tough man to play for.

Very critical, very demanding. From the McGraw school you know. But that didn't bother me. I didn't care who I played for, just so long as they gave me the chance to play, because I knew I could do the job. So I just kept my mouth shut—I was too scared to say anything anyway—and kept my eyes open.

Pepper Martin was with the Cardinals then, and so was Joe Medwick, Johnny Mize, Lon Warneke, and a lot of other good ones. Pepper Martin was quite a character. You never knew what to expect from him. We were in Boston one time and Frisch had him playing third. Pepper didn't like to play third because he hated to field bunts. Casey Stengel was managing the Braves then and before the game Pepper went up to Casey and said, "You'd better tell your guys not to bunt on me, because if they do I'm gonna hurt 'em." So naturally they started bunting. After a while Pepper got so mad that when he charged in and picked up the ball he'd throw it at the runner going down the line instead of to first base. He was zinging that ball right over their heads. He figured that was the best way to stop them.

Then Elbie Fletcher dropped one down the line that Pepper got a good jump on and when Elbie saw how quick Pepper had got that ball and saw him winding up with it, Elbie cut away from the line and ran straight for the Cardinal dugout, ducking his head between his shoulders. I tell you, that ball came like a bullet right over the button of his cap and smack into the dugout and damn near cleared our bench. That ended the bunting.

I'll never forget one day that spring, just before the season opened. We were in Springfield, Missouri. Dizzy Dean came into the clubhouse and started going around shaking hands with everybody. He had just been sold to the Cubs. His arm was bad, but everybody told me that Mr. Wrigley knew that when he bought him. The Cubs wanted Dizzy, sore arm or no, because every time he pitched there was a full house. But even with the bad arm Dizzy went out and did a fine job for the Cubs that year and helped them win the pennant. When he came up to me that day he said, "Well, I'm not going to say good-bye to you, because I'll be seeing you again soon." It seems the Cubs had offered $100,000 for me—which the Cardinals turned down. That gave me something to think about: The Cubs were willing to give $100,000 for me, and I was still only making $400 a month at that time!

I can recall quite well the day Medwick got beaned. He had been traded to the Dodgers and not long after the deal we went into Ebbets Field. We had a young pitcher named Bob Bowman on the mound, and he hit Joe in the head just about as hard as I've ever seen anybody get hit. Some people thought it was done intentionally, but I never believed that.

Three thoughtful Gas Housers in 1939. Left to right: Pepper Martin, Mickey Owen, Lon Wameke.

Chuck Dressen was coaching third base for the Dodgers at that time, and he was great at stealing signs and letting the batter know what was coming. Every time Bowman threw the curve Dressen picked it off and whistled up to the batter. So Don Padgett, who was catching, went out and told Bowman to hold the ball like he was going to throw a curve and then throw the fastball. That's one way to put a dent in somebody's head, but that's the batter's lookout. Anyway, Bowman faked the curve, Dressen whistled, and Medwick stepped into a fastball and got hit. Hit hard.

A big free-for-all broke out. That was always happening with the Dodgers in those days. I remember it well because I came running in from right field and grabbed the first guy I saw—and who do you think I wound up with? Big Van Mungo. And then Freddy Fitzsimmons collared me, and there I was, caught between two of the biggest guys on the field. I was lucky to get out of there with my head on straight.

In 1941 we battled the Dodgers for the pennant. There was lots of low-bridging, lots of brawls. Whit Wyatt would throw in tight and so would Mort Cooper. And those guys could scorch that ball. We might have won it that year, but we had bad luck with injuries. Jimmy Brown had a broken nose, Terry Moore got hit in the head, and I broke a collarbone.

I can recall it so well. We were playing in St. Louis, the second game of a double-header against Pittsburgh. In the first inning Stu Martin, who used to be a Cardinal, hit a line shot to right-center and Terry Moore and I both went after it. We were both hollering for it and at the last second I saw Terry leave his feet. He dove and caught the ball and skidded right between my legs. I tried to jump him, and as I went over I hit his shoulder and flipped and broke my collarbone.

I was in the hospital for four weeks. Dr. Hyland, who was the team physician, wired my shoulder up, because I had a compound fracture. He said if I hadn't been an athlete he would have left the wire in permanently, but Dr. Hyland was the type of physician who made every effort to keep from putting bolts and wires into you because he was afraid it would cause you trouble later. So after four weeks he pulled the wires out of my shoulder. I went from the hospital right out to the ball park, where we were playing the Dodgers. Wyatt was pitching against Cooper and beating him, 1–0. Billy Southworth sent me up to pinch-hit. Well, it would be nice to say I came out of the hospital and hit a home run. Unfortunately I didn't. Wyatt struck me out. It doesn't always happen the way it does in the storybooks, does it?

Because of all those injuries we found ourselves short of ballplayers. In September Mr. Rickey brought Stan Musial up from Rochester. We didn't catch the Dodgers that year, but it wasn't Musial's fault—he hit around .420 for the few weeks he was there.

You know, I hit at Musial when he was a left-handed pitcher in the Cardinal farm system. He started as a pitcher, but he came up with a bad arm and since they saw how well he could move that bat they converted him to an outfielder. But I don't think anybody knew what a great hitter he was going to be, because of that odd batting stance he had. I know I heard a lot of pitchers say he could be pitched to, but I never saw anybody do it successfully.

There were a lot of times when they would pass Musial to get at me. How did I feel about that? Well, I always loved to hit with men on base. And when they'd walk him to fill a base and pitch to me, it put another man on and just made me more determined to do something with that ball.

I'd have to say today that the 1942 Cardinals was the greatest club I ever played on. There was tremendous team play and desire; we felt like we just couldn't be beat. Never seemed to matter how many runs we were down in a game, we were always confident we could come back. You know, we didn't miss that pennant by much in '41, losing to the Dodgers by just a couple of games. So we were hungry. Young, talented, confident, and hungry. That's a combination hard to beat.

We had Johnny Hopp and Ray Sanders alternating at first base, Jimmy Brown on second, Marty Marion at short, Whitey Kurowski at third, and one of the best behind the plate, Walker Cooper. He'd be catching and a guy would come up to hit and Cooper would spit tobacco juice across his shoes. The guy would back out of the box and look at him, and Cooper would say, "Well, what are you going to do about it?" Here's this six-foot-four, 220-pounder, wearing a mask and chest protector. What were you going to do about it? Nothing. You got back in there and hit. He was a great guy though. Wasn't mean. Really very good-natured.

In the outfield we had Stan Musial, Terry Moore, and myself. And we had Mort Cooper and Johnny Beazley winning twenty games for us, and we had Max Lanier, Ernie White, Howie Pollett, Howie Krist, and some other good pitchers.

It was another tight pennant race with the Dodgers that year. You know, we were something like ten games behind in August, and we caught them and passed them. They won 104 games and we won 106.

That was my first World Series, in 1942. Anybody who tells you he's not nervous going into his first World Series is lying to you. Why, being nervous is part of it. If you're not nervous, then it isn't important, and to a ballplayer the World Series is the most important thing there is.

We opened in St. Louis, against the Yankees. Red Ruffing was pitching for them, and he showed us something. He had a no-hit, no-run game for seven and two-thirds innings before Terry Moore finally got a base hit and broke it up. We went into the last of the ninth getting beat, 7–0. Well, something happened then. We knocked Ruffing out and scored four runs and had the tying run at the plate before they stopped us. That rally, even though it fell short, was the turning point for us. It made us feel real good. We went into the clubhouse and said, "Well, we gave them one hell of a scare."

The next day Johnny Beazley went out and beat them, 4–3. I can recall that quite well. In the last of the eighth it was tied, 3–3. I came up and doubled and on the throw to second Rizzuto bobbled the ball and I went into third. Then Musial singled to center to put us ahead. In the top of the ninth, they had a man on first and Buddy Hassett singled to right field. I came running in and scooped it up and threw the man out at third. That broke the back of the inning and we won the ball game.

Then we went to New York and played them three games in Yankee Stadium. Ernie White and Spud Chandler hooked up together, and Ernie shut them out, 2–0. We beat them a wild ball game the next day, 9–6. Beazley came back in the fifth game. Johnny was just a rookie, you know, and he had a great season and a great Series. We were down 1–0 in the fourth inning, and I came up and hit one into the seats off of Ruffing to tie it. We went into the top of the ninth tied, 2–2. We got a man on and Whitey Kurowski hit one into the left-field seats. That gave us the game and the World Championship.

Everybody said what a great upset it was, us beating that Yankee team. But I don't think it was such an upset. Those 1942 Cardinals were a great ball club, that's all.

It was a happy moment for me, and a sad one at the same time, because on August 27 of that year I had enlisted in the Air Corps and I knew I'd be gone soon. I was finally called into service the twenty-third of January, 1943, and was gone for three years.

I wanted to be a pilot, but they said they wanted me to be a bombardier. Well, I didn't care anything about pushing a button, and I was grounded. They were going to ship me out then, but one of the colonels said they wouldn't have much of a team if they let me go. You see, we had a service league down there in San Antonio, with eight teams in it, and those officers took it very seriously. I was all set to go, had my bags packed and everything, when they got a wire the night before from the Eighth Service Command saying that they could keep me there.

I stayed at San Antonio for the next two years as a physical training instructor. I was fortunate in that I was able to continue playing baseball, keeping myself in pretty good shape. Hit .498 the first year in the service league, then the next year I fell to .420. The pitching started getting better, you see—fellows like Tex Hughson and Howard Pollett were showing up.

The 1946 Cardinal outfield: Stan Musial, Terry Moore, Enos Slaughter.

Then it turned out that the Navy was beating the Air Force pretty badly over in Honolulu. That didn't sit too well with Larry MacPhail, who had gotten himself a commission in the Air Force. So he had a hand in getting us shipped out to Honolulu. About forty-five ballplayers, mostly major leaguers and Triple-A players, were assembled in Kerns, Utah, and then sent up to Seattle where they put us aboard a ship and we all wound up in Honolulu.

Right after we got there, however, the Navy disbanded their team. That's the way things go in the service, I guess. So we never did get the chance to challenge them in Honolulu. I was stationed at Hickham Field, and on the team there we had Birdie Tebbetts, Billy Hitchcock, Pollett, Joe Marty; and then there was a team at Wheeler Field, with boys like Taft Wright, Max West, Lew Riggs, Ferris Fain, Sid Hudson, and Hughson. We played a lot of ball over there for the servicemen.

Then one day they called us all together and an officer spoke to us.

"Boys," he said, "if you'll volunteer to go out to the islands and play some ball for the fellows there, we'll see you get shipped home real fast when the war is over."

We said we'd go. We were all willing, and anyway nobody wanted to take a chance on saying no. So we got our shots and they boarded us onto a ship—the PA–101, I'll never forget it—and we landed in Saipan on July 4, 1945. Then they divided us up. I was assigned to the B-29's of the 58th Bomb Wing on Tinian. We had two teams there and one over at Saipan, in the Mariana Islands. A long way from Roxboro, North Carolina. I'll say.

The first thing we had to do was build diamonds. I got in working with the Seabees, running a bulldozer, helping to carve out the ball field. They did the same thing on Saipan, and we played back and forth. The bleachers were built out of empty bomb crates and sometimes we had as many as 15,000 troops at a game. We were drawing better crowds on Saipan than they were in Philadelphia.

You've heard what great baseball fans the Japanese are. Well, when we got to Saipan there were still quite a few of them holed up in the hills. I'll be damned if they didn't sneak out and watch us play ball. We could see them sitting up there, watching the game. When it was over they'd fade back into their caves. But they could have got themselves killed for watching a ball game. Talk about real fans!

A lot of times we'd go out and sit on the edge of the runway and watch those B-29's taking off, one after the other. You know, we were on Tinian when that plane took off to drop the atomic bomb on Hiroshima. Of course nobody knew what was up. That was the best-kept secret of the war. Later on we met the crew that had dropped the bomb. They were a pretty quiet bunch of boys.

Well, after the war they kept their word to us. They assembled us together at Guam and we got aboard a ship and headed for home. On the way back we ran into the tail end of a typhoon; our ship was supposed to be eleven days back but we wound up taking nineteen. Three of those days they kept us locked down under because the ship was doing a thirty-nine-degree angle. You never saw so many pale and sickly faces. The ship was creaking and crying and we were just praying she'd hold together. Finally when we got up out of the hole the ocean was still wild. It looked like a blue mountain that wouldn't stand still; it would be so high, and the next thing you knew you'd be looking down and not seeing bottom—that's how much that old ship was tossing and pitching. But it was okay, because we knew we were headed home.

So I came out of the service in pretty good shape, and a good thing I was, too. They were calling me an old man—I was thirty years old then. That was a laugh; hell, I had fourteen more seasons ahead of me in the big leagues. Led the league in RBI's my first year back with 130. Then we got into that play-off with the Dodgers. Ended up in a flat-footed tie. First time in baseball history that had ever happened.

It was a best two-out-of-three series. The first game was in St. Louis, and we beat them there, 4–2. Then we took that long train ride back to Brooklyn, to play the second game at Ebbets field. We jumped out to a big lead and were ahead, 8–1, going into the last of the ninth. Murry Dickson was pitching for us. They got a rally going, knocked Dickson out and the next thing we knew it was 8–4 and the bases were loaded and their big first baseman, Howie Schultz, was the batter.

Eddie Dyer was managing the Cardinals then. He brought in our lefty screwball pitcher, Harry Brecheen. Well, that Ebbets Field was a madhouse. You can imagine, in a situation like that. But that Brecheen, nothing bothered him. He worked the count full and then threw the prettiest screwball you'd ever want to see and struck Schultz out. That gave us the ball game and the pennant.

We got on the train and went back to St. Louis to open the Series against the Red Sox. They beat us the first game, 3–2, when Rudy York hit a home run in the tenth inning. Then we battled them around and after the fifth game we were down three to two. We played that fifth game in Boston and Joe Dobson beat us, 6–3. So we were in trouble. And I was in trouble myself. You see, in the fifth inning Dobson hit me with a pitch on my right elbow. It really gave me a sting, but I wanted to stay in there. I went ahead and tried to hit one more time, but the elbow had swelled up so much that I couldn't even swing the bat, and I couldn't throw a lick. So I went to Eddie Dyer and for the first time in my career asked to be taken out of a ball game.

"Skipper," I said, "I can't do you any good. I can't throw and I can't swing a bat. Better get me out of there."

Doc Weaver, the club trainer, took me into the clubhouse and put ice packs on the elbow, but it didn't feel like it was doing much good. We had to go back to St. Louis that night to finish the Series. When I got on the train Doc wrapped my arm up with a towel and epsom salt and I put on an electric jacket that the pitchers wore in the bull pen on cold days, plugged it in and stayed put on the train all the way back to St. Louis.

When we got to St. Louis Doctor Hyland took me right to the hospital and x-rayed my arm. Then he came to me with a sad look on his face.

"Eno," he said, "I'm sorry to say, but you've got such a bad hemorrhage that if you get hit on it again the chances are I'll have to amputate your arm."

"Doc," I said, "I guess we'll have to take that gamble."

So I played in the sixth game and Brecheen beat Mickey Harris to even up the Series. No, I wasn't worrying about my arm. I just played my game, that's all. Took my chances.

Then we went into the seventh game. The seventh game of the World Series. Say it aloud—it's got a *sound* to it, doesn't it? The first game is all nerves and excitement, but that seventh game, that's in a class by itself. By the time that game comes up you're a bunch of battle-scarred veterans.

We had them down 3–1 going to the top of the eighth and they got two runs. So we went into the bottom of the eighth tied up. Bob Klinger was pitching for them, a former National Leaguer. I led off the inning with a base hit. Whitey Kurowski tried to sacrifice but popped up. Then Del Rice flied out. Harry Walker was the next batter. With two out and Harry not being a long-ball hitter, I figured it might be good strategy to try and steal; then if Harry poked a hit I'd be home. I took off to steal second and Harry hit one into left center, not too hard. I had got a good jump and when I got to second and saw where that ball was going I said to myself, "I can score."

You know, there was some background to that play. In an earlier game in the Series Mike Gonzales, our third-base coach, had stopped me at third on a bad relay throw and we lost that ball game. I went to Eddie Dyer and told him I thought I could have scored easily if I hadn't been held up.

"Well," he said, "from now on if you think you've got a legitimate chance, with two out, you go ahead and try it and I'll back you up."

So that was in the back of my mind when I went around second base. I kept going. I never broke stride. I had it in my head that I was going to score. Sometimes you just make up your mind about something and everything else gets locked out. I still don't know to this day if Mike Gonzales ever gave me the stop sign or not. It wouldn't have made a lick of difference if he'd had. I rounded third and kept going. When I got ready to slide into home I saw Roy Partee, the catcher, take about two or three steps up in front of the plate and I slid across easily.

You know, they've made Pesky the goat of that Series because when he took the relay from the outfield he hesitated for a second before pegging it home. Well, I don't go along with that. Anytime an infielder has to go out to take a relay his back is to the play and it's up to his teammates to let him know where the runner is. Bobby Doerr, who was playing second for the Red Sox, told me later that with 36,000 people up on their feet yelling, nobody could hear anything. So Pesky didn't know where I was or what I was doing and nobody could tell him, because of the noise. If somebody would have told him where I was he probably could have thrown me out by ten feet. I've seen the films, and

what he did after he caught the ball was turn toward second base because Walker had rounded the bag and was coming toward second;
then he saw me out of the corner of his eye coming home, and he had to
turn again and threw off stride to home, and I was able to slide in safely.

They called it "Enos Slaughter's Mad Dash Home." I guess I'll always be remembered for that more than for anything else, and that's
just fine with me, because it was right in my style of play.

You know, a few years ago they had us back to St. Louis for the twen-
ty-fifth anniversary of the Series between the Cardinals and Red Sox.
The public relations people asked me if I could re-enact the "Mad
Dash."

"I'll try," I said. "I don't know if I can make it or not, but I'll try."

They had made every effort to get as many of the original players
back on the field as they could. Pesky was there at shortstop, Roy Partee was behind the plate, and they had Joe Dobson pitching this time.
They couldn't get Harry Walker to hit the ball because he was managing Houston at that time, but they did get his brother Dixie. So I'm on
first and when Dobson delivered the ball I broke. Well, you wouldn't
believe it, but Dixie hit the same type of ball to left center that Harry
had hit twenty-five years before. And I'm going. Huffing and puffing,
but going. Heck, I'm fifty-five years old now. I barrel around second.
Then I come into third, and I go around third. Pesky takes the relay
and throws to the plate, and doggone if his peg doesn't pull Partee up
the line again and I slide in and score, twenty-five years later. Exact
same thing. If we'd rehearsed it for a year we couldn't have done it any
more perfect. But, boy, I'll tell you, I was pooped.

Later on I told Pesky, "We'll do it again twenty-five years from
now."

He said, "You'll never make it."

You can't tell. I'll be only eighty years old then, and you know I keep
my legs in shape.

In 1954 I'd been in the Cardinal organization for nearly twenty years
and loved every minute of it. I loved the Cardinals. When Mr. Busch
took over the team, my contract was the first one he ever signed.
"Enos," he said at that time, "you're a credit to the game and you'll always be with us."

We go to spring training and I have a good spring. Then we come
back to St. Louis and are playing a preseason series with the Browns.
On Saturday I help beat Bob Turley with a double. On Sunday I'm not
in the lineup, which felt strange to me. In the latter part of the game
I'm sitting on the bench and Eddie Stanky, who was managing then,
looked at me and said, "Slaughter, go on and get dressed. The general

manager would like to see you in his office." It never dawned on me about being traded.

So I went and got dressed and went on up to see Dick Meyer, who was the general manager.

"Eno," he said, "all things have to come to an end. We've sold you to the New York Yankees."

Well, it floored me. It cut my heart out. I cried. I cried like a baby. I couldn't help it. I'd been a Cardinal since 1935, and I don't think anybody who's ever worn a Cardinal uniform was ever more loyal to it than I was or put out as hard as I did or gave as much. But you go. Of course you go. You have to. Somebody says to you, "That's baseball." You get a few handshakes and walk away from twenty years of your life.

So I joined the Yankees and, believe me, I gave them the same one hundred ten percent that I had given the Cardinals. In fact I even gave them some of my blood. There was a brawl one day, I think it was the worst I ever saw on a ball field. We were in a tough race with the White Sox and tempers were running a little high. In this one game Art Ditmar was pitching and Larry Doby was hitting. Elston Howard was the catcher, and Nellie Fox was on first. Doby was a low-ball hitter and we were trying to pitch him high and tight. So Ditmar brushed him back on a couple of pitches. Then the next one got away from Howard and went all the way back to the stands. Fox rounded second and went to third, and Ditmar went in to cover the plate. I don't know what was said, but he and Doby had a few words. Then Ditmar came back to the mound and Doby stepped in to hit.

Billy Martin was playing second base, and he came in to the mound and asked Ditmar what Doby had said. Next thing that happens Billy Martin is yelling at Doby. So Doby starts for the mound and Ditmar starts for home plate. A couple of punches were thrown. Well, you know what happens then. Both benches flared up and everybody is on the field. Bill Skowron came over and tackled Doby. Then big Walt Dropo, and I mean big—six feet six, 240 pounds—comes over and jumps on Skowron. So they're three deep on the ground there.

Well, along with everybody else, I'd run off the bench and tried to get in there. Wasn't mad at anybody, just trying to help out. You know how it is when a fight's swarming over the field. Jim Rivera grabbed me by the belt and said, "Hey, Enos, you don't wanna get in there." That was good advice and I should have listened.

Finally I got in the middle of that thing and took hold of Walt Dropo's collar and said, "Walt, get up off of them." Then somebody got hold of me and jerked me backwards while I was still holding Dropo by the collar. So now I'm choking Dropo. Man, that didn't rile him! He

"As I was going off, one of the umpires picked up my cap and put it on my head backwards."

got up snorting and ran over the top of everybody and grabbed my uniform and tried to measure me off. He never did land a lick, fortunately, because I was like a little bantam rooster, darting around under those big arms while he was swinging. He ripped my whole jersey right off of me. Then I look up and there's my roomie, Whitey Ford, up on Dropo's back, and Dropo is carrying him along like a little old bumblebee, still trying to get at me.

Well, finally we all cooled off. A couple of policemen came and took Billy Martin and me off the field. As I was going off, one of the umpires picked up my cap and put it on my head backwards. Billy and me went into the clubhouse and had a beer and sat there and watched on television while the Yankees went ahead and won the ball game.

I didn't play all that much for the Yankees; Stengel had me alternating against right- and left-hand pitchers with Hank Bauer. Then early in 1955 they traded Johnny Sain and myself over to Kansas City, which at that time people called the Yankee farm team in the American League because of all the deals that went back and forth between those two clubs. I had a good year for Kansas City, hitting over .300. Then a year later the Yankees bought me back. This is 1956 now. We won the pennant that year and went into the World Series against the Dodgers. We played a few games that Series that I'll always remember. One of them, of course, was the perfect, no-hit, no-run game that Don Larsen pitched. I was in left field in that one. That put us up three to two and we went over to Ebbets Field for the sixth game.

The sixth game was one of the finest pitching duels ever in a World Series. Bob Turley and Clem Labine hooked up and it was 0–0 all the way to the bottom of the tenth inning. The Dodgers got men on first and second with two out and Jackie Robinson was the batter. Well, what I figured I ought to do was play a medium left field, where I had a chance to throw the man out at the plate on a base hit, and still have time to go back for a fly ball. But what Robinson did was hit one of those line drives that come out there like it's shot out of a rifle. I went back as quick as I could and jumped against the wall, but the ball hit up there and the winning run scored. Some of the newspapermen wrote that I'd misjudged the ball, but that was wrong; it was hit just too quick for me to get back on it.

Anyway, Johnny Kucks shut them out in the final game and we won the World Series. We won pennants again in '57 and '58. So I got into three World Series with the Yankees. I enjoyed my years with the Yankees very much. But I guess deep in my heart I was a Cardinal, and always would be, even though they'd hurt me awful bad.

VIC RASCHI

VICTOR JOHN ANGELO RASCHI
Born: March 28, 1919, West Springfield, Massachusetts
Major-league career: 1946–55, New York Yankees, St. Louis
    Cardinals, Kansas City Athletics
Lifetime record: 132 wins, 66 losses

In his prime years with the Yankees, Vic Raschi was
known as one of baseball's finest clutch pitchers. The three-
time 20-game winner also posted five World Series victories
and in 1951 led the American League in strikeouts. Since
1900 only Spud Chandler, Whitey Ford, and Lefty Grove
have posted a higher winning percentage than Raschi's .667.

There was something special about being a Yankee back in those
years. We believed we were the best and that we couldn't lose. It
wasn't arrogance, it was pride. We used to go out there each day with
every expectation of winning. And when we didn't win, then it was
more than just losing a ball game, because it hurt our pride.

They began cultivating it in the minor-league system. They let you
know that you were part of a great winning tradition that began with
Babe Ruth and Lou Gehrig. It was drilled into you that once you made
the Yankees you would be entering that tradition, that playing for the
New York Yankees was the height of anybody's baseball career.

In 1949 the Red Sox came into New York to close out the season with
a two-game series, leading us by one. All they had to do was win once
to take the pennant. They had a rookie pitcher, whose name I forget at
the moment. Well, just before the Saturday game we overheard some of
the Red Sox talking about starting this rookie on Sunday. In other
words, they were so confident of beating us on Saturday that they were
looking forward to relaxing in the last game, figuring they'd have
wrapped it up by then. This was the way they felt. I suppose they were
entitled to feel confident; but it made us kind of mad and gave us some

added incentive—not that were weren't primed for those games to begin with.

Well, they did jump off to a 4–0 lead in that game. But we tied it and then won it on Johnny Lindell's home run and some great relief pitching by Joe Page. So we went into Sunday's game tied for first place and I guess they forgot about starting that rookie.

Ball games just don't come any bigger than that, do they? Not only are you tied for first place on the last day of the season, but you're playing the team that you're tied with.

To make things just a little more difficult for us, Joe DiMaggio had been sick for about a week with a virus and wasn't up to full strength. He couldn't run too well, but he was in there, and we wanted him in there.

I had a pretty good idea that I would be pitching that game and I was pleased about it. You have to get back to pride again; everything was riding on this one game and the team was entrusting me to win it for them. I knew that as long as I stayed in baseball, no matter how many times I went to the mound, I would never pitch a game bigger than this one.

I never talked too much before I pitched, because I had a lot of thinking to do. You've heard of pitchers psyching themselves before a game; well, it can help quite a bit, but I think it helps even more if you get a kind of sweaty feeling in the palm of your hand. That's anticipation. I had never experienced a build-up and an anxiety before a game to such an extent. And they can say what they want to, but they all get it. I wouldn't give one penny for any ballplayer who didn't get that anxiety; I wouldn't want him playing beside me.

I think it was fitting that it turned out to be a close, hard-fought game. We scored a run in the bottom of the first inning. Phil Rizzuto hit a triple and Tommy Henrich brought him in with a ground ball. After that it was nip and tuck all the way. Nothing but zeroes up on the scoreboard, and that big, big Sunday crowd sitting back and watching.

Ellis Kinder was pitching for them and he was going beautifully. But then in the top of the eighth they had to take him out for a pinch hitter. Mel Parnell came in. Henrich hit a home run and then we loaded the bases off of Tex Hughson and Jerry Coleman cleared them with a double that Al Zarilla just missed catching in right field.

So we went into the ninth inning leading by five runs. It should have been easy, but it wasn't. The Red Sox still had some kick left in them. They got two men on and Bobby Doerr hit one into deep center. Normally, DiMaggio would have caught that ball, but he was so sick and worn out that he couldn't catch up with it. It fell in for a triple. Joe took himself out of the game, right then and there. Cliff Mapes went into center and the next batter flied out to him. That was two out. But Billy Goodman singled and that made it 5–3. Birdie Tebbetts was up next, and he was the tying run.

When the ball came back into the infield after Goodman's hit, Henrich got it and walked it over to the mound. I knew he wanted to say something encouraging, but before he could open his mouth I said, "Give me the goddamned ball and get the hell out of here." Poor Tom wasn't expecting that. He handed me the ball and scatted out of there.

Well, a moment later Tom had the ball back in his hand when Tebbetts fouled out to him. We'd won a pennant.

I started the second game of the Series that year, against the Dodgers. We had won the first game, 1–0, behind Allie Reynolds. The score of the second game was 1–0 again, but we didn't win it. Preacher Roe beat me, and it was my own fault.

In the second inning Jackie Robinson doubled and got over to third, and Gil Hodges was the batter. Right here is where I made my mistake. One of the things they teach a pitcher is how to work when there's a fast man on third base. If you decide to pitch out of a windup you've got to make up your mind that the runner on third isn't going to bother you; you keep your concentration fixed on the batter. If you can't do that, if you're going to worry about the man stealing home, then you work out of a stretch position.

So Jackie Robinson was on third, and he was just about the best base runner I've ever seen. He could get away from a standing position in a flash; by his second or third stride he was going at full speed. I'd never pitched with him on base before and I was going into a full windup. But his movements were distracting me—remember how he used to agitate on the bases? You never knew what he was going to do, and he was fully capable of doing almost anything he wanted. So I decided I had better switch over and work from a stretch position. But you can see right there what happened—Robinson had broken my concentration. I was pitching more to Robinson than I was to Hodges, and as a result I threw one up into Gil's power and he got the base hit that beat me.

When I went into the dugout nobody dared say a word. I knew what had happened and everybody else knew what had happened. That was the only run of the game, and it was my own fault. I think that was the only mistake I made in that game; but you don't have to make too many when you lose 1–0, do you?

I guess I began to take baseball seriously when I was a freshman in high school in Springfield, Massachusetts. We were playing in a scholastic tournament and a Yankee scout by the name of Gene McCann was scouting it. He came up to me after the game and said he would

*Four heroes of the 1952 World Series. Top: Yogi Berra and Mickey Mantle.
Bottom: Allie Reynolds and Vic Raschi.*

like to talk to my parents and me about a career in professional baseball.

He visited the house one evening and told us what he had in mind.
After I graduated high school the Yankees would get me a scholarship
at a college and pay my way through. My only obligation was to give
the Yankees first crack at me after I had completed my college education.

Well, I wanted to go on to college, but this was during the Depression and my family didn't have much money. So, with my father's
blessings, I accepted the Yankees' offer and they arranged for me to go
to William and Mary, down in Virginia.

I'd had a few other offers at the same time. The St. Louis Cardinals
wanted to sign me, but they would have put me right into their minor-
league system. The Cleveland Indians were also interested. As a matter
of fact, they invited me up to Boston to work out with them at Fenway
Park.

I took the train to Boston, feeling pretty excited about it. Steve
O'Neill himself, who was managing the Indians, met me at the station
and took me out to the ball park. In the clubhouse they gave me a
Cleveland uniform to put on and then I went out onto the field. I was
only sixteen years old and there I was, wearing a big-league uniform,
working out in a big-league ball park, and keeping my eye on fellows
like Mel Harder, Earl Averill, Hal Trosky, Johnny Allen.

Steve O'Neill told me to loosen up my arm easily, that he wanted to
see me throw to a catcher. In a little while he brought a catcher over
and I pitched to him. I cut loose and threw as hard as I could and felt
pretty good about myself.

Then this kid walked out and started to warm up. You couldn't help
but notice him because he had this big, flashy windup. He started
throwing harder and harder. Each pitch seemed so much faster than
the previous. I'd never seen anybody throw a ball like that. Pretty soon
it sounded like it was exploding when it hit the catcher's mitt. He was
throwing bullets, just plain bullets. "Good God!" I said to myself. No
way was I going to compete with this guy.

It was Bob Feller, of course. I hadn't heard of him yet at that time.
But it was marvelous to watch him throw that ball, and demoralizing,
too. Heck, we were about the same age.

You know, I had the reputation for staring hitters down, for standing
out there and glaring at them once they got set in the batter's box. Well,
that was true, and it was all very carefully calculated. I figured if I
could break their concentration when they came up to the plate I had
them beat, or at least gained an advantage. Once you had made them
turn their eyes away you had a slight psychological edge, in my opin-

America's Most Famous
High School Graduate
Bob Feller, Boy With Million Dollar Arm,
Receives Diploma From Little Country School

ion. But there was one guy you couldn't do it to. Want to take a guess who? That's right—Ted Williams. Well, what do you do with a guy that's been staring at *you* from the moment he's left the dugout to go out into the on-deck circle, and keeps his eyes on your eyes when he steps into the batters' box. How long can you stand out there and stare at a guy? The ball game's got to go on, doesn't it? He was the one man I couldn't stare down. You see, Ted's concentration up at the plate was so intense I don't think he even knew what I was trying to do.

I don't know how I would have fared trying that on Joe DiMaggio. I was fortunate in having Joe as a teammate and so never had to face him. He was the greatest all-around ballplayer I ever saw. He was a quiet leader on a ball club. Never said much, never argued. But at the same time he evoked tremendous respect and inspiration. A great team man.

You almost never saw him say anything to an umpire, and if he did, it was usually quietly, so that the fans never knew it. When he got mad he would give the dirt a little kick—that was the extent of it, that little kick at the dirt. When they threw at him he'd never say anything. He wouldn't come back to the dugout cursing, asking our pitcher to deck somebody in retaliation. Did they throw at him much? Sure they did, especially in Detroit. Detroit had some pretty mean guys on their staff. Dizzy Trout would throw at you, and so would Virgil Trucks and Freddy Hutchinson. But Joe never complained. Personally, I never thought it very good strategy to throw at guys like Joe or Ted Williams. They could beat you when they were happy; get them mad and they'd kill you.

We talked about Bob Feller before. Well, of course I got to pitch against Bob later when I was with the Yankees. One game will always stand out in my mind. It was a night game in Cleveland, back in 1950, in August. Bob and I hooked up in a real duel. We were leading, 1–0, in the eighth inning, and I was on third base with one out and Phil Rizzuto was the batter.

They put the squeeze play on. Phil laid the ball down just right, and I was slow getting away from third—I wasn't the fastest thing on two feet anyway. Luke Easter fielded the ball and threw home, and there's Jim Hegan waiting for me. Well, I slid in and all I could see was shinguards—Hegan knew how to block the plate. I was out, but we won the game anyway, 1–0.

At about three o'clock in the morning I woke up with a terrific pain in my right knee. It turned out I had torn the cartilages on the outside of that knee. We didn't tell anybody, though. We kept it quiet for two years because they didn't want anybody bunting on me and taking advantage of the bad knee.

Joe DiMaggio and Mickey Mantle in 1951.

I had a lot of trouble running and tried to stay off the bases as much as I could. But finally they had to operate on that knee, and it was a successful operation. A few years later, during the winter, I slipped and sure enough, tore it up again. It finally led to my giving up baseball.

George Weiss was the general manager when I was with the Yankees and he was a tough man. A little while ago we talked about staring a man down; well, here was someone who would never look at you. You'd talk to him and he would be looking everywhere but at you. You always got the impression he was thinking, *What's this guy want and how can I get rid of him in a hurry?*

When it came to negotiating a contract he would let you know that the whole Yankee organization had had a hand in winning the pennant. Talking to him, you felt your own contribution getting smaller and smaller. What used to irritate him when we talked salary was my not quibbling over my earned run average, my wins, my shutouts, etc. I never talked to him along those lines. The only thing I would ever discuss with him was my value to the ball club. Was I valuable to the Yankees or wasn't I? This irritated him, because he had nothing to come back on, no counterarguments to make.

After winning 21 ball games three years in a row I dropped down to 16 in 1952. That winter I went in to talk contract with Mr. Weiss.

"Didn't have such a good year, did you?" he said.

"Yes," I said. "I know that."

"I think we'll have to cut your contract," he said.

"I don't think that's fair," I said. "Look at the years I've put in. I've had a bad knee and still went out there. I had a bad knee last year and still won sixteen ball games, and we won the pennant."

We argued back and forth and didn't get anywhere. Finally I left, telling him I'd see him down in spring training. This made him mad; he liked to have everything settled before camp opened. When finally we agreed and I signed a contract, it was on terms that were more satisfactory to me than they were to him. After I had signed, he said to me, very sternly, "Don't you *ever* have a bad year."

I won 13 games that year and he sent me a contract calling for a twenty-five percent cut. Same thing. I told him I'd see him in spring training. I went down to St. Petersburg and never saw him. The next thing I knew, newspapermen were coming out to the cottage where I was staying.

"You've just been traded to the Cardinals," they said.

That's how I found out about it. Weiss never told me. I'd had the bad year he had warned me about—if you want to call 13 and 6 a bad year— and he got rid of me. I was awfully disappointed about it. I'd been a Yankee for a long time.

I decided I'd better call my mother and tell her, rather than have her hear it over the radio. When I got her on the phone, I said, "Mom, I've got something to tell you. I was just traded from the Yankees to the St. Louis Cardinals."

"That's wonderful," she said. "I'm happy, really happy."

I was dumbfounded. "What do you mean, you're 'really happy'?" I asked.

"I never wanted you to be a Yankee," she said. "I never liked the Yankees."

"You didn't?" I asked.

"No," she said. "I always wished you could be a Boston Red Socker."

How do you like that? All those years my mother was wishing I was with the Red Sox.

MONTE IRVIN

MONFORD MERILL IRVIN
Born: February 25, 1919, Columbia, Alabama
Major-league career: 1949–56, New York Giants, Chicago
    Cubs
Lifetime average: .293

Because of the color barrier, Monte Irvin did not reach the big leagues until he was thirty years old. In a few short years, however, he established himself as one of the National League's premier right-handed hitters. In 1951 he was the power hitter behind the Giants' remarkable drive to their "miracle" pennant, batting .312 and leading the league in runs batted in with 121.

In 1973 Irvin was elected by a special committee to the Hall of Fame in recognition of his outstanding play in the Negro Leagues.

I got out of the service in September, 1945. I had been away from baseball for a few years, so I went down to Puerto Rico to sharpen my skills a little bit. A few months later we heard that the Dodgers had signed Jackie Robinson.

Yes, it came as a surprise. Originally we had heard that Branch Rickey had signed Jackie to play for a team called the Brown Bombers in Brooklyn, to play in Ebbets Field when the Dodgers were on the road. But then the straight story came out, that he would be given a chance to play for Montreal and that if he was good enough he'd move up to the parent club. I was delighted for Jackie, and it gave hope to a lot of us. Hopefully he was going to open the door for other black players to follow.

So we followed Jackie's progress very carefully. There was a lot at stake, and not just for Jackie, not just for the other black ballplayers, not just for baseball; it went beyond that. We knew, of course, that he was going to have to take an awful lot. I guess we knew better than anybody else what he was going to have to put up with.

It was nail-biting time. If Jackie had not been able to stand up under the pressure, I don't know what would have happened, I don't know where it would have gone from there. But you know the story. Under all the pressure—and the pressure was tremendous—he handled himself well. He was a great ballplayer, a dynamic ballplayer, and every day that he played he pushed that door open just a little bit wider for the rest of us who were waiting to get through.

The amazing thing about Robinson was that during those first few years he was very stoic about what he was undergoing, accepting the abuse and the insults without saying a word. Then, after he had made it and been accepted, you found out what kind of fires he had inside him, how explosive and aggressive he really was. Those first few years must have been hell for him. I understand that Branch Rickey was talking to him all the time, telling him to keep that temper under control, not to provoke any incidents.

As I said, I followed Jackie's progress very carefully. I was only twenty-seven at the time, and I was hoping that the opportunity to go into organized ball might come my way.

I was born in Columbia, Alabama. My family moved to New Jersey when I was about eight years old. So I remember very little about Alabama; all my memories are, for the most part, about New Jersey. We were sharecroppers in Alabama and we couldn't make a decent living there. My older brother and sister had come to New Jersey and they found out how much better the opportunities were. So the rest of us decided to follow. This was around 1927.

It was great growing up in New Jersey. There were ten of us, living all together in the same house. Of course we were as poor as everybody else, but we were healthy, hard-working, and just one big happy family.

It was rough making a living during the Depression. We had just the bare necessities. But my father and brothers worked at a dairy, so we had plenty of milk. And my father had a green thumb, so we had a garden and lots of fresh vegetables. We all pitched in. When I was old enough I worked in a bowling alley, setting up pins. Later on I got a job helping to deliver milk. In those days they delivered milk by horse and wagon. I liked that, because not only was I earning money, but I was building up my legs, going up and down that wagon all day. I was about twelve or thirteen years old then.

I was always interested in athletics. My best sport when I was growing up was football. But at that time the door hadn't been opened in football either. Also, I knew that as far as injuries were concerned, you were less likely to hurt yourself at baseball. So I took the baseball route. I'll tell you, I had a lot of confidence in myself. I didn't think anybody could beat me at playing baseball. I could run, I could throw, I could hit the ball as far as anybody. In fact, they still talk about some of the balls I hit when I was playing around New Jersey. I was a short-stop then, and I had a real good arm; sometimes, if the pitcher didn't show up, they'd send me out to the mound. I remember pitching against Hank Borowy when we were high school kids. But I loved to hit. I always had a lot of power.

There was a man operating a team in Newark, named Abe Manley. He'd heard about me and thought he would come up and take a look. I guess he liked what he saw, because he said he wanted to sign me. There was no bonus, of course. In those days you had to consider your-self lucky if you were asked. So I jumped at the chance. This was in 1937. I had to play under an assumed name and only on the road, be-cause I was attending college at the time—Lincoln College, in Penn-sylvania. I was majoring in history, with hopes of teaching someday. Actually, what I wanted to do was become a dentist, but I didn't have any money and didn't have any hopes of getting any. So in 1939 I left college after two years and became a full-time member of the Newark Eagles.

I didn't know back then whether or not I'd ever get the chance to play in organized ball. I was always optimistic, but I couldn't be sure, because if you weren't around at that time, you don't know how in-tense feelings about it were. The mood of the country was completely different then. You know, I starred at Orange High School for four years. High school athletes generally are regarded fondly in their hometown, right? Well, the night I graduated I went with a date and another fellow and his date to a restaurant two blocks away from the school—and we were turned away. They wouldn't let us in. This is pretty hard to take. But there wasn't anything we could do about it.

After the war things began to change for the better, particularly in or-ganized baseball. But before that happened, there were a lot of good black ballplayers who passed from the scene without ever having had the right opportunity. I'm not talking about just the men we've put in the Black Hall of Fame already, but many others, men like Willie Welles, Oscar Charleston, John Henry Lloyd, Ray Dandridge, Leon Day. These men would have been outstanding, if those barriers hadn't been up against them.

Sure, there was a lot of talk among the players at the time about the color barrier. We just couldn't understand why the feeling against us was so intense. Everybody had gone to school together, done a lot of things together—so why couldn't we play professional baseball togeth-er? We hit the same ball, ran the same way, threw the same way, played by the same rules—so what was the difference? When we weren't play-

Monte Irvin with the Newark Eagles.

ing league games we played exhibition games against white teams, and a lot of the white players used to tell us that some of us should be in the major leagues. They knew the barrier was wrong, an awful lot of them did. But it wasn't time yet.

In 1947, a short while after Jackie made the big leagues, I signed with the Dodgers. But then Branch Rickey couldn't get together with the Newark ball club for compensation. Mrs. Manley, who pretty much ran the club's business, wanted a certain amount of money for my contract, and Rickey didn't want to give it. She raised such a fuss about it that the whole thing was dropped. Then Horace Stoneham came along. He'd seen that the Dodgers were signing black players, so I guess he figured he had better start thinking in those terms, too.

This wasn't until early in 1949. I was playing ball in Cuba that winter. A Giant scout named Alex Pompez approached Henry Thompson and myself. He told us we'd get the minimum salary—about $5,000 then—but that the Giants thought we had the ability to play in the major leagues. He wanted to know if we were interested. We sure were.

I was excited, naturally, but at the same time a little apprehensive. I didn't know what it was going to be like. Jackie had had a few unpleasant incidents, which we knew about, of course. We figured it was going to be rough, but it was an opportunity and at the same time something new was happening and we wanted to be part of it. There were some rough moments, especially in the South, but we were young, and we so badly wanted the opportunity to play in the big leagues that we were willing to put up with whatever came our way.

I started off the 1949 season with Jersey City and did all right. After about a half season I was hitting .373 and they brought me up, along with Hank Thompson. Leo Durocher was managing the Giants then. He couldn't have been nicer. He welcomed us very warmly and introduced us around. Then he talked to us privately.

"Fellows," he said, "it's no different from what you've been doing everywhere else. Just go out and play your own game and you'll be all right."

The following spring the Giants decided to go with Don Mueller as their right fielder and sent me back to Jersey City for a little more seasoning. I played there for about a month and was hitting .510. I guess they figured that was seasoning enough and brought me back up. I went into the regular lineup then and stayed there.

Willie Mays? I think most anybody who saw him will tell you that Mays is the greatest ballplayer that ever lived. He could do everything: run, field, throw, hit, hit with power, steal bases. I don't think there was ever a center fielder, be it Tris Speaker or Joe DiMaggio or Terry Moore or anybody else, who was better than Willie in going and get-

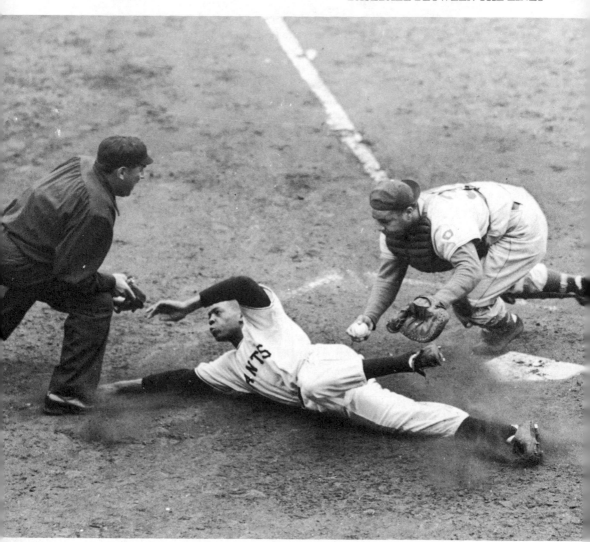

Giants' center fielder Willie Mays slides into the plate in the fourth inning, September 2, 1951, only to be tagged out by Dodger catcher Roy Campanella.

ting a ball. He would play shallow, catching the line drives and would-be Texas Leaguers, and at the same time you couldn't hit anything over his head. At the crack of the bat he was gone. And of course he had an arm like a cannon; you could never take an extra base on him.

Willie joined the club a month or so into the season in '51. They brought him up from Minneapolis, where he was hitting .477. Leo assigned him to room with me and we became good friends. He was a fine young man, with a wonderful, happy-go-lucky disposition. No inhibitions. All he wanted to do was play ball. He was a tonic to have around, and not just for his great ability. Everybody was extremely fond of him.

Playing alongside Willie every day was exciting. He kept pulling one miracle after another and as many times as you watched him you still never quite got used to it. One day he made this unbelievable catch in Pittsburgh, off of Rocky Nelson. He was playing in close and Rocky got hold of one and drove it way out into that big center field they had in old Forbes Field. Willie whirled around and took off after it. At the last second he saw he couldn't get his glove across his body in time to make the catch, so he caught it in his bare hand.

Leo was flabbergasted. We all were.

"I've never seen anything like that in my life," Leo said.

Then Leo decided to have a little fun with Willie. He told us to give Mays the silent treatment when Willie came in after the inning. You know, you do that sometimes, after a guy has done something spectacular on the field and is expecting the big noisy reception when he comes in. So when Willie came back to the dugout nobody said a word. We just sat there with our arms folded and stared out at the field, ignoring him completely. Willie was puzzled. He sat there looking around waiting for somebody to say something. Finally he couldn't contain himself any longer.

"Leo," he said, "didn't you see what I just did out there?"

Durocher didn't say anything.

"Leo," Willie said. "Didn't you see what I did?"

Leo turned around and looked at him, poker-faced. "No," he said, "I didn't see it. So you'll have to go out and do it again before I'll believe it."

And then there was that great catch he made on Vic Wertz in the 1954 Series. I never thought he had a chance to get even close to it. You know, he likes to play that catch down. But let me tell you, that's one of the greatest outfield plays I've ever seen. I was going out there to play the rebound, hoping to hold Wertz to a triple. That ball was *hit*. But Willie caught it. Don't ask me how. But there he was, going a mile-a-minute, his back to the plate. When the inning was over and we were on our way in, I said to him, "Nice going, roomie. I didn't think you'd get to that one." Very casually, he said, "I had that one all the way. Had it all the way." And I said, "Oh, you did, huh? Well, okay."

But you talk about World Series games, why, we played twenty-two of those each season—every time we played the Dodgers. Those games were always something special. It didn't matter where we were in the standings—though in those years we were usually both right around the top—it was always a battle.

We'd look at the schedule, see the Dodgers were coming up and a terrific sense of anticipation would begin to build. We were always up for those games. You couldn't help it. It was a traditional rivalry, and if you ever forgot it, then the fans reminded you in a hurry. If we didn't win the pennant, then beating the Dodgers was the next best thing.

In 1951 we did it all—won the pennant and beat the Dodgers head-on in doing it. That was the strangest kind of season, 1951, any way you look at it. We won our opener and then lost the next eleven. We just couldn't seem to do anything right. It didn't look like we'd ever get squared away. But then we did; we started playing good ball later in the summer, but by that time it looked like it was too late, that we'd given away too much ground to make up. It was the middle of August now, and we were 13½ games behind the Dodgers.

We had just lost three in a row to the Dodgers in Ebbets Field and were in the clubhouse after the game. The clubhouses there were pretty close together and we could hear some of the Dodgers yelling through the wall at us. They were on Leo particularly; some of them didn't like him and were really giving him a raking. They were letting him know that it was all over as far as they were concerned.

Well, somehow that struck a chord in the whole team. I can't explain what it was; maybe it simply was pride. It was like right then and there every man made some private decision—the same decision—that we were going to make a run at it, no matter how hopeless it looked. From then on we really started to play some ball.

We were a good ball club. There was nothing flukey about what we did. Willie had joined us after the season was underway and went to center field, and Bobby Thomson switched from center field to third. Then Leo made a key move; he took me off of first base and put me in left field, and took Whitey Lockman out of left and put him on first. Also, we had Alvin Dark, Eddie Stanky, Don Mueller, Wes Westrum, Henry Thompson. And those good pitchers—Sal Maglie, Larry Jansen, Jim Hearn, Dave Koslo, George Spencer. It was a very well-balanced ball club. I think the Dodgers might have had a better team, man for man. Why, they practically had an all-star club, with Robinson, Duke Snider, Pee Wee Reese, Roy Campanella, Gil Hodges, Billy Cox, Carl

Furillo, Andy Pafko. And that made it all the sweeter, of course, beating a club as good as they were.

We had great leadership and inspiration going for us. We were coming from behind, all season long. I think that probably makes a difference. You can't let up for a minute, not for a game or an inning or a pitch. Every day you go out and you know you've got to make up ground. Somehow we never really got discouraged. I've got to go back to that kid we had in center field: he was one of the big things we had going for us. Day after day he kept coming up with those great plays and throws to save a game, or the hit that won it. And remember, he was just a rookie that year, playing in the biggest baseball pressure-cooker of them all—a Dodger-Giant pennant race.

In addition, Durocher was making fantastic moves, taking the pitcher out at just the right moment, putting up the right pinch-hitter, moving men around in the field as if he just *knew* where the ball was going to be hit. He was uncanny. Personally, I think he must have won six or seven games for us by his strategy.

Leo kept prodding us on. We didn't know if we would ever come close or not. We never mentioned winning the pennant. We just didn't like the idea of letting them run away with it. So we figured we'd give them a fight for it, let them know we were in the league. Then they started to lose and we started to win. The Dodgers didn't play bad ball coming down the stretch—they were around .500, I think, which isn't championship baseball, but isn't a total collapse either. But the thing was, we hardly lost a game after the middle of August. We won 39 of our last 47 games. At one point we put together a sixteen-game winning streak.

We finished the season in Boston, winning our games there. When our game was over we were in first place by a half game and the Dodgers were battling the Phillies in Philadelphia. We were listening to that game on the radio. They went into extra innings, and I remember one spot when the Phillies had the bases loaded with one out and Del Ennis was up. "Hit it, Del," we were yelling. "Hit it anywhere." Hell, we were a fly ball or a ground ball away from a pennant. But Newcombe struck him out. Then Eddie Waitkus lined one that looked like a sure hit, but Jackie made that great diving catch on it. Then Jackie came up in the fourteenth inning and hit the home run to win it. We were on the train back when we heard about it.

So there was going to be a play-off. The first game was in Ebbets Field, and Jim Hearn won it for us, 3–1. I hit a home run and so did Bobby Thomson. We beat Branca. Not many people remember that Bobby hit two home runs off of Branca in that play-off, and each one was a big one.

Then we moved over to the Polo Grounds and Clem Labine shut us out, 10–0, throwing that great sinker and that jug-handled curve ball.

So there was one more game to play. It was inevitable I guess, typical of what we'd been going through—always that one more game to play, the one we just *had* to win. And it was true; they'd all been big games. But this was the biggest one of them all.

Big Newcombe started for them, and he came out throwing bullets. He went along strong for eight innings, and going into the last of the ninth we're down, 4–1. Well, I don't have to look in the record books to tell you how it happened. Dark was up first and he singled. Then Mueller got a base hit. Two men on. And I'm up. The tying run.

Now, I'd had a good year, and a particularly good second half. Got a lot of key hits. Hit over .300, had twenty-four home runs, led the league in runs batted in. Mr. Clutch. But what did I do? Popped up to Hodges in foul ground, right near the railing. Well, I *could've* hit into a double play.

Whitey Lockman was up next. He hit one down the left-field line for a double. That made it, 4–2, and put the tying run on second, with one out. When Mueller slid into third he hurt his ankle and they had to take him out and put in a runner. While that was happening, Charley Dressen, who was managing Brooklyn, got on the phone to the bull pen, where they were throwing. He asked who looked good down there. Well, Erskine was warming up, but it seems he was kind of wild; he'd bounced a few curves. Branca was throwing strikes and was really popping the ball. So Dressen asked for Branca, and Ralph took that long walk in.

Branca's first pitch to Thomson was a fastball for a strike. It was just the kind of pitch Bobby liked to hit, inside and a little high. But he took it. Now let's just hold it there for a second while I tell you where, in my opinion, we had got a good break. Campanella had injured himself in that last game in Philadelphia and wasn't playing. Rube Walker was behind the plate. But I'll tell you what I think might have happened if Campy had been in there. He would have called time, even though the pitch was a strike, and gone out to Branca and said, "Hey, wait a minute. We've got to keep this ball down. Don't let him hit a home run. Keep it down." But Campy wasn't there.

So Ralph threw him the same pitch. And Bobby was ready for it, and he whacked it. You know what happened. Would I say it was the biggest single moment in baseball history? Well, I don't know. What would you say?

We were stunned for a moment. Nobody said anything, nobody moved, even though we saw that the ball had gone in the stands. Then it struck us: We'd won. It sank in. We began jumping up and down and

His teammates waiting at home plate for Bobby Thomson, Ralph Branca (right) departs. Jackie Robinson is in foreground. Polo Grounds, October 3, 1951.

yelling. All that joy and excitement flooded into us like so much nervous energy and I think if we hadn't started yelling and jumping we would have exploded. We started grabbing each other and laughing; we just couldn't find words. It was chaos. Happy chaos. And then pandemonium broke loose throughout the whole ball park. One thing I'll always remember though: Jackie Robinson was standing there watching Bobby circle the bases, making sure he touched each one.

Then we were all at home plate, waiting for Bobby. Our next problem was getting from home plate to the clubhouse in center field. The fans were swarming all over the field, patting us on the back, shaking our hands, pulling at us. Too many well-wishers can be scary. Finally the police came and helped us get through.

We celebrated in the clubhouse with warm champagne. Somebody had forgot to chill it. I guess when we fell behind in the game they figured we were licked. Can you imagine that?

GENE CONLEY

Donald Eugene Conley
Born: November 10, 1930, Muskogee, Oklahoma
Major-league career: 1952–1963, Boston and Milwaukee
Braves, Philadelphia Phillies, Boston Red Sox
Lifetime record: 91 wins, 96 losses

An unusually endowed athlete, Gene Conley was the first man to play two major sports in the same city—basketball for the Boston Celtics and baseball for both the Boston Braves and Boston Red Sox. Conley's best year was 1962, when he won 15 games for the Red Sox. Two years later a bad arm forced him into retirement.

I went to Washington State College and played a couple of years of baseball and basketball. During the summer in my sophomore year I started pitching for a semipro team in Walla Walla and was going real well; there were scouts out at just about every game. I knew they were there to watch me and I guess I liked the idea. It made me bear down harder.

My family didn't want me to sign a contract until I had finished school, but you know how it is—a career in professional baseball looks very glamorous, and in addition you can't help wondering just how good you really are. So when the Boston Braves offered me a $3,000 bonus, I took it.

My first year in the minors was 1951. I pitched for Hartford, in the Eastern League. I was making only $300 a month, was married, my first child was on the way, and I needed some money. One day I got a call from Bill Sharman, who had just joined the Boston Celtics. He said he'd seen me play basketball out in California, against UCLA, told Red Auerbach about me and that Red said to ask me if I was interested in trying out for the Celtics.

"Since your graduating class is '52," he said, "the Celtics would be able to draft you."

"Well," I said, "that's very interesting. Can you make any money?" That was my chief concern.

"You can," he said, "if you make the team."

So the Celtics drafted me and after the baseball season was over in '52 I went up to Boston and tried out. And I made it; I wasn't on the first team, but I made it. I was delighted and a little bit surprised; after all, I'd had only one year of varsity basketball in college. The salary was $4,500, which was a big-league basketball salary in those days.

The Braves didn't seem to mind my playing basketball then. I was still nothing more than a minor-league prospect and they weren't particularly interested in what I was doing.

Then I had a good year pitching for Toledo in the American Association—I won the Minor League Player of the Year Award—and got set for another year of basketball. That was when the Braves wanted to know what was going on.

"Look," they said, "we're thinking of bringing you up next year. We're concerned about your getting injured."

"I played with the Celtics last year because I needed the money," I said, "and I have to play again this year for the same very good reason."

"Well," they said, "if you won't play we'll give you a thousand dollars."

I thought that was pretty nice. Same as getting a thousand-dollar bonus. And since the chance to make the big club was what I was after, I decided to take the thousand, get a job that winter and not play basketball.

I came up to stay in 1954. Had a good year and was runner-up to Wally Moon for Rookie of the Year. Once I'd made the big leagues I gave up basketball.

You know, spring training had been kind of rough. The Braves had some hard-nosed veterans who weren't overly cordial to rookies. Every rookie was a potential threat to somebody's paycheck; that was how they looked at it. Some of the fringe pitchers in particular, guys who were battling to hold their jobs, surely weren't going to give you any help. Sometimes the resentment was quite open. When they saw you were scheduled to pitch, you heard remarks like, "Let's see what the pheenom is going to do today." It was understandable, I suppose; after all, I was there to try and take somebody's job. If you pitch a good game or two you're going to send some guy to the bull pen, or even off the team. This inside competition on a ball club is a real thing, especially in spring training and during the first few weeks of the season. That's when jobs are at stake.

So there wasn't much support or encouragement from anybody, except the coaches. Charlie Root, the old Chicago Cub pitcher, was the pitching coach when I joined the club. He was a real rough, tough character. "Don't worry about those other guys," he'd say. "the hell with them. Do your job, take their bread and butter away from them. They've been there long enough." And knowing Charlie, he probably went up to those older pitchers and told *them,* "Don't let that kid take your job. He doesn't know anything. Bear down. Keep him outa there."

Charlie always had a chip on his shoulder anyway, because of that Babe Ruth episode in the 1932 World Series. Charlie was pitching when Ruth supposedly pointed to the center-field bleachers and then hit the ball there. He used to tell me that there was no way Babe Ruth could have done that to him and gotten away with it. "He was raising his arm to straighten out his sleeve or something," he said. Charlie Grimm told me the same thing. "Root would have put that next pitch right into Ruth's ear if Babe had tried that on him," he said. Root was that way. He had a reputation as a head-hunter. And he would tell us young pitchers to be the same way. "Don't let these guys take the bread out of your kid's mouth," he'd say. "Don't let them dig in at home plate. Knock 'em back, knock 'em down."

Generally, I never threw at hitters. Dispostion is part of it; I never liked doing it. It just wasn't my style of pitching. But when I was told to do it, naturally I did. I remember a time when we were playing a game in St. Louis. I'd been hit pretty hard my last few times out and just before I went out to warm up Charlie Root came over to me.

"Now, Gene," he said, "your stuff is all right, but they've been digging in on you. What I want you to do tonight is set a couple guys down on their butts."

"Okay, Charlie," I said.

"I'll give you a word of advice," he said. "When Musial gets up there, sit him down and that'll straighten out the whole bunch.

Then he walked away, and I'm standing there thinking to myself: I'm going to knock down Musial, in *St. Louis,* in front of thirty thousand people. I couldn't believe it.

Around the third or fourth inning Musial is leading off. Perfect time to knock him down. I stood out there telling myself how foolish this was. Then I turned around and happened to glance out toward the bull pen and I could see Charlie standing up with his hands cupped around his mouth, yelling something at me. I couldn't hear him, but I had a pretty good idea what he was saying.

So Musial got in there and, boy, did I flip him. I really flipped him. As a matter of fact I thought the ball went through him. I really did. Del Rice was catching and he came out to the mound. "Gene," he said, "I thought the ball came out through his ear, I swear." So did I, and I

Gene Conley with the Milwaukee Braves; with the Boston Celtics.

was scared stiff. I had to take a minute or so to regain my composure. The fans were booing and yelling. Musial? Never bothered him a bit. He got up, dusted himself off, went into that funny little stance and stood there peeking out at me just as if nothing had happened.

Remember when Joe Adcock hit four home runs and a double in one game against the Dodgers in Ebbets Field? Well, Joe had been blasting the Dodgers all year, and we sort of expected they'd come bearing in on him sooner or later. Sure enough, a day or two later somebody hit him in the head. I was starting the next day and Adcock came up to me and said, "Get one of them for me, will you?" I said okay.

For some reason or other the guy I picked out to floor was Jackie Robinson. I knocked him down a couple of times. Then he started dropping bunts along the first base line, but they went foul. I didn't even realize what he was trying to do until I picked up the paper the next day and saw Jackie quoted as saying he wished he could have got one fair so he could have stepped on me at first base. And all the while I thought I was getting a break because Jackie was trying to bunt instead of swinging away. I didn't realize that I was getting an even bigger break when those balls rolled foul. But Robinson played that way.

Jackie was a remarkable ballplayer in so many ways. He was always a factor when he was in the ball game. One night I was pitching against Carl Erskine in Ebbets Field and we went into the bottom of the twelfth in a scoreless tie. It was one of the finest games I ever pitched in the big leagues. With one out Jackie got on first base and Carl Furillo came up. I figured in that situation Robinson was almost certainly going to try and steal. I threw over there a few times, but he kept getting right back off again, not cutting his lead at all.

Then I got set to throw a curve to Furillo, but even as I went into my motion and began my delivery I was watching Jackie, to see what he was going to do. The moment I released the ball I realized I didn't get a good snap on it and I could just see it doing nothing as it went up there. You seldom get away with that kind of mistake, and I didn't get away with it that night. Furillo jumped on it and hit a line drive into the lower deck in left and I'm beat, 2–0, in twelve innings.

Carl Furillo got all the headlines the next day, and he deserved them, because he did the job. But *I* knew that it was Robinson who had distracted me just enough to get me to hang that curve.

We won pennants in '57 and '58. Spahn and Burdette were our big guns those years. Lew had ice water in his veins. Nothing bothered him, on or off the mound. He was a chatterbox out there. I've never seen anybody like him. He would talk to himself, to the batter, to the umpire, and sometimes he would even talk to the ball. Lew would throw at a batter on occasion, and sometimes just as he was delivering the ball he would yell, "Look out!" and then throw one of his dinky little sliders on the outside corner while the batter fell back. He didn't have what you would call great stuff—he threw sliders and sinkers and spitters, but he had great control, and he would battle you. He always knew what he was doing out there.

Sure he threw spitters. Everybody knew it but they could never catch him at it. He would drive the third-base coaches crazy, loading up the ball so that they could see him doing it and then wiping it off when they yelled, or sometimes pretending to wipe it off and throwing a loaded pitch up there. Then he'd turn around and grin at them. He knew how to agitate.

One time in Cincinnati they kept a movie camera fixed on him throughout the whole game, trying to catch him in the act of loading up the ball. I'll bet it must have cost them a few thousand dollars. Lew really enjoyed himself that night, going through all his motions, touching his cap, face, mouth. I believe he shut them out. I asked him later in the clubhouse if he'd thrown many that game. "No," he said. "Only about sixty percent." And that camera didn't catch one of them.

Spahn loved baseball and he loved to pitch; you got the feeling sometimes that pitching was his whole life. I always thought he got kind of a raw deal after he retired by not getting a job as a big-league manager. With his knowledge of the game, he would have been a good one. But as a rule, it seems that not too many former pitchers become managers; certainly not in recent years anyway. I don't know why that should be so. When you figure that approximately two-fifths of every big-league club is composed of pitchers, you begin to wonder why the percentage of former pitchers managing is so low.

Spahn hated to miss a turn. He expected to pitch every fourth day no matter what. If your turn was rained out and he was due the next day, then you sat it out and he pitched. I remember one time it didn't work out that way and they started me and held Spahn back a day. He didn't like that at all. I heard he went up to the front office and got it squared away. He didn't want to miss a turn. And I'm not being critical of him; to the contrary, I think his attitude was great. He knew what he wanted to do, he knew he could pitch and win, and he wanted to do it, without having anybody step on his toes.

Spahn once told me something about Yogi Berra that I thought was interesting. He pitched to Yogi quite a bit over the years and he used to deflate the legend about Berra being a bad-ball hitter. "He guesses with you," Spahn said. "That's what he does." So if a guy is guessing on a pitch and he gets it, then it doesn't matter if he's hitting at a bad ball, because he's ready for that pitch, he's already timed it.

I remember the scouting reports we had on Yogi in the World Series.

They said he'd swing at anything, a ball in the dirt, or over his head, or wherever, and that to be careful when you got ahead of him, because he'd go after the bad pitch. But Spahn said, "I don't want to listen to that story." He said that in a tight spot, when Berra was really bearing down at the plate, he wouldn't offer at pitches that were just off the corner, that you had to throw him strikes.

I believe Spahn was right about Yogi being a guess hitter. I pitched against him in a Series and I threw him a curveball that dropped around his feet, and he hit it for a single that drove in a run. Well, as far as I'm concerned, there was no way he could have hit that pitch if he wasn't guessing on it and was set for it.

The only basketball I played in those years was in the Y in the wintertime, just scrimmaging. I did this until 1958. I had a real bad year in '58. I didn't pitch all that much and when I did I wasn't very effective. When I say a bad year, that's putting it mildly: I was 0–6. It wasn't a matter of arm trouble, it was just that I started off poorly and never got the chance to get squared away. You see, we had a very strong staff and once I was dropped from the rotation I couldn't get back in. We had Spahn and Burdette, plus Bob Rush, Carl Willey, Joey Jay, Juan Pizarro. So they put me in the bull pen and forgot about me. I got lost down there. How can a guy who's six feet nine get lost? Easy.

Then I got into the doghouse. Deep. One night in Los Angeles I went to one of these fancy poolside Hollywood parties, with Red Schoendienst, Burdette, Frank Torre, and another guy, whose name escapes me at the moment. Frank Torre threw somebody into the pool; there was a little heat about it and a couple of tables were broken and a few people went flying around here and there. The next day in the Los Angeles *Times* there was the headline: FIVE MILWAUKEE BRAVES PLAYBOYS INVADE BEL AIR HOME. Under it were our pictures.

Well, there wasn't much they could say to Schoendienst, or Burdette, or Frank Torre, who was having a good year at first base. But I'm sitting there with an 0–5 record. Fred Haney, who was managing the club then, came up to me and said, "Gene, you can't afford this." So that put me even deeper into the doghouse, so deep I never got out.

At the end of the season they told me I was going to get a salary cut, which didn't surprise me. So I started thinking about the Celtics again. They'd just got Bill Russell and some of those other outstanding players and were beginning to launch that great dynasty. I'd been away from it for a long time, but I got to thinking about what would happen if I got in touch with them to see if I could get started again. I called up Red Auerbach and asked him if he could use an old washed-up pitcher.

"You think you can still play?" he asked. "You know we play it a little differently now." He reminded me about the twenty-second rule and some of the other changes. He reminded me, too, that they had a pretty good team, with Russell, Bob Cousy, Tom Heinsohn, and guys like that. I told him I'd like to give it a whirl and he said I was welcome to come up for a tryout. I did that and doggone if I didn't make the team again, five years later.

They got into the play-offs that year and those games overlapped with spring training. Birdie Tebbetts, who was general manager of the Braves, called me up.

"Play-offs or no play-offs," he said, "you're going to have to leave the Celtics. You're still a baseball player."

He said that even though I'd had a lousy year they felt I could still pitch. Then he told me they were cutting my pay twenty-five percent. That seemed like an awful lot.

"I realize you've got to cut me," I said, "but I don't appreciate the dimensions of it."

"Listen," he said, "you're going to take the cut and you're going to come to spring training." Birdie could be a pretty tough guy.

"I don't know if I can make it to spring training," I said. "We're into the play-offs now and I can't leave them. It wouldn't be right."

We left it at that, and when I mentioned it to Auerbach, he said, "Oh, no, you can't leave this club now. You're playing a little and you're good relief for Heinsohn and you're helping us. We've got a championship team here. Stick around and enjoy it." Then he gave me a few thousand to help me make up my mind.

So I kept writing Birdie, telling him I'd be there, but that I'd be a little late. I stayed with the Celtics right to the end and we won the championship, we won the whole works, which was a tremendous thrill. I'd been on pennant winners with the Braves in '57 and '58 and then on a championship team with the Celtics right after that. So I was pretty excited.

The day after the Celtics had won it all I joined the Braves in spring training. And there was Birdie.

"Forget it," he said. "You've been traded to the Phillies."

At first the Phillies didn't seem to care if I played basketball or not. Then one day Bob Carpenter, who owned the ball club, called me in and said, "Gene, I don't think I want you to play basketball."

"Mr. Carpenter," I said, "you don't know how much fun I'm having. The Celtics are a great bunch of guys, plus we're winning championships."

"That may be so," he said. "But we're paying you pretty good money, and I think you ought to give up basketball."

"I can't do that," I said.

"What will it take to keep you from playing?"

"Well," I said, "I'll have to think that over. After all, I've played two years with them and I'm helping them and they want me."

"Name a figure," he said.

"Twenty-five thousand," I said.

"I'll give you twenty."

"Make it twenty-five."

"Twenty," he said.

"Twenty-five and I'll quit," I said.

That made him mad. "You'll either take what I offered you," he said, "or get out."

"Then I'll get out," I said.

I went to Auerbach and told him what I'd done.

"Good for you," he said. "Now you're talking like a champion. Stick with us and you'll have a lot of fun."

"That's all right," I said. "But the least you can do for me now is give me a two-year contract."

"No problem," he said.

Frankly, I was astonished when he said that. They just weren't giving two-year contracts to anybody at that time. Russell, Cousy, none of them had two-year contracts. I was the only one.

Then the Phillies traded me to the Red Sox and the Red Sox—always generous with salaries—gave me a five-thousand-dollar increase over what I'd been making with the Phillies. As luck would have it, Dick O'Connell, the Red Sox general manager, was a red-hot Celtics fan and he was delighted that I was playing for them. I guess that's what I'd needed all along—a general manager who was a basketball fan.

The differences between baseball and basketball are tremendous. In baseball there's much more individual responsibility, especially if you're a pitcher. You're alone out there on the mound, really isolated, and nobody can help you throw the ball over the plate. The only comparable moment in basketball is the free throw; that's when you're really on the spot. Otherwise you're always working as part of a unit every moment, hitting the open man, looking for an opening, always playing together. Also, I'd say there's more room for error in basketball, more room for making a mistake and getting away with it.

Conditioning in basketball is harder. It's unbelievable the shape you have to be in. That's because you're always in motion when you're out there; there's no standing still. But at the same time don't underestimate the stamina you need, say, to pitch a nine-inning game in St. Louis in the middle of August when it's over a hundred degrees on the field. That is simply an incredible ordeal. You lose from twelve to fifteen pounds and for the next day or two you feel sick.

So playing both sports I was always in top condition. There was no way I couldn't be. And since those seasons overlapped by three weeks at each end I used to get the feeling I was playing some kind of ball for thirteen months each year.

I roomed with Robin Roberts for a while when I was with the Phillies. He was something like Spahn, in that he'd pitch all day and all night, throwing out of that easy motion. Fast ball across the knees. That was Robby. Speed, control, stamina. Sometimes I got the feeling he had only two signs: fast ball and pitch-out. But what a great pitcher! He was something special out there. You give Robin Roberts a run or two lead in the late innings and there was no way anybody was going to take it away from him. He could reach back when he had to.

I asked him one time, "Robby, when you've got a runner on third and you need some extra on the ball, do you find yourself pushing off that mound a little harder?"

"No, Slim," he said. He called me Slim. "I pitch the same all the time. The first pitch goes in the same way as the last one."

"That can't be true," I said, "because I notice when there's a man on third and less than two out, that ball pops a little better."

"Well," he said, "you can't see what I'm doing, Slim. That comes from within."

That was his way of saying it, and I think what he was saying is the very essence of the great pitcher, or the great athlete in any difficult situation. He didn't *look* like he was doing anything different, but, boy, he was doing it when he had to. Bill Russell was like that. He was the type of guy, in a basketball game, who was always involved in the key moment. If it meant a blocked shot, a shot that might beat you, his timing seemed always to be just a little better. He'd be in the right spot, getting just high enough to get a piece of the ball. Jackie Robinson was like that too. Doing it when it had to be done. You'd look back later and ask yourself: How the devil did he do that? You couldn't answer it. I don't think they knew themselves. They just did it.

Ted Williams had just retired when I joined the Red Sox, so I never had the opportunity to be a teammate of his; but I did pitch against him a couple of times here and there. There was no better swing. I pitched against him in 1952, when the Braves were still in Boston, in a city series. I'll never forget Ted coming to the plate. You talk about a guy putting you back on your heels on the mound. He dug in, and he looked so *big* up there and the bat looked so light in his hands, and he didn't swish it around, he *snapped* it back and forth, and he looked so darned anxious, as if he was saying, "Okay, kid, let's see what you've got." Confidence just oozed out of him. He took something away from you even before you threw a pitch.

You know, he claimed that no one could hit him with a ball. He could pick up a pitched ball that quick and his eyes and reflexes were

Ted Williams shaking hands with Jimmie Foxx after a 1942 home run. ". . . he looked so big up there. . . ."

so good that he never had a problem getting out of the way. Speed never bothered him; you couldn't throw a fastball by him, so you have to believe he was seeing that ball the moment it was released. I've heard a lot of guys say that a pitcher who was particularly fast and a little wild, like Herb Score, for instance, never bothered Ted. If a ball came at his head all he did was step back easily and let it fly past, that he never staggered or fell away, the way most batters do when the ball is at their head. Ted knew right away what it was and where it was going.

I had arm trouble off and on for several years. My last year with the Red Sox was '63. I went to spring training in '64 but could hardly throw the ball. My arm was completely gone. A few days after the season opened, Pinky Higgins, who was the general manager then, called me up and gave me the bad news. It came as no surprise, of course, but still it hit me pretty hard. I'd been in baseball for fourteen years and suddenly with a one-minute phone call it's all over.

My arm was dead, there was no question about it. But I thought that maybe I could fool myself. So I made a phone call to Gabe Paul in Cleveland.

"Gene," he said, "we're fixed for starters, but we could use a guy who can go a few innings in relief. Do you think your arm might come around?"

"I think it just might," I said.

"Would you like to come to Cleveland now and do some throwing?"

Well, at that very moment my arm was hurting so bad I could hardly hold on to the telephone.

"I'd better work out some more before we do that," I said.

"All right, Gene," he said. "I'll tell you what. I'll pay your expenses if you want to go down to Burlington, North Carolina."

There had a club there and he suggested I go down into that warm weather, pitch a few games and see how I felt. I said okay. Still trying to fool myself. So I went to North Carolina, to a bush league, after spending ten years in the big leagues. It was like going from the top shelf to a dusty old drawer at the bottom of the bin. I tell you, sometimes you can't get out until you've been humiliated and embarrassed and gone right down to the very dregs of your pride.

They gave me a uniform that made me look like something out of the 1920's, with the pants reaching only to the knees, like knickers. There were holes in the socks. But it was the best they could do. And I was riding that rickety bus, going to ball parks where the fields were lumpy and the lights were unbelievably bad. But I figured I'd make the best of it.

I took cortisone for the pain in my arm and did some throwing. After a few days the manager asked me if I wanted to try it in a game.

"Do you think I ought to?" I asked. I was dreading the idea of it.

"Why not?" he asked. "Does your arm feel all right?"

"It feels as well as it's going to," I said. The pain was killing me.

So I started a game. We were playing Greensboro, North Carolina. Those kids came up to the plate and started knocking line drives all over the place. I tried flooring a few of them, but they weren't impressed; I didn't have enough on the ball to scare anybody. After four or five innings they had to take me out.

I called Gabe Paul the next day.

"Gabe," I said, "I tried but I can't do it."

"I thought that might be the case," he said. "I guess you just had to get it out of your system."

"Well," I said, "it's out."

When I walked away from that telephone I was really shocked. There was no more fooling myself. It was all over and I knew it. Not only that, but I didn't have a job, nothing to go back to. The basketball was about over, too. So I was pretty depressed.

I wandered around for a while, a lost soul on the streets of this town in North Carolina. Then I walked into a church and sat down in the back, all by myself. There was a service going on. After the singing this Baptist minister started preaching. All of a sudden it hit me real hard and I caved in and started crying. I just sat there in that last row and cried and cried, trying to keep my head down so as not to upset anybody. Then I felt a hand on my shoulder and I looked up. An elderly Southern gentleman was standing there gazing down at me.

"What's the matter, son?" he asked. "Did you lose your mother?"

I shook my head, the tears still running. "No, sir," I said. "I lost my fastball."

TOMMY HOLMES

Thomas Francis Holmes
Born: March 29, 1917, Brooklyn, New York
Major-league career: 1942–52, Boston Braves, Brooklyn
Dodgers
Lifetime average: .302

In 1945 Tommy Holmes set a National League record that has not come close to being topped: He hit safely in 37 consecutive games. In addition to the streak, that year Holmes led the league in home runs, doubles, hits, and slugging average, and had a batting average of .352. In 1947 he led the league in hits for a second time. From 1944 through '48, Holmes' batting average never went below .309. His batting eye must be rated among the best of modern times, for even though he often went to bat over 600 times in a season, Holmes never struck out more than 20 times in any one year.

I grew up in the Borough Park section of Brooklyn, which was a hotbed of baseball. But even though I played a lot of baseball as a kid, I began training early on to be a professional fighter. I loved the ring and really thought I could make a go of it. I could spend hours on the punching bag, and even when I was a kid I won all kinds of prizes for my skill on the bag. But my father, who had been a second for a lot of great fighters, put a stop to all that. "My son will never be a prizefighter," he said. He was pretty definite about it, and so that was that.

I started to draw some attention as a ballplayer when I was going to Brooklyn Tech. I had a few good years there when I hit for averages like .613 and .585. That can't help but to attract the scouts, even if it's only high school. Then I started playing semipro ball on Sunday for five dollars a game.

Living in New York City I wanted to be a New York ballplayer. Being a Brooklyn boy, the Dodgers naturally were my team, but they never did show much interest. It was the Yankees who came around with a contract. In fact it was Paul Krichell, their top scout, who signed me. Even though I was a Dodger fan, I found it flattering to be offered a Yankee contract; they were the glamor team back then.

I went to Norfolk, Virginia, in 1937 and began my professional career. I managed to hit the ball and always had good percentages. I played five years in the Yankee farm system and my averages were .320, .368, .339, .317, and .302. Pretty good hitting, right? But you never saw me in a Yankee uniform, did you? It was murder playing in that organization then.

I'll tell you what my problem was. I was a center fielder and the Yankees already had a guy out there named Joe DiMaggio. And to make matters worse, they had a couple of other guys in the outfield named Tommy Henrich and Charlie Keller. But Mr. Weiss, the Yankee general manager in those days, said to me, "Tommy, if we see we can't use you we'll send you to a club where you'll be able to play." That was the promise he made to me and he kept it, because they finally sold me to the Braves and I had a chance to be a regular.

Casey Stengel was managing the Braves at that time, and even though we weren't a winning team we had some good veteran ballplayers on that club. Paul Waner was one of my teammates on the '42 Braves. We talked hitting a lot, naturally. He used to tell me, "Look, there are three men in the outfield; why should we hit it where they are?" He used to preach shooting for the foul lines. If you missed, he said, it was just a foul ball; if you got it in, it was a double. "And if it goes in the stands," he said, "don't worry. We don't pay for the baseballs." If they tried to cover the lines on him, then they were opening gaps in right- and left-center and he would put the ball out there. This is what he taught me. And while I wasn't a power hitter, I used to get around thirty-five or forty doubles a year, from following Paul's advice.

Paul had his habits, as everyone knows. It's no secret that he drank. One day during the war the ball club traveled to an army camp somewhere in New England to play a game for the soldiers. The whole ball club went. We were riding in army trucks, standing up and holding onto the straps in the back. It was a hot day, a real scorcher. The perspiration was running off of us. One of the guys said to Paul, "Say, Paul, what would you give for a shot right now?" Paul smiled. He had a fountain pen clipped to his breast pocket and he took it out, opened it and darned if he didn't have a shot of whiskey in it. He drank it, screwed the pen together again and clipped it back onto his pocket, and I think that truck must have been shaking, everybody was laughing so hard.

Ernie Lombardi was there too. What a hitter! You know, that poor

Tommy Holmes as Brooklyn Tech's .600-hitting first baseman in 1933.

guy was severely handicapped by being terribly slow afoot. How he ever hit for those .320 and .330 averages I'll never know. Stengel loved him, and loved to kid him. One time we had a big lead in the late innings and Lombardi is on first. Stengel stands up in the dugout and yells, "Steal it, Lom!" Everybody starts to laugh. But on the next pitch, Lombardi starts moving. He was going to prove something. I think everybody in the ball park, fans and players alike, froze. Nobody could believe it. Here's big Ernie Lombardi heading out to steal second. The catcher was so startled he couldn't throw, the second baseman was so startled he was late covering. Lombardi could have taken it standing up, but he went in sliding, in a triumphant cloud of dust. When he stood up he had the biggest grin of satisfaction on his face. He played seventeen years in the big leagues and in all that time stole only about a half dozen bases, and that was one of them.

I remember one time we got on the train to take our first western trip of the year. We had a few rookies on the team and in those days they weren't making much money, maybe six hundred a month. They were pretty excited about making their first western trip. Well, Lombardi—bless him, I'll always remember him for this—went around to all the kids and said, "Hey, kid, got enough money?" And without waiting for an answer he'd push a twenty on them. Just wanted to make sure they had a few extra, to tip porters and waitresses, or buy themselves a beer, and so on. He wanted them to be able to feel like big leaguers. That was the kind of guy Ernie Lombardi was.

You look back and you remember those things, those acts of kindness, the men like Ernie Lombrdi. And you remember, too, the men who taught you and who helped you and you realize that this is what the game is all about—one man passing along his advice and his insights to the next. This is what helps make baseball a tradition, along with the memories and the base hits and all the marvelous things that take place out on that field. Do I sound like a sentimentalist? Well, maybe I am. But I'll always remember the Paul Waners and the Casey Stengels, and all the others who did so much to help me. And I suppose that in a way I'm remembering the men who helped *them,* men I never knew. Today I try to help young players whenever I can, passing along whatever helpful tips and advice I can. And so it goes along, it never stops.

But talk about great ballplayers, what about Pete Reiser? There wasn't a thing he couldn't do on that ball field. When I came up in '42 he had already led the league and was well on his way to doing it again when he suffered that injury, running into the wall in St. Louis. I always admired him, from the first moment I saw him. We were both center fielders, both built about the same. But I'll be frank—that's where the resemblance ended. He could hit a ball twice as far as I could, he could run twice as fast as I could. It's just a sin that he never became the .340 lifetime hitter that he should have been, or the base-stealing champion that he should have been. The feeling about him in 1942 was that he was as great a star as there was in the game.

Nineteen forty-five was a year when everything I tried, everything I did, worked out. I led the league in home runs, hits, doubles, slugging average, and just missed winning the batting crown by a few points. Phil Cavaretta edged me out, .355 to .352. Later on, somebody pointed out something else that I wasn't aware of: I was the only man ever to lead the league in home runs and also have the least strikeouts for a regular; I struck out only nine times that year.

Also in that year I got real lucky and went on a tear throughout the month of June and into early July, hitting in thirty-seven consecutive games. That set a National League record and I'll be darned if it hasn't stood up now for more than thirty years. The previous league record was thirty-three straight games, by Rogers Hornsby.

I had thirty-two straight games when the Pirates came into Boston for a double-header. I needed hits in both of those games to set a new record. Frankie Frisch was managing the Pirates then and he came up to me before the first game and said, "Good luck, Tommy—I'm throwing two left-handers against you." What he was telling me was there was no sentiment in our business. The lefties were two good ones, too—Al Gerhauser and Preacher Roe. Frisch wasn't giving away anything that day.

But I was hot. I didn't waste any time. First time up in each game I doubled, on the first pitch from Gerhauser and on the second pitch from Roe. A photographer snapped a picture just as I was hitting that double off of Roe and setting a new record. Later on I asked everybody on both teams to autograph it for me.

You know, it wasn't until after I'd broken the record that I realized how much tension and pressure I'd been under. A sigh of relief went out of me so huge that I felt like a collapsing balloon. Up until that moment it had never bothered me; but, boy, it had been building.

It finally stopped at thirty-seven, in Chicago. Hank Wyse shut me out. I didn't even come close to a hit. But I guess that hitting streak is the thing I'm proudest of, and do you know why?—because when they talk about hitting streaks they say DiMaggio in the American League and Holmes in the National. Anytime they link you up with Joe DiMaggio, you know you're in with the big leaguers.

In 1948 we won the pennant and went against Cleveland in the World Series. That opening game is one that people still remember. Bob Feller pitched for the Indians and Johnny Sain for us, and they hooked up in a beauty. There was no score going into the bottom of the eighth and Feller was pitching a one-hitter. It looked like we were going to be playing all day and all night before somebody scored.

Then Feller walked Bill Salkeld to open the inning. Phil Masi went in to run and we sacrificed him over to second. Johnny Sain was the next batter and he made out. That left it up to me. There then occurred one of the most controversial plays ever in a World Series, one that you can still get an argument about today.

Johnny Cooney was coaching third base for us and he was yelling to Masi to be careful with his lead; at the same time he wanted Masi off the bag in order to get a good jump if I happened to get a base hit.

Now, Johnny Cooney told me this. He was watching Lou Boudreau, who was playing shortstop and who was trying to keep Masi close. Boudreau was crouched over, his hand on his knee, his fingers spread. He turned around and looked at Walter Judnich in the outfield. Noth-

ing happened. Then Boudreau did the same thing, turned around to
Judnich, but this time his thumb closed against his finger. Cooney
spotted that and yelled to Masi, "Back!" You see, they had put on a
timed pickoff play. From the moment Boudreau brought his thumb in,
a count was on—one, two, three. At the count of three, Boudreau was at
the bag and Feller was wheeling to throw. Masi broke for the bag when
Cooney yelled, Boudreau was breaking with him, and Feller was turning and throwing. Masi hit the dirt and it was a close play, and Bill
Stewart, the umpire, called him safe. Boudreau argued long and loud,
but the decision stood, of course.

Phil Masi was my roommate and I asked him later, "Phil, were you
safe or were you out?"

"Tommy," he said, "he tagged me behind the shoulder, but my hand
was touching the base. I was safe."

Now, someday I'd like to ask Lou Boudreau if that was in fact the
sign, that movement of the thumb, because that's what we believed it
was, and when Cooney saw it he yelled. That made the difference, that
enabled Masi to get back, on a very close play.

So then play resumed. I'm still up, remember. Now, if I had made
out, that whole thing would have been forgotten. But I didn't make
out. Feller threw me a fastball high and outside—one of the few he put
out there on me all day. I hit a low line drive past Kenny Keltner into
left field; two skips and she was out there. Masi scored easily. Biggest
hit of my life. Sain held them in the ninth and we won the game, 1–0.

Whenever I tell people about the 1948 World Series they say, "That
was the one with the pickoff play, wasn't it?"

"That's right," I tell them.

"When Bob Feller lost the heartbreaker."

"That's right," I say. "But never mind that; let's talk about who got
the hit."

Tommy Holmes connecting for the hit that established a new National League record for consecutive-game-hitting streaks. Forbes Field, Pittsburgh, July 6, 1945. Holmes later had players of both teams autograph the picture.

Tommy Holmes
S. P. Frizzette
Dick Culler
Rev Wm Young
Max Butcher
Truett Sewell
Dick Yurcenich
Al Lopez
Jim Russell
Walter Beck
George Barton
X Roseegus
Al Sionfield
Frank Gustine
Lloyd Waner
Frank Colman
Vic Barnhart
Artie Cuccurullo
Bill Sackell
Jake Flowers
Dino Jorgensen
Al Geihearus
Jack Saltzgaver
John Barri
Preacher Roe
Ken Sable
Bob Elliott
Babe Dahlgren
Pete Conquest
Frank Fienk
Bill Brumrey

HERB SCORE

HERBERT JUDE SCORE
Born: June 7, 1933, Rosedale, New York
Major-league career: 1955–62, Cleveland Indians, Chicago
  White Sox
Lifetime record: 55 wins, 46 defeats

Herb Score was one of the most brilliant young pitchers ever to come to the major leagues. In 1955 he set an all-time record in strikeouts for first-year men: 245—it was also a league-leading figure. The following year he struck out 263 to lead the league again, coupling this with a 20–9 won and lost record. Score's future seemed limitless, but his career was aborted by a series of injuries, leaving baseball fans to speculate upon "what might have been."

One night in the spring of 1957—my third year in the big leagues—I was heading back to the hotel. It was just at curfew time. When I walked into the lobby there seemed to be something going on—it was awfully crowded, with lots of people standing around, including newspapermen. Hank Greenberg, the general manager of the Cleveland ball club, was there too. Boy, I said to myself, am I glad I'm getting in under curfew.

When they saw me they all came running over and I got concerned because I thought something had happened.

"Herb," somebody said, "what do you think of it?"

"What are you talking about?" I asked.

"You haven't heard?"

"Heard what?" I asked.

By this time everybody was standing around me. I couldn't for the life of me figure out what was going on. Then somebody said: "The Red Sox have offered a million dollars for you."

"What?" I said. I thought they were kidding me. A million dollars is a lot of money today, but in 1957 it was really a ton.

Herb Score in 1956.

"It's true," somebody said. "A million dollars. Cash."

Greenberg told me later that it was a bona fide offer, that Tom Yawkey was ready to sit down and write out a check for a million dollars. "We told them no," Greenberg said. And that was that.

A few weeks later, though, I'll bet they wished they'd taken it.

I can honestly say the only thing I ever wanted to be was a baseball player. I was just fortunate in being physically able to do it. That physical ability is the whole thing, of course—you either have it or you don't, you either can do it or you can't. An athlete is endowed by the good graces of mother nature; after that it's simply up to him to polish that talent.

I was born in Rosedale, Queens, in New York City, but when I was in high school we moved to Lake Worth, Florida. That's when the scouts started to take notice of me. I pitched a no-hitter in my freshman year and that caught some attention. Then I began averaging pretty close to three strikeouts an inning, and that made them curious.

Cy Slapnicka of the Cleveland Indians wintered in Lake Worth, and one day somebody suggested he come out to see me pitch, and he did. He began showing up at the games, watching me. By my senior year in high school there were a lot of scouts coming out to the games. We got to know who they were and we'd spot them and everybody would start buzzing. No, it didn't make me nervous to know they were out there watching me; nothing ever made me nervous out on the mound; I was never happier or calmer than when I was standing out there. I loved it and I enjoyed it.

The scouts weren't supposed to talk to a kid about signing until he was out of high school. But some of them, especially the older ones, were very ingenious when it came to getting around the rules. In my case, Slapnicka used to take my mother, my sisters and me out to dinner, and never once would he talk to me about signing or do or say anything he wasn't supposed to. But he did talk about the Indians and their organization. Very quietly and effectively he sold me the idea that Cleveland had a good organization with a history of fine pitchers; at that time they had Lemon, Wynn, Garcia, Feller.

Slapnicka had signed Feller, you know, and I'm sure that fact impressed me. He talked a little bit about it, about how he had gone out to Iowa to see this unknown farm boy pitch, and how exciting it had been the first time he saw Bob kick and fire that fastball. There's no getting away from it—when you're talking with the man who signed Bob Feller, and he's interested in signing you, you pay attention.

So after high school, when it came to deciding with which club to sign, I chose Cleveland. I wanted to go with them. They gave me a bonus of $60,000, while I had three other offers that started at $80,000, and one club in particular that told me to come to them last and they would top any offer I had received. But I didn't want to do that; I didn't want to make it seem like an auction; and anyway I had pretty much made up my mind to go with Cleveland, and I don't think I made a mistake.

I would say that the two men who had the greatest influence on my playing career were Mel Harder and Ted Wilks. Mel taught me how to throw the curve, and Wilks was the pitching coach at Indianapolis, where I played in 1954. He really turned me around and got me to the major leagues. I was wild, just as wild as a pitcher could be. There was no question I could throw hard, but that wasn't doing me much good if I wasn't getting it over.

In the spring of '54 I was pitching an exhibition game for Indianapolis and threw 44 pitches and only four of them were for strikes. Hank Greenberg was at the game and later on he pulled me aside.

"Look," he said, "there's no reason for you to be this wild. I know you're willing to work hard, and with the stuff you have, if you can't get it over the plate it's just going to be a waste."

Then he told me that Ted Wilks, who used to be with the Cardinals, was coming to the club to work with the pitchers. Hank gave me strict orders to listen to Wilks.

Ted was a garrulous type of guy. He also was very tough-minded and stubborn. The first thing he said to me when we got together was, "Now, don't tell me you can't. Whatever I tell you to try, I want you to try. I don't want to hear you say 'I can't.'"

"Okay," I said.

"The first thing I want you to do is cut down on your leg kick."

"I can't," I said.

We looked at each other and laughed.

Ted worked with me every day, even when I was in a game. I'd be out there pitching and I'd hear him in the dugout calling me every conceivable name, cursing me out when I wasn't doing what I was supposed to. I'd hear that voice: "You dumb so-and-so. Bend your back. Keep your head still." He never let up. He never stopped drilling those lessons into me. I'll always be grateful to him. Thanks to Ted Wilks I had a good year, winning 22 games and chalking up 330 strikeouts.

I came up to the big leagues in 1955. In spite of the great year I'd had at Indianapolis it still wasn't easy breaking into that pitching staff. They had Bob Lemon, Early Wynn, Mike Garcia, Art Houtteman, and the best one-two punch I've ever seen coming out of the bull pen, Don Mossi and Ray Narleski. Feller was still there, it was his next-to-last year. Meeting him and becoming his teammate was a great honor.

When I came up Feller had lost that tremendous speed, but he still had the great curveball. His curve was really remarkable. He had terrific spin on it—that's what makes the curveball. You could almost hear the seams biting into the wind.

Of course people would start trying to make comparisons between my fastball and Bob's. They would ask him about it, and what could he say? What can anyone say? As far as I'm concerned, you take the real hard throwers, like Feller, Koufax, Nolan Ryan—there's not that much difference between them. But you take guys like Feller and Koufax, they also had outstanding curveballs. Thanks to Mel Harder, I had the good breaking ball, too. You strike out as many batters with your curve as with the fastball because when you can throw that hard the batter has to be geared up to get around on it, and so you can catch them off stride with the breaking ball.

I had a big follow-through; I really drove off of the mound when I delivered the ball. In fact, I used to wear a basketball players' kneepad on my right knee because when I'd follow through, very often I would hit my left elbow against my right knee. That's how hard I was throwing; I used to put so much behind each pitch that my body was swung way out of position after I delivered the ball. I used to throw balls that I never saw reach the plate, and when they were hit I had to look around to see where they were going. Very often I simply didn't see the ball after I'd let it go.

I suppose that's what happened when I was pitching to Gil McDougald that night in Cleveland. I had retired Hank Bauer and Gil was the second batter of the game. He hit through the box a lot, but I never worried about a ball being hit back at me; I just never allowed myself to.

So I fired it in there, heard the crack of the bat, looked up and I can remember seeing the ball coming right into my eye. Boy, it had got big awfully fast and it was getting bigger. There was really nothing I could do about it. It hit me flush in the eye and as soon as it hit I remember saying to myself, *"Saint Jude, stay with me."* I went down and I knew enough not to move; I just lay there. I never lost consciousness. I could hear everybody around me. I knew I was bleeding because I could taste the blood. I remember putting my finger in my ear to see if I was bleeding out of the ear, since I knew that if you had a concussion or a fractured skull you'd be getting blood out of your ear. My nose and my mouth were filled with blood and I remember somebody sticking a towel in and I said, "Hey, get that towel out, you're going to choke me." I was conscious the whole time, and lucid, and calm; I think I was the calmest one out there.

They carried me to the clubhouse and put some ice wrapped in a towel over my eye. The team doctor came in, took the towel away and

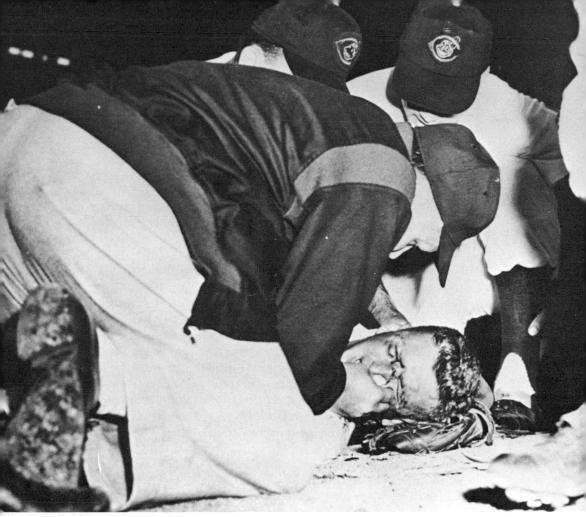

Moments after being hit by McDougald's line drive.

looked in the eye with a light. While he was doing that I closed my other eye and couldn't see the light.

"Do I still have an eye?" I asked.

He didn't say anything. The clubhouse was very quiet. The grand-stands were pretty quiet too, even though there were a lot of people in the ball park. Play had been suspended while another pitcher warmed up to take my place.

"I can't see that light, Doc," I said. He had it right in my eye.

"Look," he said, "you've got so much bleeding and swelling in there I'm not surprised."

Then he covered up the eye with a bandage and I went to the hospital. When I got there they still couldn't tell me if I'd lose the eye or not;

there was too much hemorrhaging in it for them to be able to determine the extent of the damage. They told me it would take a few days.

Fortunately, I didn't lose the eye, but I had to lie absolutely still for eight days, with both eyes covered. It was while lying in the hospital those days, in the darkness, that I had a chance to reflect a little about myself, about life, about all the things that were important to me. In many ways it was a maturing experience. You learn something about values, yours and other people's. That eye injury was not the worst thing that ever happened in my life.

You know, people think what happened to me that night cost me my career. But they're wrong. That had absolutely nothing to do with me losing my effectiveness. The following spring I was pitching as well as I ever did. Then I was pitching in Washington. In the third or fourth inning my arm started to bother me. I didn't say anything. I figured it would work out. These are the mistakes you make when you're young.

Then in the seventh inning I threw a pitch to somebody and it actually didn't reach home plate. I called out Bobby Bragan, the manager, and told him I thought I'd hurt my arm, and he took me out. The next day the thing had swelled up so much I couldn't get it through the sleeve of my coat. It turned out I had torn the tendon in my elbow. I was advised to rest for thirty days. They thought that would help, but it didn't.

I pitched the rest of the year with a bad arm. I'd missed a whole year in '57 bcause of the eye injury and didn't want to miss any more time. So I kept throwing with a sore arm. I used to tell myself not to change my delivery to compensate for the soreness. But you do change your delivery; what once was natural becomes unnatural. After the soreness went away and I could throw without pain again, I never had quite the same motion.

I could still throw the good curve, but I couldn't throw the fastball like I used to anymore. It was gone, and with it a lot of the fun of the game went for me.

The last couple of years I pitched I was terrible. I just couldn't put it all together anymore. I went back to the minor leagues for a while and tried it there. The reason I did that was to prove to myself, once and for all, what I could do or what I couldn't do. I didn't want to go into middle age later on saying that I could have pitched some more if I'd tried. I tried. I probably worked harder in those last years than I ever did, until I had finally proved to my own satisfaction that I couldn't pitch anymore. Some people asked me why I went back to the minor leagues; they felt I was humiliating myself. But I never felt humiliated. There was no disgrace in what I was doing. The disgrace would have been in not trying.

BILLY GOODMAN

WILLIAM DALE GOODMAN
Born: March 22, 1926, Concord, North Carolina
Major-league career: 1947–62, Boston Red Sox, Baltimore
  Orioles, Chicago White Sox, Houston Astros
Lifetime average: .300

Billy Goodman must rank as baseball's greatest utility man. In his career he played 624 games at second base, 406 at first base, 330 at third base, and 111 in the outfield. But wherever he played, he hit. Five times he hit over .300 and six times over .290. In 1950 he led the American League in batting with a .354 mark—while getting into games at a half dozen different positions.

I n 1950 I led the American League in batting with a .354 average and when I came to spring training the next year I was considered a utility man. No, I didn't complain about it. That never bothered me. I knew I'd be playing someplace, be it first base, second base, or the outfield. I had a contract and that's all that mattered.

You see, you have to remember what kind of ball club the Red Sox had in those years—an all-star at just about every position. If I had been strictly an infielder or strictly an outfielder I may never have got a decent opportunity to show what I could do. But by being willing, able, and eager to place anyplace they asked me to I was able to get that opportunity, and I made the most of it.

I remember one time Mr. Yawkey called me into the office and asked me if I had a preference where I wanted to play. I told him, "Wherever they need me." That's about how I felt.

Going way back to when I was a kid, when we had these little old pickup teams back home, playing on Saturdays in the cow pasture, you didn't have a regular position. Sometimes you'd play infield, sometimes you'd play outfield. You shifted from one place to another. Hell, I figured if you can do it, do it. In baseball you're supposed to use to

BASEBALL BETWEEN THE LINES

the utmost what abilities you have. A fast man steals bases, a power hitter goes for the long ball. And if you have the ability to be versatile on a
ball field, then you use it. Am I right or wrong?

I was born on a dairy farm, in Concord, North Carolina. I milked the
cows, chopped cotton, plowed cotton, did just about a little of everything. That old versatility again, huh? I don't know if I would have
stayed a farmer if it hadn't been for baseball. I just never thought about
doing anything else except playing baseball. It was an ambition of
mine right from the beginning.

A scout from the Atlanta Crackers saw me playing semipro ball in
Concord and signed me to an Atlanta contract. It was an independently
owned ball club then. I played in Atlanta in 1944, went into the service
for a year, then played there again in 1946. Earl Mann, who owned the
team, told me if I had a good year he would sell me to a big-league club
and give me a little of the money. Well, I had the good year—hit .389—
and he sold me to the Red Sox, and sure enough I got a check in the
mail from him. Earl Mann is the only man I ever played for who kept
every verbal agreement he ever made with me. That's not much of a
commentary on human nature, is it?

I went to spring training with the Red Sox in '47 and there he was,
Ted Williams. Best hitter I ever saw, period. No, I didn't talk to him
then. I was a rookie and wasn't supposed to say anything.

I stayed with the Red Sox until June and then finished up the season
at Louisville. I'd played first base and the outfield in Atlanta, then
shortstop and outfield at Louisville. In 1948 Joe McCarthy made me
the regular first baseman. I played under a lot of good managers, but
McCarthy was tops. He was first class. He treated me great. A great
handler of men.

That was my first full season in the majors, 1948, and I stepped into a
terrific pennant race. We tied with Cleveland at the end of the regular
season and played them in the first pennant play-off ever in the American League. It was a one-game play-off, in Fenway Park.

McCarthy started Denny Galehouse in that game for us. A lot of people were surprised by the choice, myself included, I guess. Denny was
a good pitcher, but he wasn't our ace that year. But I don't think we had
a hell of a lot of options; we were up against it for pitching that day.
Remember, we'd just come charging down the line to get into a tie and
we had a lot of tired arms. Mel Parnell, Jack Kramer, and Joe Dobson
were our aces and they were about worn out. So I think that no matter
who McCarthy started in that game he would have drawn criticism.
What he did was his decision and it was good enough for me, then and
now.

Gene Bearden started for the Indians. He had a great year for them.

Billy Goodman in 1950.

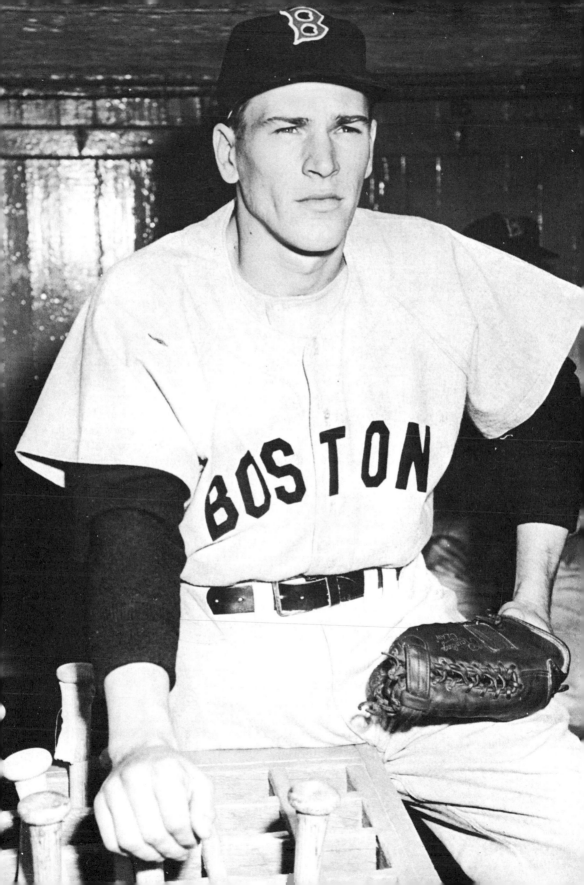

He won twenty games, which he had never done before and which he never did again. He was a left-hander and his best pitch was a knuckleball. The next year the hitters started laying off the knuckler, which wasn't always a strike, and he had to start coming in with other pitches, which didn't work too well for him and he never had much success again. But in 1948 he was great. He beat us in that play-off game, 8–3. Lou Boudreau hit two home runs for them.

We might have done better that year, but it was just about then that Tex Hughson's arm went bad and Dave Ferriss' arm went bad. You lose two pitchers like that at the same time and you're going to hurt. Hughson was some pitcher when he was right. He had a good fastball, and he could throw just about any pitch you can name. We thought we were fixed for pitching for at least five years, but then those two hurt their arms.

The next year wasn't much different. It came down to the last game of the season at Yankee Stadium. We'd come in there with two games to play and needing just one to clinch it. We lost the Saturday game and that put us in a tie with the Yankees. We started Ellis Kinder in that last game and they went with Vic Raschi.

I remember something Ellis Kinder said on the bus after the Saturday game: "You get me three runs tomorrow and you've got yourselves a pennant." Well, if we would have done that for him we would have won. We went into the top of the eighth inning losing, 1–0, and had to take Ellis out for a pinch hitter. Then in the bottom of the eighth the Yankees scored four more. In the top of the ninth we scored three off of Raschi. Those were the three Ellis had asked for, and if we would have done that while he was still in there we would have taken it, because he was pitching great ball. But it wasn't enough and we lost, 5–3.

So that was two of them we'd lost on the last day of the season. I was beginning to wonder if there was such a thing as a pennant. It's really frustrating to come so close and go away empty. Look at it this way: in 1948 we tied, in 1949 we lost by a game, and in 1950 we lost by four games. That's missing three pennants by a total of five games. We just didn't have that little extra in pitching. Cleveland had Lemon, Wynn, Garcia, Feller. The Yankees had Raschi, Reynolds, Lopat, and then Ford. We never seemed to have that extra depth, particularly that big man coming out of the bull pen to put the cork in the game.

I had my biggest year in 1950. Everything broke right for me. It happens like that once in a while. I woke up in the morning feeling great, went out, got my base hits, and kept it going for a whole season. Ended up hitting .354 and leading the league. The funny thing about it was that we had such a powerful club in 1950 that I still had a problem breaking into the lineup.

I opened the season at first base but then chipped my ankle and was out for three weeks. So they brought up Walt Dropo and he got hot and stayed hot all year. When I was ready to play again there was no place to put me, even though I was able to play almost any position on the field. We had Dropo, Bobby Doerr, Vern Stephens, Johnny Pesky, Williams, Dom DiMaggio, Al Zarilla. And every one of them was hitting hard. Doerr was low man among the regulars that year, and he hit .294. The club average was over .300. I think it's going to be a while before you see that again.

Then Williams broke his elbow in the All-Star game and I went into left field. When Ted came back I started filling in wherever they needed me. I played outfield, third base, second base, first base. But I still can't break in regularly anywhere—and all the while I'm leading the league! But it really didn't bother me. I didn't think that much about it. I just tried to do whatever they wanted me to. When you're on a great ball club you tend not to think about yourself that much; there are too many interesting things going on, like every time Ted Williams comes to bat, for instance.

We lost Williams for nearly half a season in 1950 but still made a run for the pennant. We missed out by just a few games. But that's a hard man to replace. Ted was some kind of man to have in that lineup, especially in a close game. You were always in it as long as you knew Ted was coming up. He could rock it all of a sudden and everybody knew that. It had to be on the mind of the opposing pitcher; he just had to be giving some thought to Ted's coming up. It's hard to measure that kind of advantage, of course, but it has to be a factor.

With Ted in there we often had to play a different game; the guys batting ahead of him did, anyway. We never did steal much, because with him hitting behind you you didn't want to take a chance on getting thrown out, and neither was it always a good idea to open up a base because they were apt to put him on. Also, you had to have your wits about you when it came to taking an extra base; you never tried it unless you could put it in your hip pocket, because again you were leaving an open base and didn't want to tempt them into walking him. I'll tell you another thing you had to think about when you were on first and he was up: You had to keep your eye on him, because he could scald that ball, and not just in the air either. I've never seen anybody hit a ball on the ground the way Ted did. It seemed to pick up speed every time it bounced, like there was a little rocket in it trying to take off.

When you're talking about Williams' hitting there's another thing you've got to remember—he was doing it in what was probably the most difficult park in the big leagues for a left-handed batter. The stands break away sharply from that foul line in right field and the power alley is a long way back. And when that wind was blowing in it was really rough. When he got hold of the ball it usually didn't make much difference; he could ride it out. But you had to be as strong as Ted was to do it consistently.

I'd have to say that Herb Score was the hardest-throwing left-hander I ever batted against. It was a damned shame what happened to him, getting hit in the eye the way he did. He seemed to lose something after that. He and I were teammates for a while, on the White Sox. I remember one time, he was pitching and I was playing third. A guy swung at the ball and rolled one up on the grass off to the side of the mound. Score never moved. I had to come way in and field it, and of course by that time the man was on first base.

I said, "Herb, you've got to field that ball. You've got to come off that mound for those."

He said, "I didn't see it."

Well, I knew then that there was something the matter. Either he was throwing the ball so hard that he couldn't pick it up after it was hit, or he was having a problem seeing. Whenever he was pitching I was scared to death somebody would hit another one back at him. If he wasn't seeing those little rollers, then you knew he wouldn't see one that was shot back at him.

Bob Feller was another guy who could throw that ball. I don't have to tell you that. I'll never forget the first time I saw him pitch. That was in '47, first year I was up. Cronin sent me in to pinch-hit. "Make him throw you a strike," he said. I did better. I made him throw three of them, all in a row. I went back and sat down and said to myself, "Man, you're in the wrong league." I'd never seen anything like that. Then after the game I hear some of the guys saying in the clubhouse, "He's lost it. Doesn't have it anymore." I thought, *Lost it?* If he's lost it then he sure as hell doesn't miss it. If he had more stuff before the war, as some of them told me he did, then I'd hate to have seen him. As Satchel Paige used to say, "If anybody threw that ball any harder than Rapid Robert, then the human eye couldn't follow it."

But I'll tell you something—Feller wasn't the toughest pitcher I ever batted against. At least when he threw that fast ball you knew it was coming, you had some idea where it was going to be, and now and then you'd get your bat on it and it would go. You'd get your shots off of him. But if I had to pick myself one guy that I wouldn't want to hit against when he was right, it would be Hoyt Wilhelm. It was a battle just to get the bat on that knuckleball. You know good and well, how in the hell is a man going to hit a ball that the catcher can't even catch? I've heard guys pumping somebody up about how Wilhelm knew

Bobby Doerr.

which way the ball was going to break. Well, I thought if that was so, then Wilhelm would have got together with his catcher now and then and let him in on the secret, especially with a man on third base.

In June '57 I was traded to Baltimore and after that season I was traded again, to the White Sox. Then all of a sudden, after so many years, I got lucky. Found myself on a pennant winner. The 1959 White Sox. We had a good bunch of boys there. They played together, as a unit, better than any club I ever played on. We were a fine defensive team and we had phenomenal pitching. Four good starters—Early Wynn, Bob Shaw, Billy Pierce, and Dick Donovan. And then there were those two guys coming out of the bull pen all year, Turk Lown and Gerry Staley. They were exceptional.

They called us the Go-Go Sox. Remember that? We had a lot of Punch-and-Judy hitters. Now and then somebody would hit one hard, but not too often. But we did everything that the book says you're supposed to do, bunt them over, hit and run, make the good plays in the field. We hit fewer home runs than any other team in the league and had one of the lowest batting averages. But we had the great pitching, the good defense, and speed—we were way ahead of everybody else in stolen bases. A completely different team from those great Red Sox teams. And we won ourselves a pennant.

We won it because we were able to dominate our chief contenders—Cleveland. We worked the Indians over real good. We played them a four-game series in Cleveland at the end of August and swept them four straight. I think that broke their backs. But you talk about a team doctoring an infield. They knew we were a running team—we had Luis Aparicio, Nellie Fox, Jim Landis, and a few other guys who carried that mail around the bases for you. Well, the Indians had that infield plowed up with loose sand lying around, I swear it was a few inches thick, to stop us from running. Didn't do them any good. After we took Cleveland those four straight nobody could stop us. The feeling on the team was, *We's in business.*

Along with Aparicio, Fox, and Landis, we had Bubba Phillips, Earl Torgeson, Jim Rivera, Al Smith, Jim McAnany, Sherman Lollar. That Lollar was a great guy. You know, you've generally got one guy on a club that fixes gloves. He'll restitch them or lace them if somebody asks him to. Sherm Lollar was the guy who did it on our club. One time Clint Courtney, the catcher, came into Chicago. He wanted some work done on his mitt. Lollar took it and worked on it. Then, just for the hell of it, when he was finished Sherm took a big block of limburger cheese, cut off some pieces and stuffed them up into the glove. When he went into the dugout to hand Courtney the glove, he had the rest of the cheese concealed in his hand.

"Here you are," Sherm said. "Go get 'em now."

While Courtney was examining the job Lollar had done, Sherm gave him several friendly pats on the back, smearing that cheese all over Courtney's shirt.

Then the game started and Courtney went behind the plate. It was a hot day and that stink started rising off of his shirt. You couldn't get within ten feet of the plate without smelling it. If I'm not mistaken, the umpire finally made him go in and change it.

Ted Kluszewski joined us late in the year and without him we would have been hurting. They tried to stop him with left-handed pitching, but he damn near killed some of them. Ted was right on top of the plate and they tried to burn him inside, but, boy, did he hang some out. He

hit some line drives through the box that I'll bet are still giving some
pitchers nightmares. Of course Ted is big and strong; he's got to be one
of the strongest men I ever met, and also one of the nicest.

When he joined the team they assigned him to room with me. "Bill,"
he said, "sometimes I do some heavy snoring. If it bothers you, just
give me a kick."

Sure enough, that first night he starts snoring, real loud. I can't sleep.
I'm lying there looking over at him, at this big, big guy. He had told me
to kick him. And I'm thinking: *Kick Ted Kluszewski?* Suppose it just
happens that tonight he doesn't feel like being kicked? I thought it
over for a long time, and then wrapped that pillow around my ears and
went to sleep.

Getting into the Series finally after so many years was a real thrill.
Boy, you don't know what that's like until you're in it. The phone was
jumping off the hook with everybody calling for tickets. I never knew
how many third and fourth cousins I had. "Hey, Billy old buddy, don't
you remember me?"

We bombed the Dodgers 11–0 in the first game. Then they beat us
some tight ball games. Drysdale beat us one game, but the guy who really stopped us was their relief pitcher, Larry Sherry. He won two in
relief and snuffed us out in two others.

The Dodgers were using the Coliseum out there as a home park,and
that was the worst place I ever played in, as far as seeing the ball was
concerned. In fact I got hit with a ball I didn't even see. Sherry hit me
in the knee with one, I never saw it.

They beat us in six games, but we never disgraced ourselves. We
weren't the greatest team in baseball history, but we played ball together like we thought we were. And I'll never forget those pitchers. What a
staff! I'll tell you, if we would have had those guys in Boston during
those big years we would have had some fun. We could have closed
shop in August and gone fishing.

ROBIN ROBERTS

ROBIN EVAN ROBERTS
Born: September 30, 1926, Springfield, Illinois
Major-league career: 1948–66, Philadelphia Phillies, Bal-
timore Orioles, Houston Astros, Chicago Cubs
Lifetime record: 286 wins, 245 losses

Robin Roberts was one of the greatest pitchers in National League history. A power pitcher with remarkable control, he hit his peak in 1952, winning 28 and losing 7. From 1950 through '55 Roberts was a 20-game winner; he led the league five consecutive years in complete games, five consecutive times in innings pitched, twice in strikeouts, twice in shutouts, four times in victories.

There are 31 post-1900 pitchers in the Hall of Fame. Roberts was voted into the Hall of Fame in January, 1976.

W hen I was in grade school in Springfield, Illinois, I went to a little two-room school called East Pleasant Hill. There were two teachers; one taught the first four grades in one room and one taught the next four grades in the other room.

In my eighth-grade year, when we were graduating, we had a sports night. At that time Grover Cleveland Alexander was living in a hotel in Springfield. I guess he was sort of down and out at the time. One of the teachers asked him to come to the sports night and talk to us, and Alex said he would. We had our dinner and afterward Alexander got up to speak. We knew who he was, of course, that he had pitched for the Phillies and the Cardinals and was one of the greatest that ever lived. So when he stood up to say a few words you could have heard a pin drop. This is what he said: "Boys, I hope you enjoy sports. But I will warn you about one thing: Don't take to drink, because look what it's done to me." And he sat down. That's all he said. That's all the man said.

That was a long, long time ago. I've never forgotten the sight of that man, that great pitcher, standing up and baring his soul in front of a bunch of awestruck kids. If anybody had told me that night that I was going to grow up and become a pitcher for the Philadelphia Phillies and break a lot of the club records that Grover Cleveland Alexander had set, well, you can imagine what I would have told them.

I grew up just outside of Springfield, in farming country, though not on a farm. But we did have two acres and wherever we had dirt we grew something edible. I was one of six children—four boys and two girls. My dad was a coal miner. He came over from Wales after the First World War and settled in Springfield.

I guess you might describe us as poor, but we never thought about it; we were a close family and we had a good time together. We used to take Dad's Bull Durham tobacco sack and fill it full of grass and hit it with a cricket stick that he had for some reason brought over with him from Wales. That was the first bat we used. That's really how I started playing baseball.

I always thought about playing sports, but never particularly about a career in professional baseball. In those days we didn't have television; we listened to the games over the radio and basball seemed out of reach for most kids at that time. It was all a dream. We just couldn't imagine ourselves as major-league ballplayers, whereas today you can see it on television and it has greater reality to kids. I think, too, that in a curious way it was a little easier to be a ballplayer in those days because it *was* all a dream, and so you stayed natural and enjoyed yourself. Today kids of twelve and thirteen start trying to make it and I think they run the danger of becoming too self-conscious and lose some of their naturalness.

When I was nineteen I went to Michigan State on a basketball scholarship. After my freshman year I went into service, then I came back and played basketball at Michigan State in my sophomore year. I had always played a lot of football and a lot of baseball, too. When I went out for baseball at Michigan State they were surprised that I could play, because I was there on a basketball scholarship. I had played third base and the outfield in high school and on the sandlots. I pitched only when they needed somebody; I could always throw the ball hard, but I had never given much thought to pitching.

So when I came out for the baseball tryout the coach was a little surprised and said to me, "What are you doing here?"

"I think I can play baseball," I said.

"What do you play?" he asked.

"What do you need?"

"Pitchers."

"That's what I am," I said. "A pitcher."

I figured it made sense to go out for what he needed. So from age nineteen on I concentrated on pitching. As I said, I could throw hard, and I could throw strikes; even as a kid I could always throw strikes, and I seemed always to have that smooth delivery.

So I started pitching for Michigan State. Then I played college-league ball in Vermont for two summers, for Montpelier. The scouts started coming around in Vermont that second summer, in 1947. I received six invitations to come and work out in September. Let's see, there was the Phillies, of course, and the Yankees, Red Sox, Tigers, Athletics, and Braves. I had a schedule mapped out to meet these clubs in different towns. The Phillies happened to be first, and I worked out with them in Chicago.

After the workout they said they would give me $10,000 to sign. Now, I had no great understanding of bonuses then, although Curt Simmons had received a big one that May from the Phillies. I just didn't figure myself for a big bonus. I was so anxious to get into baseball that I didn't worry about that. I would have been happy to sign for two thousand.

I told the Phillies, however, that I felt a loyalty to my promise to work out with the other clubs, who had made arrangements for me. The next day the Phillies said they'd pay me $15,000. Well, I was still loyal, but loosening up now. The third day they pushed it up to twenty-five thousand.

Now, that was a lot of money, particularly back in 1947. So I had something to think about. You know, when I was a kid my parents were often on me for playing baseball and not helping my brothers work. I'd read where Lou Gehrig had bought his mother a house out of his baseball earnings, and I'd always thought what a nice thing that was and wished I could do the same for my mother someday. So when Babe Alexander, the Phillies' traveling secretary, told me they would give me twenty-five thousand, I said, "That would buy a nice house, wouldn't it?"

"It sure would," he said.

"Okay then," I said. "Let's go."

So I never did work out with the other clubs, and you can't help but to wonder how high it would have gone if I had—the big-league clubs were throwing around some mighty fancy bonuses in those years. But I signed with the Phillies and have never regretted it.

The first thing I did was buy my mom that house. I think it cost around $19,000. Then I bought myself a car and a couple of new suits. It was great. I was on top of the world. The problem was, I didn't know anything about money, specifically about taxes. I ended up having to borrow from my father to pay my income taxes. It took most of what he'd saved all his life. Everybody thought I was so rich, but I wound up owing money. I paid my father back with my Series check in 1950. It took me two years to get even.

I started the 1948 season with Wilmington. I pitched there for two months, compiled a 9 and 1 record and was called up. The date was, I think, June 17, and I pitched against the Pirates the day I came up. I pitched against Elmer Riddle and he threw a low-hit shutout against me and I lost, 2–0. This was a little more than two years after the coach at Michigan State asked me what position I played.

Naturally I was thrilled about coming up. Surprisingly enough, and I can't explain this, I felt I belonged, right from the beginning. I felt I could pitch in the major leagues. I think it was knowing I could throw knee high and that I could throw hard. I'll tell you though, I might have had second thoughts after facing my first batter. He was Stan Rojek. I was very nervous and threw four of the wildest pitches you've ever seen. The next batter was Frankie Gustine. I went to a full count on him, and then struck him out on a bad pitch. From that moment on I was never nervous in the major leagues again.

I don't think anyone was ever able to concentrate in a baseball game any better than I was. I stood out there in total isolation, just throwing that ball as well as I could. Nothing bothered me. I can remember those good ball games in the early fifties when we played the Dodgers in Philadelphia. Generally it was Newcombe and me, and there would be around 35,000 people in the stands. After the game I would be driving home with my wife and I'd say, "Was there a big crowd tonight?" "It was jammed," she'd say. Not once, not warming up, not pitching, had I ever looked at the crowd. Nor did I ever hear them. That's how intensely I concentrated.

In fact, I would concentrate to the point where I would not even see the batter; I would only see the bat as he swung. When I was pitching well I saw only the catcher. I was telling some young pitchers that once, in spring training. They thought I was kidding; couldn't convince them. Well, that fall in the World Series Spahn pitched a two-hitter against the Yankees, and in the write-up the next day Spahn told the reporters, "I knew I was going to be good because I didn't see anything but the bat early in the game." I cut that baby out and next spring showed it to those kids and said, "Look, Spahn and I say the same thing."

I guess it's hard for anyone to imagine that kind of concentration. But I'm sure there were other pitchers who worked the same way. Did you ever watch Vic Raschi pitch? I'm sure he concentrated like that. Most guys that are fastball pitchers must concentrate that way, because if you don't follow-through all the way it takes just a little bit off your fast ball. You've got to finish throwing the ball, you've got to throw it by them; you can't stop at the batter, you've got to go on to the catcher. I was always pitching the full way to the catcher; as far as I was concerned that was where the ball was going—to the catcher, not the batter.

Robin Roberts in 1948.

Whenever I threw a home-run ball, and Lord knows I threw plenty of them, I usually knew as soon as I saw that full swing what I had done wrong. Of course, when they hit them to opposite fields or over my head to center field I never felt bad. I'd tell myself, "Well, he hit a good pitch." But whenever they would pull them, I'd know I'd made a mistake. That's why I was never upset by a home run, because I knew immediately what had happened and was able to correct it; because as soon as I saw a guy getting his full body into a swing I knew I hadn't finished throwing the ball the way I should have. It was never a mystery to me what had happened.

I was never impressive as a pitcher. I just got them out. I wouldn't strike out more than three or four in a game, but two of them would be with a man on third and one out. Listen, that's when you'd *better* strike them out. I could always throw the ball just a little harder when I had to.

Was I ever sorry I hadn't signed with the Yankees? No. I think one of the most unfair things is people belittling the ball club with which I compiled my record. From 1948 until 1956 the Phillies were a real solid baseball team. A lot of people say I won 286 games pitching primarily with an inferior Philly club, and that's not only unfair, it's untrue. You don't win that many games without getting a lot of help, I don't care how good you are. I won 28 one year; you don't do that with a bad ball club. We had fellows like Granny Hamner, Willie Jones, Richie Ashburn, Del Ennis, Andy Seminick, Eddie Waitkus. They could play ball.

Being with the Yankees wouldn't necessarily have meant that many more wins, because how many can you win? Beginning with my second full year my win totals were 20, 21, 28, 23, 23, 23, 19. Remember, I led the National League six years running in games started; if I'd been with the Yankees I might not have gotten the opportunity to pitch that often. I was so happy to be with who I was with that I never had any regrets. Of course from '56 on we were not a good ball club, and to be frank, I was part of that decline, I was not as good a pitcher as I had been. So those years are not good memories. But as far as those early years with the Phillies are concerned, I wouldn't want to trade them for anything.

When I joined the team Schoolboy Rowe was still there. He was about through then, but still a beautifully coordinated athlete. Big, graceful guy. We were on the staff together for only about a year or so and then they released him. I was working out in the outfield before a night game, and I look up and here he comes, carrying his bag. He was leaving.

"Robin," he says, "I've been released. I'm leaving. But before I go I just want to tell you that you're going to be some pitcher; though there's something you want to look out for—you give your curveball away. I thought I would tell you that before I leave."

I thanked him, wished him well, and watched him walk away. But wasn't that curious? As long as I was on the staff with him, in a sense competing with him, he wouldn't tell me I was tipping my curve. But when he knew he was leaving, he told me. I guess baseball was that way in his day—he came up in the early thirties, remember. When you were on a pitching staff you were rooting for your team of course, but at the same time you were competing with other pitchers to stay there. That was a good illustration, I think, of the old-time attitudes.

The Eddie Waitkus incident? Sure I remember it. It happened in July of '49. I'd been with the ball club a little over a year at the time. I didn't know anything about it until the following morning. I was having breakfast in the hotel dining room and somebody came up to me and asked how Waitkus was.

"I guess he's all right," I said. "Why?"

"He was shot last night," the guy said.

That was the first I heard about it. I'll tell you exactly what I was told and what I believe. Eddie roomed with Bill Nicholson. Eddie was a bachelor. He was out on a date that night—this was in Chicago—and he came in at about a quarter to twelve. While he was out a girl had called the room. She asked for him and Nicholson told her he wasn't there. She left a message, asking Nicholson to tell Waitkus that so-and-so from his hometown was there in the hotel and wanted to say hello. She even gave a street address that was near Eddie's home.

When Eddie came in Nicholson gave him the message. The room number was included. So he went up to her room. This is the way Waitkus told me what happened: He knocked on the door and the girl said "Come in." When he walked in there was nobody in the room. He looked around, and all of a sudden the girl jumped out of a closet with a rifle and shot him. Just like that. She just missed his heart.

You could make a different story out of it, but how does a guy get shot with a rifle if there's anything going on? It had to happen the way Eddie said it did. It turned out that the girl wasn't from his hometown at all. They say she used to hang around the ball park in Chicago all the time.

Waitkus was injured very seriously; I believe he was on the critical list for a while. But he recovered and came back to play the next year and helped us win the pennant.

We finished sixth in 1948, then third in '49. So while a lot of people may have been surprised when we won the pennant in 1950, that didn't include us. We were an improved club. We were a relaxed, cocky bunch of guys; we knew we could play ball. Bob Miller joined us, Curt Simmons became an outstanding pitcher that year, Bubba Church had a good year. Mike Goliat came in and became the second baseman we'd been needing. And of course Jim Konstanty had a big year coming out of the bull pen. We just put it together in 1950. But more than anything else, and I don't think we appreciated it until later, was the leadership given by Eddie Sawyer, our manager, and a wonderful person.

They called us the "Whiz Kids." But that was a little misleading. Although a lot of us were young, we had our share of experienced players, like Seminick, Waitkus, Ken Heintzelman, Konstanty, Dick Sisler.

Coming down to the end of the season it looked easy for us. We had a seven-game lead with nine days to go. But before we knew what was happening we were in Ebbets Field on the last day of the season, having to win that game to avoid a play-off with the Dodgers. People talk about a collapse, except they don't know what they're talking about. We got hurt badly in September. Church got hit in the eye with a line drive off the bat of Ted Kluszewski and was out for the rest of the year. Then Miller suffered a back injury. And to cap it off, Simmons left in the middle of the month to go to military service. So we wound up playing our last ten games with one regular starter available—me.

The lead began to melt away, until that last day. We have to win it, or else we're tied with the Dodgers. It was going to be my fourth start in eight days, and for some mysterious reason, whether it was youth or enthusiasm or whatever, I had as good stuff on that eighth day as I'd ever had. I should have been worn out, but I wasn't.

That was the biggest game I was ever involved in. As I say, I had good stuff all the way, and, incidentally, so did Don Newcombe; it was just one fine baseball game.

We were ahead 1–0 until around the last of the sixth. Then Pee Wee Reese came up and hit one out to right field. Talk about oddball things happening. On top of the right field wall was a screen and where the screen came down to the wall there was a ledge. Well, he hit one against the screen and it dropped straight down to that ledge and just lay there. After that game they changed the ground rules and made it a double; but at that time it was all you could get and naturally Reese, with the ball just sitting up there, got four bases. I'll never forget the sight of Del Ennis standing there looking up at it, waiting for it to come down. But it never did. That tied the game at one apiece.

Did I get the feeling the gods were against me when that happened? No. I can honestly say that I never let anything upset me on the mound. Not errors, not bloop hits, not anything. And I think that good disposition probably helped me as much as the good throwing arm. After

Reese had circled the bases I simply got another ball and went back to work.

We went into the last of the ninth still tied. Let's set the inning up. Cal Abrams led off and I went to three and one on him. I threw him a pitch inside, low and inside. Larry Goetz was the umpire, one of the two or three best umpires I ever saw. Larry called it a ball. I remember my reaction at the time—I didn't think it was a ball, but it was close. So I walked Abrams. Reese came up. Twice he tried to bunt and fouled them off. Now, in a situation like that you go inside, to keep the guy from hitting behind the runner. I went inside and Pee Wee hit a rope to left field, a real shot. So now they're on first and second and Snider is up, and Robinson is next. This is getting serious.

Snider's got to bunt, right? That's the way you're supposed to play it, aren't you? Now, I don't know if Ashburn was moving in a little bit in center field. If he was it was because he, like me, was anticipating a bunt and wanted to be ready to back up a play at second base. But there was no pickoff on; that's all story. If there was a pickoff on I didn't know about it, and I had the ball. So I think Richie probably thought Snider was going to bunt, and so did I. Consequently, I didn't throw the ball hard. I was more intent on getting off the mound and fielding the ball and trying to keep Abrams from getting to third.

To my surprise, Duke swung away. I'll never forget it. When he hit it I thought it was a line drive to Goliat at second; but it was to Goliat's right, into center field. I think Abrams might possibly have got a little bit of criticism that was unjust, because I can remember turning and seeing him holding up, and I think he thought too that Goliat might catch it. It was a vicious shot, but it wasn't high in the air. So Abrams had that late jump and Ashburn was in close and caught the ball on the first or second hop in running stride. Richie was not known for his throwing arm, however, so the third base coach sent Abrams in. As it turned out Richie threw a one-hopper to Stan Lopata and Abrams was out by fifteen feet. It wasn't even close.

The runners had moved up, so now it was men on second and third and one out and Robinson was up. Sawyer came out and said put Robinson on. Which made sense. So we walked Jackie to load the bases and that brought up Furillo. Sawyer told me to keep the ball down be-

Dick Sisler (Number 8), being welcomed after his pennant-winning home run.

cause Furillo was a high-ball hitter. My first pitch was eye-high, but I got away with it because Carl popped it straight up. The next batter was Hodges and he hit an easy fly to right field. Del Ennis came in, and a lot of people don't know this, but the ball got into the sun and Del had to fight it a little and caught it right against his chest for the third out.

It wasn't until I walked off the mound after that inning and sat down that I realized how petrified I'd been.

So we went into the tenth inning. I was the leadoff hitter. And I singled up the middle, which not many people remember. I started that tenth inning with a base hit. It wasn't a hard-hit ball, it was a seeing-eye baby that went through the middle. Waitkus came up and Sawyer let him hit away. He hit a looper to right center that dropped in and I went down to second base. Ashburn tried to sacrifice but I was thrown out at third.

So now we had men on first and second and one out. Dick Sisler came up. He'd already had three hits. Well, he tagged one very hard, a line shot into the left-field seats. That put us up, 4–1. I still had to get three more outs in the last of the tenth, and there was no doubt in my mind then that I would. I got them, one, two, three, and Philadelphia had its first pennant since 1915—thirty-five years.

After pitching four games in eight days they couldn't start me in the World Series opener because I'd had only two days rest. Konstanty started and he lost, 1–0. I pitched the second game. I was a little shaky at the beginning and gave up a lot of hits, but they got only one run. Then we tied it up. We went into the tenth inning and DiMaggio came up. He had popped out four straight times. When he came up in the tenth it was the only time that day that I wasn't leery of him. I assumed after getting him out four straight times that I was handling him all right. I think I might have been just a little bit overconfident with him that last time. The moment I saw the pitch going in I knew it didn't have the drive it should have had and I saw DiMaggio's whole body moving into it, and he hit it upstairs. That was the ball game.

They beat us four straight, in four low-scoring ball games. They scored only eleven runs in the Series, but that was enough.

You know, in 1951, for the third year in a row the Dodgers and the Phillies played extra innings on the last day of the season to decide the National League pennant. In 1949 they beat us in ten to win it over St. Louis; in '50 we beat them in ten to win it; and while we weren't in it ourselves in '51, they had to beat us to gain a tie with the Giants. That was the year the Dodgers lost a 13½ game lead in the last six weeks. When they came into Philadelphia for that final series they were in trouble.

On Saturday night I pitched nine innings against Newcombe and he whipped me, 5–3. When I lost a ball game I really took it home with me. I brooded. I couldn't sleep. So, not being very good company and not wanting to bother my family, I lay down in a hammock in my backyard with a half dozen cans of beer and just sipped and rocked all night and watched the sun come up.

When I went to the ball park on Sunday I figured I'd be the last guy they'd want to call on; what the hell, I'd pitched nine innings the night before. So I sat down in the bull pen and relaxed. The game was back and forth all the way. By the eighth inning, in spite of all the excitement, I was getting awfully sleepy. Then Sawyer called down and said, "Tell Roberts to warm up." So I got up and started throwing. Then they brought me in. We were leading by a run, the tying run was on second, and Furillo was the batter. He hit a shot to left field that tied it up. Then I got them out.

The game went on into extra innings. By this time Newcombe was back in it. In the last of the twelfth we loaded the bases with one out. Ennis came up and Newk reached back and struck him out. That brought up Waitkus, and he hit a low screaming liner. Jackie Robinson went in back of second and dove for it. Now, I was on third base, looking back as I ran. I saw Jackie dive for it, get it and then throw it back over his head. I still to this day think he trapped that ball, and he knew it, and in desperation was trying to get a force play at second. When I touched home plate I thought the game was over, but then I looked back again and the umpire was signaling that the ball had been caught. I've always wondered why Jackie, if he'd caught it on the fly for the third out, tried to throw the ball to second. Years later I met him at some function or other and I said, "Jackie, did you really catch that ball?" He laughed and said, "What'd the umpire say?"

Then in the top of the fourteenth Jackie hit one upstairs. After saving the game for them, he won it. That put them in the play-off, and set it up for Bobby Thomson. Not even Jackie could do anything about that.

But Robinson had that flair. He was something special on a ball field. I remember something that our coach, Cy Perkins, said to me once. After he'd watched Jackie for about five years, he came up to me one day and said, "You've heard all those stories about Ty Cobb, Robin?" I said yes. Cy had played against Cobb for quite a few years. "Well," he said, "that's the closest thing to Ty Cobb I ever saw. Jackie Robinson."

Jackie was probably as fine a baseball player as I ever saw. Sometimes he looked a little stiff and awkward out there—he was not a graceful performer—but what a base runner, what reflexes, and what a competitor! And he was tough. Nothing describes him better than just plain tough.

Cy Perkins, our coach, who I just mentioned, was a tremendous person. He was a wise and compassionate man who'd been around base-

Jackie Robinson.

ball a long time—he came up with Connie Mack's Athletics around the time of the First World War. He worked quietly with us and was always honest with us.

He was there when I first worked out with the ball club in Chicago. When I was working out that first day I heard somebody behind me say, "Don't let that kid get out of this park." I turned around and it was Cy Perkins, and that was the first time he had ever seen me.

In 1950 while I was warming up for a spring training game—after just one and a half years in the big leagues—he said to me, "Kid, you look great." He always called me "Kid."

"Well, I feel fine," I said.

"I want to tell you something," he said. "I've been in baseball for thirty-five years and the five best pitchers I've ever seen are Walter Johnson, Lefty Grove, Herb Pennock, Grover Cleveland Alexander, and you."

I laughed. My lifetime record at that time was 22 wins and 24 defeats.

"I'm not kidding you," he said. "You've got the best baseball delivery I ever saw. You're our next three hundred game winner."

He never told me how to pitch, he never told me how to do anything. "Do it your way," he used to say. Occasionally I would get knocked out in the first inning and he would say, "Hey, don't worry; they're big leaguers. They're going to do that to you now and then." There was never criticism, always the attitude that he considered himself lucky to be able to work with us.

But he never looked upon me as being a special person because I was a good pitcher; I was a good pitcher by the accident of natural endowment. He felt it was ninety percent gift and ten percent effort. And he would make sure you knew that. He kept it all on a beautiful keel.

When I won a game I never saw him. He felt that I had the stuff and should have won the game; he'd never come over to congratulate me. But when I lost he'd always be there and never let me get morose or despondent about it. As I said, I never slept when I lost. I'd see the sun come up without ever having closed my eyes. I'd see those base hits over and over and they'd drive me crazy.

One night I got knocked out in the first inning. We left town that night and I was in a roomette on the train. I knew I was in for a rough night.

Perkins knocked on the door and came in.

"How are you doing?" he asked.

"Cy," I said, "how can I be doing?"

He sat there for a while and then started to reminisce. Very casually, in a detached sort of way. He went back to the days when he was playing with the Athletics, when they were battling the Yankees. Mr. Mack—they all called him Mr. Mack—had Lefty Grove primed for this big game. Watching Grove warm up, Cy said he'd never seen him throw harder, which must have been something, because Grove could really fire. The A's went out in the top of the first and Grove walked to the mound. Well, the Yankees ripped him for seven runs in the bottom of the first. Perkins said he couldn't believe it. *Nobody* was supposed to hit Lefty Grove like that. Finally Mack had to take him out.

That's the story Cy told me that night while the train was barreling along and I was lying there feeling sorry or myself. Then he left. And I began to think: "Lefty Grove got knocked out in the first inning. What the hell am *I* worrying about?"

But that's the way Cy Perkins was. He didn't say, "Look, if it happened to Grove it can happen to anybody." He just went away and let it sink in on its own.

He was a very quiet man. He did the same thing for all the guys that he did for me, but always very quietly. The players all had tremendous respect and affection for him, but the owners barely knew he was there; they couldn't appreciate what he was doing.

One day in September, 1954, he came up to me and said, "They're getting rid of me." I thought he was kidding. But he wasn't. So the next day I went to see Bob Carpenter, who owned the club.

"Mr. Carpenter," I said, "Cy Perkins told me you're getting rid of him."

"Cy's getting old," he said.

"Don't get rid of him," I said.

"What do you mean?"

"I don't think you appreciate how much help he gives us," I said.

"You're kidding," he said.

"What does he make, Mr. Carpenter?"

"Why?"

"I'll pay his salary," I said. "That's what he means to me. And I know he means the same to the other guys."

He didn't believe me. They wouldn't listen and they got rid of him.

I had a reputation for not throwing at hitters. That was not entirely true, but most of the time it was true. If they knocked our guys down I would throw at their guys. But generally I didn't throw at anybody. Perkins said to me one day, "Robin, they've been getting on you for not knocking hitters down, haven't they?"

"Yes," I said.

"You never think of it, do you?" he asked.

"No," I said. "It never enters my mind."

He said, "It never does to the good ones."

Why should I have knocked them down without provocation? Here's a man I respect, a man who respects me, telling me not to worry about it. I just never gave a thought to getting involved with that stuff.

So Cy left in 1954. I stayed with the Phillies until 1961. I went to the Yankees in '62, but never pitched for them. They released me at the end of April, which is a bad time to get released, since everybody is pretty much set. So I came home. I didn't know what to do. I was thirty-four years old.

I get a phone call. It's Cy.

Cy Perkins. "You'll be pitching shutouts when you're forty."

"What are they trying to do to you, kid?" he asks.

"What do you mean?"

"Don't you let them drive you out of this game. You'll be pitching shutouts when you're forty."

"Cy, you son of a gun," I said.

"I'm telling you, kid, don't you quit. There's no way that you can't keep pitching."

So I went to Baltimore and had some fine years there. My first year in the American League I was second in earned-run average. I pitched another five years in the big leagues—thanks to Cy's phone call.

Cy passed away a year later, but his encouragement had helped get me back into the big leagues, so I guess you could say he was still influencing my life.

I guess there are times when you do worry a little about getting old. Well, I'm nearly fifty now, but if I would have known how much I was going to be enjoying life at this age I would never have worried about getting old. But it would have been a great help, knowing at twenty-five how much I was going to enjoy being fifty. I don't have any reason whatsoever to look back with any regrets. What happened, happened, and I'm very proud of a lot of it and disappointed in some of it. But I wouldn't change any of it.

Regrets about not winning 300? No, not really. A lot of people thought I was striving for 300 wins. But what I was really striving for was to pitch until I was forty-four or forty-five years old. I knew if I could do that the wins would take care of themselves.

I stayed with Baltimore until August of '65, when I went to Houston. I pitched well there, but found my arm swelling up when I threw curve-

balls. I had an arm operation that winter to correct the problem. The next year I tried to pitch but the arm wasn't right. So they released me and I went to the Cubs and finished out the year as a pitching coach. They wanted me back the next year, but I didn't go.

After resting all winter, my arm felt good. So I decided I'd go to Reading in the Eastern League and pitch until June 1 and if nobody picked me up, then I'd go home and pack it in. I was forty years old now. I did all right, won five, lost three, pitched a shutout. But June 1 came and nobody had picked me up. So I quit.

As I was driving home that night I knew it was over. I thought about Cy. I thought, "Well, Cy, you son of a gun, you said I'd pitch a shutout when I was forty, but you didn't tell me what league it was going to be in."

So I came home smiling.

INDEX

Entries in italics refer to illustrations.

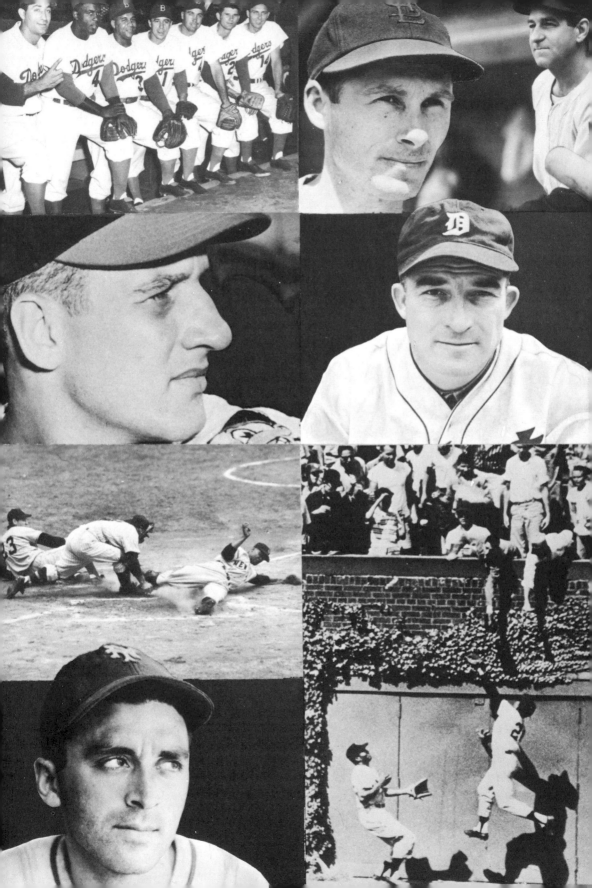